No Room for Secrets

No Room for Secrets

JOANNA LUMLEY

MICHAEL JOSEPH
an imprint of
PENGUIN BOOKS

MICHAEL JOSEPH

Published by the Penguin Group

Penguin Books Ltd, 80 Strand, London WC2R ORL, England

Penguin Group (USA) Inc., 375 Hudson Street, New York, New York 10014, USA

Penguin Books Australia Ltd, 250 Camberwell Road, Camberwell, Victoria 3124, Australia

Penguin Books Canada Ltd, 10 Alcorn Avenue, Toronto, Ontario, Canada M4V 3B2

Penguin Books India (P) Ltd, 11 Community Centre, Panchsheel Park, New Delhi – 110 017, India

Penguin Group (NZ), cnr Airborne and Rosedale Roads, Albany, Auckland 1310, New Zealand

Penguin Books (South Africa) (Pty) Ltd, 24 Sturdee Avenue, Rosebank 2196, South Africa

Penguin Books Ltd, Registered Offices: 80 Strand, London WC2R ORL, England

www.penguin.com

First published 2004

3

Copyright © Joanna Lumley, 2004

Set in 13/16 pt Monotype Bembo
Typeset by Rowland Phototypesetting Ltd,
Bury St Edmunds, Suffolk
Printed in Great Britain by Clays Ltd, St Ives plc

A CIP catalogue record for this book is available from the British Library

ISBN 0-718-14682-4

This book is for Jamie, Tessa and Alice

Contents

Prologue

I may have been in your life for many years, as a vaguely remembered name, or as a shadow on a flickering television screen in the background; or this may be the first time we've met. In any case I've been in your home – but through an appalling oversight I have never invited you into my house until now. You can't say you really know someone until you've seen where and how they live. My house is my home, where all my life is assembled; all thoughts and memories from my earliest days up to this very moment are here, and this book will be a tour of . . . well, to be frank, me.

Q. Can we ask questions?

A. Of course you can. I prefer to talk to people like this, one to one, heart to heart – and we can go at your speed because you are a welcome visitor.

Q. In that case, where is your husband?

A. I want you to know that my husband Stephen is not in the house at the moment. He is far away in Chicago, working on an opera, so we can get this show on the road and poke about without disturbing him. He's rather private, actually, and although I know he's very happy that you're touring

I

my heart, my life, my home, he cannot be here. I thought we'd start at the beginning of my life in the hall, and end up in the attic, which is as far as we can go without climbing on to the roof tiles. Just as rooms contain all sorts of different things, so this book will hop from memory to memory; in effect it will be in real time – and because I speak rather fast, I think we can cram it all in during this one precious visit. But look! I'm talking like this and you haven't even got over the threshold. Please come in.

Hall

I was born under Taurus, on the evening of the 1st of May 1946, a year before the Partition of India and in one of the loveliest countries in the world: Kashmir. The nursing home in Gupkar Road, Srinagar, is still there, with its painted verandas and quiet garden shaded by tall plane trees. The old city sprawls comfortably among the Dal and Nagin lakes, criss-crossed with tree-lined canals and paddy fields; the colossal mountains of the Karakoram and Himalayan ranges roar away into the sky; kingfishers dip amongst the tethered wooden houseboats where small boats called *shikaras* sell their wares: vegetables, jewellery, cloth and chickens.

My parents had met and married in Kashmir; on both sides of my family India had been home for several generations. James Lumley, my father, had joined the Gurkhas almost as soon as he'd left Sandhurst; his having been born in Lahore – where his father, my grandfather, had been a banker – meant that India had got under his skin for ever. As a very little boy he had been sent back to boarding schools in England, as were his elder sisters. He was always called Jimmy; good at games, a fine horseman and polo player, he was quite slight in build, about 5 feet 10 inches tall, with a tremendously high, broad forehead: my sister and I used to call him the Educated Egg. My mother's parents had married in Rangoon: Leslie Weir, a Scot born in Ghazipur, and Thyra Sommers, a Dane born in New Zealand . . .

Q. Please get on with it.

A. . . . and my mother, Beatrice, only missed being born in Persia – as it was – by days, as her family moved from this to that diplomatic posting. We were all used to travelling all the time. England was 'home' even though they didn't live here: England was in fact 'school' and later on 'leave'. My mother was seven years younger than her sister Joan Mary, which meant she was brought up mostly as an only child, at boarding school when the family was travelling in Bhutan, Sikkim and Tibet, and then returning when she was 17 to the country she loved and felt most at home in, India. Look at this huge map: it's almost the first thing you see as you come in through the front door, 'Kashmir and Jammu and Gilgit Region, 1940', traced with little red pencil lines where my mother had trekked, being a passion-ate hillwalker. The hall is covered with pictures, photo-graphs and drawings. The floor is uncarpeted – the house was built in 1847, and the Victorian fashion was for these tiny tessellated tiles set in a pretty pattern.

Q. Are they meant to clink like that when you walk on them? Some of them are loose.

A. No, of course not, and thank you for asking. They get a lot of wear and tear and I've tried to glue them down and cement them in but it's fairly hopeless. I like the idea of bare floors, and I like the slip–slap of a foot on an uncarpeted ground. Some of this comes from the enjoyment of a cool floor in a hot country, from my earliest memories. Anyway, my father met my mother in the hill station Gulmarg when he was on leave: she, rather a tomboy by nature, was doing a headstand on the grass, and when she turned the right way up with all her black hair tumbled round her face he thought, 'I must marry that girl.' My sister, Ælene, was born in what is now Pakistan, in Abbottabad, two years before my story started. So I had the luckiest of all beginnings: an excellent ready-made family, a May Day birth, a Himalayan background and what I thought was a 'Monday's child fair of face' gift. I swear my mother said I was born on a Monday – but I have just now discovered it was really a Wednesday, which has absolutely shaken me. All my life I have thought of myself as a painted clown and an optimist whose duty is always to be cheerful, and suddenly I am 'Wednesday full of woe' and it has set me back. (I have only known this for the past six months.)

We left India for ever a year after I was born when the Partition of India took place. Those days are now so remote from the way life is lived today that it's very hard to believe they're within living memory. Journeys were made by ship, taking many weeks, and it wasn't uncommon when children were sent back to school in England for them not to see their parents for several years. It didn't mean that families were any less loving or concerned – it was simply the custom, rather like sons' unquestioningly following their fathers into the coalmines. It was expected. But when my parents married and we were born, they decided they didn't want us to have the same fractured upbringing they had endured. We all packed up and followed the flag, or bugle, or in fact marching orders, and travelled like so many service families to wherever we were sent. As soon as we arrived, my mother would make our nursery or bedroom familiar: a Kay Nixon print of red squirrels, Beatrix Potter pictures, and books, a Chinese rug and the toy-basket. I can't remember ever feeling sad at leaving a house – the future and the unknown always eclipsed any regrets. Even now, the moment you're at the departure gate, or when the train pulls out of the station, you turn your face and mind to the journey ahead while the immediate past streaks away like smoke in the wind.

These suitcases stacked up here like a hall table have labels hanging off them and glued to their sides: BOAC, ancient hotels in Cairo, triangular stickers saying 'Biarritz'. They give me a thrill and a sense of security, of certainty that 'travel' will soon be here again, even if it's not for good. The idea of stopping travelling fills me with an immeasurable dread; but Stephen has grown heartily sick of the protracted torture of air travel, where cramped seats, delays and jet-lag rather smash you flat before you set foot in the new destination. Here's a picture of him when he was at the Choir School, and lots of old family pictures, and a huge Maltese clock which I can't remember to wind up; it strikes in code, in clusters of three and four, and gains about half an hour a day, so it has limited practical use – but it's very beautiful, with its pictures of Valletta harbour and hand-painted flowers. The troop-ships always stopped at Malta on their way to and from the Far East: Gibraltar, Malta, Suez, Port Saïd, Colombo, Singapore, Hong Kong. Five weeks. Please put your coat on this rush-seated hall chair and follow me.

Study

This is my study. It used to be Stephen's music room, fantastically crammed with the Steinway B grand piano, the harpsichord, all his sheet music, records, CDs, tapes, old 78 rpm gramophone records, music boxes and so on. Now it still looks completely crammed, but with books, and pictures leaning against the walls, and boxes of photographs, and paintings all hugger-mugger almost up to the ceiling. I know where everything is. I have the mind of a filing clerk and can retrieve almost anything in about two minutes. I keep old scripts now; I used to throw them all away. I keep letters and bills and stationery in this cupboard, which used to hold Jamie's clothes when he was little. I've painted it lichen-green, with an orange interior. I've just noticed that all my preceding sentences start with 'I'. This is something to be careful about. In letters of support or commendation, which I write very often nowadays, I make sure the sentences don't start with 'I'. But I'm in a whirl of me, an ego-trip like a runaway train, I, me, my, mine, *ego, me, mei, mihi, me.* I started learning Latin at St Mary's in the Michaelmas term in 1957 – my first term, as a new girl yet again, thrilled to the core by the vast winding corridors, smell of incense, gas lights and chapel bells. I can't remember much Latin now, but I still love it.

Q. Where did Stephen go with his music? And why are we calling him Stephen all of a sudden? Don't you call him Stevie?

A. Yes, yes I do; but for strangers reading this book who don't know him – or me, come to that – it seems a bit familiar. I've always known him as Stevie, but most of his music colleagues know him as Stephen. Or Maestro. What happened was this: by the side of our long thin garden runs a garden wall, behind which – attached to which – was a little printing works. You could hear the machines starting up, and the flump and whirr of a thousand pamphlets or invitations or whatever it was being printed. One day it came up for sale, and we and three neighbouring households clubbed together, bought it and divided it up. We got the part that was behind our garden wall. We put in a huge steel and glass door, a wooden floor, a kitchen, lavatory and a spacious study; and in went all Stevie's music things, the instruments and all his paraphernalia.

Now he can play the piano with the lid open, singers can sing out, coffee and tea can be made, and it's changed our lives. It's a great big airy space with sandblasted brick walls and skylights, and the glass door opens on to the garden, which in turn lies beside all the other gardens, making a leafy flowery oasis, full of birds, squirrels and foxes. Standing at my study window I can see the path leading down past the fishponds and the pear tree, down to the new music room. We couldn't be luckier. When he's composing he can't bear to hear another sound. London is never completely quiet, but the music room is remarkably silent.

Q. All these volumes of Pushkin . . . have you read them?

A. No, only two so far. It was the first time all his work had been translated into English so I bought the set. Marvellous! I can't wait to have enough time to catch up on all the books I want to read – I'll never do it, there is so *much* to be known; I'll go to my grave with books in my coffin.

Q. Some nice carved African guinea fowl, and a Bafta Award jammed into this shelf with a chess set and some Snow White playing cards.

A. I can't tell you what it meant to me to win a Bafta. It was for playing Patsy in *Absolutely Fabulous*; I can remember hearing my name called out and then going deaf and ice-cold, and walking in a dream to collect it. Because I'd never been to drama school, had indeed started my career as a lowly model, I always felt as though I was an outsider, someone who didn't deserve to do well. In my heart, I'd always felt like an actor, right back to the days in the Army School ('she is very good at dramatic art'), through a special Honours Certificate for music and drama, and parts in all the school plays; I *felt* I was an actor, but what I did and looked and sounded like seemed to be completely different from what was going on in my head. It is hard to get away from self-consciousness and insecurity. I talked too fast, had poor projection and suffered from stage fright. But I loved it – no, I didn't love it, I just knew that it was all I wanted to do with my life.

Age 15; St Mary's, 20 May 1961. Letter to my parents:

I am in the school play this term, A Midsummer Night's Dream, *the Pyramus and Thisbe scene. I am Pyramus viz*

9

i.e. e.g. Bottom and am prepared to make an utter chump of myself.

We have got our GCE O level timetables and I haven't got more than one exam on any day except for English Grammar I and II and French I and II which is rather marvellous.

I went to see Sister Barbara about the sixth form and she says I have got to stay 2 years in the VIth and take German, English, Italian, French and Latin at A level. It's a query about the last: I don't really want to take Latin. She said I couldn't possibly stay only one year as I am not clever enough to take English in one year. Then she went on to say that I was quite brilliant and nowhere but university is good enough for me . . .

Q. It doesn't sound like the Sister Barbara I knew.

A. I think I was exaggerating – I do know that they wanted me to go to university but I realized that unless I *worked* at my subjects, in particular the set books in the three modern languages, I wouldn't have a chance. I was extremely lazy and had only managed to get this far by blagging (a good word I only learned from Neil Morrissey much later). My sister took English in one year and passed easily. I was incapable of studying and couldn't seem to force myself to concentrate.

St Mary's, 18 June 1961. Letter home:

Thank you very much for the 4 leaf clover; do you know I have never found ONE. I expect I will fly through all my exams now. I have done complete revision of Biology. Until the exams start I'll do Latin, History, Latin, History etc. These are by far my worst subjects. Miss Hortin-Smith says I will get English Lit and Language easily, so I am not revising much for those.

*French and German you can't do much for and that's the lot
. . . I have decided what I want to do when I leave (I only
want to stay on in the sixth form for one year) and I want to
go to a dramatic school if they'll accept me. I truly don't want
to go to university, no more than being a secretary. And acting
though hard work is good fun. Longing to see you . . .*

Q. Did you take your five subjects at A level?

A. No, I took three, with French at scholarship level, and
only got one. I got Latin *again* at O level and passed French.
German I failed utterly. This left me with eight O levels
and one A level.

Q. Can't you see how boring it is to read this? Exam results
which had no effect at all on your future life?

A. My point entirely. I cannot believe it's right to concentrate
on exam results so much today; pages of national newspapers going on for days on end, league tables, UCAS forms,
it's all an utter waste of time. A well-rounded education is
what a child needs, not paper qualifications. If you spend
like a kicking horse on early education, you won't need to
send 50 per cent of our young ones to university to get
degrees in subjects that are neither valued nor needed.
Most of this country is run, owned, organized and operated
by people who haven't been to university. University is
for brainboxes, studying specialist subjects like . . . er . . .
science and ancient history and music and engineering,
languages, higher mathematics . . . er . . .

Q. I can tell you didn't go. Didn't you get in? Those exam results are pretty indifferent.

A. Well, obviously I never even applied. I wasn't a fool but I didn't need or want to go to university at the age of 17 when I left school. I was burning to escape into being a grown-up; exams were something to be avoided for ever, if possible, and the dreams uppermost in my brain were of adventure, travelling, wearing nail varnish, trying to speak French like a Frenchwoman, driving a sports car, in fact anything that didn't involve working on my own in a study. London, a distant Camelot, flickered and beckoned: it seemed impossibly alluring and terrifying and therefore attractive beyond measure. Much as I loved being at school when I was young, the duties and regulations began to chafe as I grew older. Rereading my old school letters, I get the impression that I turned very quickly from a cheerful cheeky monkey of 11 into a lippy, aggressive, sneering teenager, rude to people who were kind to me, shallow, bumptious and fairly repellent.

Excerpts from St Mary's school reports, 1954–1963:

> Her manner of speech needs care.
> Joanna must learn to speak politely when her requests are refused.
> Fairly good: still rather aggressive.
> We hope for better things next term.
> Still rather noisy.
> She should try to be more unobtrusive.
> Joanna has shown too little work for any comment to be made.
> Joanna has avoided work as much as possible.

Q. Ghastly. I expect you've edited out all the positive remarks for dramatic effect.

A. There were lots of lively, kind, encouraging comments: 'very good, excellent, has very good ability, extremely good, could be very good if she concentrated a little more, still very headstrong' – oh dear, we're going downhill again – 'has shown little interest, Joanna must take more trouble and not rely on ideas of the moment, good as they are . . .' At the same time, I've got to say, I was transparently happy; perhaps I was only as dreadful as I remember I was in my own mind. These are my school reports . . . they go right back to when I was four. My parents never threw anything like that away – or anything that we did or made or painted for them. There are two old suitcases full of our letters and home-made Mothering Sunday cards, poems, essays and paintings. When my father was in Malaya and we were at boarding school in England, we wrote two letters every Sunday: one to my mother here, and one to my father in Sungei Patani – on an aerogramme, I think they were called. He kept them all as well. It was incredibly touching to open these suitcases recently and find this treasure trove of one's young life.

At six, I was a clever child. Look at these results: 100 per cent in all subjects except maths, first in class, reading age of four years ahead of my age, 'excellent', 'most intelligent', 'hard-working' . . . I was, at the ages of six and seven, a year younger than the form average and still came top. Even my maths was graded at 96 per cent. I've never been so clever again. When we sailed back to England in May 1954 I must have left something of my confidence behind in the Far East. We were sent to a little boarding school in

Kent called Mickledene. There were about 70 children at the school, of whom only 15 were boarders. Some of the classrooms were in twin oast houses, the round kilns used for drying hops. I was eight; now the reports say, 'she finds it a little difficult to work or play with others', and 'Jo has not enough confidence in her own abilities', 'tends to be self absorbed', 'must learn to overcome difficulties on her own'. Here we are, though – aged nine, summer term 1955, still a year younger than the others, 'Joanna acted extremely well in the school play'. That's encouraging.

Q. And here: 'found knitting rather difficult'. But look, you're still first in lots of subjects – English, French, dictation, good, excellent, very good indeed. I can't see what the problem is.

A. There wasn't a problem. Reports never really seemed to reflect the reality of life. Teachers only knew you as a pupil, they couldn't know what was going on in your mind. They had us in their pastoral care, though, and must have noticed when we were out of sorts or homesick.

Q. Were you homesick?

A. Of course. There's not a child who's been born who doesn't feel their world tear apart when they're sent away from home. I got over it; I can't remember how quickly, but I was gregarious and chirpy and it only came back in waves at the crucial times of saying goodbye to your parents at the beginning of term. The terrible ache, and sense of dread: I can almost feel them now.

Q. And yet 20 years later you sent your only child away to boarding school. Why?

A. Because I had got through it and had a happy life at both boarding schools, and because it was still considered a normal, even desirable thing to do, and because being a single mother who had to work I felt I couldn't provide a stimulating and secure home life when I was away filming . . . I don't know. I can't bear to think of it, taking Jamie off to school with the trunk in the back of the car, pretending to be cheerful and reassuring and stopping in a lay-by to sob my heart out, thinking of him. But the truth is this: somewhere in life, somewhere in the strange process of growing out of being a baby and into a grown-up person there will always be dreadful, frightening, even tragic events, and at some stage you have to learn how to cope with them on your own.

I suppose this thinking gets passed down from generation to generation – that you must try to become self-reliant and resilient as soon as possible. Don't forget both my parents had been sent back to England from their homes in India to go to boarding schools, and in those days such children often didn't see their parents for *years*, not just weeks. So our school lives were a great improvement on theirs. These were customs, this was the way it was done. It took so long to get to India or the Far East by ship, and children were expected to thrive in an English climate, where their health wouldn't be threatened by tropical diseases. Young children became stoical at a tender age. It may seem unthinkable now, but the world has changed beyond recognition since then. If you read Rudyard Kipling's autobiographical story 'Baa Baa Black Sheep' you will get a piercing insight into the life of two small children sent away ostensibly for their own good. We were very much loved by our parents, and the longest I was away from my father was a year and a half, and from my mother six months.

Look: I've just turned up the last report my headmistress at the Army School, in Malaya, wrote in the section marked 'Notes on General Ability and Attainment and Special Aptitudes and Interests'. I wanted to include this because my parents didn't show it to me at the time – or ever, come to think of it. 'Joanna is helpful and very popular with her class, and care must be taken that she does not get spoilt by too much adoration. She has a great sense of fun, but she must realize that she cannot always be first. She is inclined to sulk if she cannot have her own way.' I never knew I was adored, never knew I sulked.

We had arrived in Malaya when I was just five, at the time of the Emergency. Communists from the North had been moving down the Malay peninsula and the British Army were there to prevent the terrorism that threatened the villages, or *kampong*s as they are called. Movement around the country was restricted and we, the army children, were sent to a large school just outside Kuala Lumpur, the capital. It catered only for children of the army so there were no Malays, no Chinese as far as I can remember. It was rather like an equivalent of the Lycée or the American School in London. We could speak a little Malay, kitchen Malay I suppose. Our housekeeper, or *amah*, was called Ah Feng and she was Straits Chinese, but we could remember a bit of Hong Kong Mandarin and she could speak a little English. My father, of course, had fluent Gurkhali: I say 'of course' because you weren't allowed to become an officer in a Gurkha regiment unless you could speak the language. My mother had – still has – fluent Urdu: it was almost her first language, and she and my father would speak Urdu and Gurkhali when they didn't want us to understand. The school wasn't far from our bungalow, which was within an army settlement called HQ Malaya.

Every day we walked to school early in the morning. We were in assembly at 8 a.m. and lessons for the day finished by lunchtime, when it was too hot for anyone to work. Even though we studied for only half a day, we came back about a year ahead of our British contemporaries. We wore blue and white cotton dresses made up, from a choice of patterns, on my mother's Singer sewing machine. Our long hair was plaited; we wore just a cotton dress and cotton pants – but we'd be soaked through with sweat after walking home in the scorching tropical sun. Sometime about then, I think, was born my passion for views of baking blistering heat seen from a dark interior. Dark trees or verandas, shadowy cloisters and outside dusty white roads or white-hot pavements; if you're lucky, a yellowish-black sky with a colossal storm brewing. That's the stuff of paradise.

Q. You don't have to write letters when you are at a day school, as you were then. Can you remember it all clearly? Without anything to remind you but photographs and these school reports?

A. I remember that we went swimming almost every day at the Selangor Golf Club. I've been back there; with hindsight, I think you should never go back. The top diving board, which seemed to me, at six, to be of an Olympian height, was lowish. The pool was small, the hibiscus hedge was modest. The flat empty countryside through which the long straight drive led to the clubhouse has quite naturally turned into part of the gigantic modern city that Kuala Lumpur has become. No one could remember where HQ Malaya had been, or identify the location of the school. It was as if it had never been. Every school I have ever been to has now disappeared: not a good thing or a bad thing; but a thing nevertheless.

The change – the difference between Malaya, where we had been for three years, and Kent, where my next school Mickledene was – couldn't have been greater. Everything in my life changed; most of all the country where I thought I belonged. You always think fairly simplistically as a child: if I like you, you're bound to like me; if I like eating it, it's good for me; if I like living here, wherever that is must like having me. One of the hugest differences was the colour of everything. Malaya's palette was extreme and vivid – skies were hot blue, flowers boiling red, storms black, moons white. Monsoons were thunderous, lightning zigzags of tungsten brightness. I used to dream of Malaya, get sudden flashes of a road turning uphill into a rubber plantation, or feel the fat wet heat of the monsoons. The stories of Somerset Maugham got it right on the button – the Malaya he knew, the civil servants, planters and traders were not my Malaya, but the place was; the temptation to go back was irresistible. In 1989, Stevie and I packed and went.

I wrote it all down:

We used to arrive in Singapore on a troop-ship, either from Hong Kong, or, after a month at sea, from England.

The ship, slowly nosing through the islands dotting the huge harbour, docked at the quayside, and after an eternity the great gangways would be wheeled up as we hung over the rails, fidgeting about in the sweltering heat until it was time to disembark.

Now, more than 30 years later, we flew in a Canadian 747 into Changi airport with its marble halls and air-conditioning, elaborate fountains and cool efficiency. In my pocket I had the fourth volume of Somerset Maugham's *Collected Short Stories*. In the preface he noted: '*They were written long before the Second World War and I should tell the reader that the sort of life with which they deal no longer exists.*' I had marked out some passages from *A Casual Affair, The Letter, The Outstation* and *Neil MacAdam*, descriptions that coincided with my own memories. I would find out if distance had lent enchantment to the scene and if my sort of life, as a small English girl during the Emergency in the early 1950s, had vanished entirely as well.

From the top of Mount Faber you can see over the harbour, out towards Sentosa Island, where the cable car, swooping across from Singapore, joins a green monorail. I cannot think where our battered old troop-ship put in: there is mile after mile of container ports, island after island; tugs, cruise ships and oil tankers swarm in the docks.

'*Outside the quay the sun beat fiercely. A stream of motors, lorries and buses, private cars and hirelings, sped up and down the crowded thoroughfare and every chauffeur blew his horn.*' There is no speeding now, no tooting of horns; you are liable to be fined on the spot for going too fast or for carrying fewer than three passengers in the rush hour.

'*Rickshaws threaded their nimble path amid the throng . . . coolies, carrying heavy bales, sidled along with their quick jog-trot and shouted to the passers-by to make way.*' I remember the coolies running, a smooth, bendy-kneed run, with their cone-shaped straw hats and bulky loads on a pole over their shoulders. All the coolies have gone, both in Singapore and in (what is now) Malaysia; and the rickshaws have gone too, to be replaced by trishaws, which are rather like the fiacres drawn up outside the Uffizi in Florence: overpriced and used only by tourists.

In Orchard Street, where the low stucco colonnades have been ousted by vaulting spotless emporia, young men accost the pink-skinned newcomers with slim, brown, outstretched wrists brandishing counterfeit Rolex watches. As the sudden night fell, a cool, dark veranda with a clinking glass beckoned like an oasis. We found it, the Tiger Tavern, after shouldering our way through the throng in the front part of the elegant Raffles Hotel, where scantily-clothed holiday-makers sweated over umbrella-laden drinks and jostled for a place in the Writers' Bar. (Here's to you, Maugham: you would recognize the building, but not the people or their purpose; and many of them, in their beach shorts and with their burnt arms, would not know your name.)

Impatient to recognize something, anything, we engaged Keder Bakas, a Muslim taxi driver, to drive us about the city for a day. Little India still sells spices in Serangoon Road: cumin, chilli, turmeric, cardamoms and cloves, stacked in sacks up to the ceilings of the low houses.

Maugham was considered a menace in Singapore, and was dreaded at drinks parties where he would glean gossip and rewrite it, so thinly disguising it that the real-life characters were immediately recognizable. He knew the Victoria Memorial Hall, which stands unchanged, the cricket club, the post office – all now overshadowed by a tall hotel, the Western Stamford. And there, shabby and resolutely unpainted, the FMS Railway Station that took us to and from the Federated Malay States, over the causeway to the Malay peninsula.

This time we drove by car, a Proton Saga made in Malaya ('Malaysia, Malaysia,' snapped the official at the border; 'Malaya not used since 1957'). Johore Baharu is as unprepossessing as its customs men. We drove on to Malacca, now spelt Melaka. Banana and oil palms line the dusty road, whose hard shoulders are made of orange laterite earth and are frequented by lorries overtaking on the inside. The driving has to be seen to be believed. On road signs, a motoring skeleton warns 'AWAS' – BEWARE.

Melaka has sprouted some tall, modern hotels. From the swimming pool on the ninth floor of the Ramada Renaissance, you can see the old town sprawling comfortably beside the Indian Ocean. The buildings, huddled in narrow streets and hanging over the torpid winding river, show Portuguese influence. At night the town comes alive.

'*They came to bazaars, narrow streets with arcades where the teeming Chinese, working and eating, noisily talking as is their way, indefatigably strove with eternity.*' The bright lights of the little shops lit the throngs of people shopping, eating and chattering like starlings in the evening. A pearl had fallen out of my engagement ring; in an open-sided shop, a Chinese jeweller found a matching pearl and fixed it in, price about one pound. Anything can be made or copied or mended in the Far East. In the West, our computer-tapping fingers have atrophied, and skills seep away for ever.

I had never been to Melaka before but this I remember from Kuala Lumpur: the night sounds of the tropics, the smells of open drains, sweet frangipani, joss-sticks and, in season, the durian, a fruit which has an aroma that could fell a donkey in its tracks at 50 yards. In the hotel there is a sign prohibiting the eating of durians in the bedrooms, penalty $500. In each room, an arrow on the ceiling marks *Kiblah*, the direction of Mecca: north-west from Melaka. Islam is the official religion. In newspapers, anyone who is not Malaysian is called a foreigner. Foreigners are prohibited from buying land, but foreign investment in industry is encouraged, in a country where government policy states that the population must increase from its present 16.5 million to 70 million to create a home market for palm oil and rubber. Newspapers are refranchised every year. If a paper were to criticize the government, its franchise would not be renewed. As in Singapore, drug traffickers are executed, unlike Maugham's 'Jack Almond' who, rejected by Lady Kastellan in *A Casual Affair*, dies in drugged squalor, a victim of opium's own death sentence.

There are no bullock carts; no attar of roses; no moon-flowers, whose lemony scent was so prized; no satin Chinese slippers. The Heath Robinson tin mines on spindly legs, trickling water and ore down their wooden chutes, have been bulldozed to make way for housing developments that would not look out of place in Hemel Hempstead.

The sky boils with black clouds as we approach Kuala Lumpur on the new motorway. Rubber plantations tremble in the torrential downpour. And now the greatest shock of all: I cannot recognize the town where I lived for three years. True, some old buildings remain in the modern city, but the old Central Market, once buzzing with fish and meat stalls, now has air-conditioning and sells gimcrack crafts to the tourists, while the elaborate and beautiful station, with its domes, arches and minarets, watches flying ring roads bringing traffic jams and chaos.

'If they lived where the climate was exhausting they sought the fresh air of some hill station not too far away.' Fraser's Hill, only an hour and a half's drive from Kuala Lumpur, is reached by a steep one-way road. The journey is spectacularly beautiful. We used to go to Fraser's Hill during the long summer holidays. We drove in our Wolseley 6/80, not stopping in the little *kampong*s, as bandits could be anywhere in those days. As the car climbed up, the air became cool; each hairpin bend brought views over treetops, over the rocky riverbed to endless jungle-covered hills.

'At last they reached the primeval forest, huge trees swathed in luxuriant creepers, an inextricable tangle, and awe descended on them.' Monkeys whoop in the morning mists, which nestle so closely that you have the impression of being on an island floating in a sea of clouds. The excitement of wearing cardigans in the evening, of wood fires burning in the fireplaces, and walking on the perfectly groomed golf course: it seemed to me aged six that this must be like England.

Now more houses have been built, but most are

shielded from the road by electric gates and long drives. They teeter over sheer drops, their windows turned to face the setting or the rising sun. Lush gardens surround them; they belong to rich industrialists and merchant banks. The small dispensary which I remember with dread is still there: bottles displaying bats' claws, snakes and a double-headed chicken have been joined by tiny unborn babies in yellowing formaldehyde, lizards and toads suspended in eternal innocence.

Once, we stayed at the Lodge, the Governor's residence, magnificently positioned on the spur of a hill, stone-clad and magisterial with well-tended gardens of dahlias and roses. This time, it was the Merlin Hotel, which although charmless to look at served an excellent Malay/Indian curry for supper.

The Cameron Highlands are four hours to the north. I had never been there before, never seen the trim Boh Tea estates rippling their green fantastic patterns over the foothills. More mock-Tudor houses, with names like Fair Haven and Dunhelen, nestle down Camberley lanes. Market stalls sell strawberries and asparagus. It is hard to believe we are six degrees north of the equator.

In the panelled hotel bar, a log fire roars in front of deep armchairs, and blowpipes and masks hang on the wall next to faded photographs of my time, Maugham's time. We call for gin *pahit*s: in the background the band tiptoes in, anxious to fill every moment with sound. 'You ain't nothin' but a hound dog', they sing at us, smiling hugely.

'*The fireflies, sparkling dimly, flew with their slow and silvery flight.*' Where are the fireflies? And mosquitoes?

And why so few geckos, and no tock-tock birds – is my memory mad? That night I woke suddenly and there on the ceiling was just one firefly, shining its calm, small light in the blackness.

'*Every morning Neil and Munro started out separately, collecting. The afternoons were devoted to pinning insects in boxes, placing butterflies between sheets of paper.*' Up in the hills, the butterfly farms have them ready-boxed for you: green, black, yellow, blue. The iridescent, shimmering creatures are pinned stiffly like little balsa-wood aeroplanes behind glass, rather as Maugham impaled his characters on their stories and displayed them for public examination as they squirmed and struggled to escape identification. Well, they are all safely gathered in now, Maugham too; and I am only slightly shocked to see that my childish ghost has joined them, skipping along in the fading twilight of the British Empire.

Q. I hope it's not always going to be like this, a sort of sour regret about places changing – with implications, for the worse.

A. Well, I hope it's not always going to hurt so much. When I came through Customs from Singapore to Malaysia they were really horrid to me, when they heard that I'd been a child there during the Emergency. I burst into tears, which astonished me and them: I had longed to return to what I thought of as home and they had made it plain that the episode of the British in Malaya was shameful and to be forgotten or written out of their history.

Q. Do you find that odd or unpredictable?

A. No, not now, not upon reflection. People hate having foreigners in power in their own land, even if their presence is benevolent. It's just that it was my home and I loved it with all my heart, while all the time it was hating me. That was the shock. And yes, I do think it's better to have jungles and rainforests than a shaved country with only the short-lived palm tree to hold the laterite earth to the rocks. It's a terrible and thorny problem, though: when I raised the subject of excessive logging and all the damage it did to the Ibans and Punans, and all the tribes living in the Sarawak forests – quite apart from the gradual extinction of their wildlife, especially orang-utans, the pollution of the rivers, loss of jungle medicine, loss of topsoil – they countered with the fact that we in Britain have cut down virtually all our forests; our wildlife – bears, wildcats, wolves – is gone: so how dare we preach to them? Aren't our rivers polluted by chemical waste, factory and farm effluent? Isn't our countryside turning towards the American prairie-style farming where the topsoil blows away into the sea?

Q. Let's drop this now.

A. What I loved about going back were the sounds of temple bells, the friendliness of people in the streets; and muezzins calling, and the smells of spices and frangipani blossoms, the sounds and smells of the bazaars, earth after rain. A month on a troop-ship with its own unforgettable smell of Vaseline . . .

Q. Surely not Vaseline . . .

A. No, but ships' engines smell like that; and the oranges we ate each day, chucking the skins into the sea, watching for land . . . and then England in June, full of such soft sweet scents of roses and wallflowers.

The smell of roses still takes me straight back to our little Kentish boarding school, Mickledene, with dark polished floorboards and the smell of box hedges and honeysuckle. It wasn't built as a school. The boarders lived in what had been a Georgian farmhouse, with a tennis court, some wild land with lupins and buttercups, watercress growing in the stream, tall dark yew trees, small orchards with molehills and cowslips. Everything you had used to be able to say to your parents now had to be written down: every Sunday before we walked the mile to Rolvenden Church we sat at tables in the boarders' house with our fountain pens and Basildon Bond writing paper, trying to think of news – it had to go over the page, one side was not accepted. Our letters were checked to make sure they were well spelt and didn't say, 'I'm homesick, come and save me.' I got to like school: I would make a good institution dweller. I made close friends, and our busy lives became the whole world, full of yearning for ponies, playing at houses, dancing, reading and mucking about.

17 May 1957 (I was just 11):

Darling Mummy,

Thank you very much for your letter. I hope you had a nice time in Bath. In literature we are reading about some people in Bath. Please, please, please will you let me go riding for the rest of the term if I don't take ballet when I go to St Mary's. If I can ride, will you send my hat. I do so want to ride because I think the people who run it are giving a gymkhana. It will be the first gymkhana I have ridden in. The fees come to about £3.15s. 6d. It is only 8/6d for a ride for just over an hour. I am terribly glad petrol rationing has stopped even though it has only gone down 1/1d. In Arithmetic we are doing Grafts [sic] they are awfully nice. A bat and ball attached to it by elastic is the craze this term. It is called Rat-a-tat-tat, Smash Hit or Jokari. My record is five-hundred-and-ninety-seven. My library book this week is called At the Back of the North Wind. *In Rest, Miss Clark is reading a book called* Silver Skates. *It is jolly good. Please do you think you could send me some presents, for there are five birthdays this term. Send just little things please. In Nature, Nikki, Michaela and I are studying birds. It is very interesting as I found an old chaffinch's nest when I went to tea with Mary Steele. She is hoping to get a pony from the Blue Cross. In Current Affairs we are making book covers. Mine is of all different things which happen in the world, like studying astronomy, tossing the javelin, aeroplanes and steamships. This morning I brushed all the riders' hats until all the dust was taken off. Please don't forget about sending me my ballet tunic pattern. I am now 5ft and I weigh precisely 6 stone 4 lbs! Please do you think you could send me my Norwegian fancy dress. It will be very useful in the play. I have not got a letter from Daddy yet. I hope he writes soon. Patricia Cohen has just been demonstrating Hebrew. It is very queer but pretty. All this term we have had very decent breakfasts, cheese-on-toast, baked beans, scrambled egg, boiled egg and bacon. Nikki and I often play what you might call tennis, hitting the ball to-and-fro with intense strength. Vicki gave me a little plaster-of-Paris rose she made for my late birthday present. I wear it on my dressing-gown. It looks very pretty. I can play my piano piece quite well now but I cannot play the last bar with both hands. It sounds nice on the staff room piano but apauling [sic] on the Hall piano which is slightly out of tune. In our dormitory on the mantelpiece we have got a horseshoe for luck and a luminous beetle also a Scottish doll in a kilt. Nikki has a blue zip dressing-gown. Oh by the way, my pink prayer book is very useful in church. I took it last Sunday. I must write to Daddy and Ælene now. Tons and tons of love from Jo.*

Q. That's an extremely long letter.

A. All the rest are very short. There must have been a competition to see who could write the most. Every Monday morning like clockwork the post arrived bringing two letters for me – one from my father, one from my mother. You never think of your parents missing you. Daddy's letters were on the regimental paper, pale grey with crossed *kukris* and the address embossed in green.

> *Depot the Brigade of Gurkhas, Sungei Patani, Kedah.*
> *Sunday, June 23rd, 1957*
>
> *Darling Jo,*
>
> *I'm so happy to think of you riding and loving it so much. I think Beauty sounds a lovely pony. Piebald ones always look so fine. Who else goes riding with you? And have you got your riding hat, and crop? Do you wear jodhpurs or corduroy trousers? Don't forget to write and tell me all about it, because I am very interested. Also, how are the piano lessons going? I suppose you find it quite easy now to read all the notes. I have still got the lovely clay horse's head which you made for me. Do you remember? I use it as a paperweight because it is always so hot here that you have to have a fan blowing – and that blows all the paper away if you haven't got a paperweight. Unfortunately*

the tip of his ear has chipped off. Otherwise he's as good as new. I'm longing to hear all about Sports Day. Do you think you can remember to ask Mummy to take photographs to send to me? Thank you darling, for saying you are glad that Mummy and I are going to have a home in Malaya. You will come out to it for next year's Summer holidays and I promise you we won't leave you alone in England for very long. I am longing to see you. With very much love from Daddy.

Q. Where was Ælene?

A. She being two years older had already gone on to St Mary's. She wrote to me often. St Mary's sounded thrilling and very grown-up, with trips to Hastings to swim, a new chapel being built, and grapefruit for breakfast on Ascension Day. The school uniform included a black velour hat, navy knickers, a gabardine raincoat, a panama hat for summer and gloves, preferably white. We had to have two pinafores for domestic use, a school tie, three table napkins and a lacrosse stick. These things were obtainable from Daniel Neal and Sons, School Outfitters, in Portman Square in London.

Q. Sounds like something out of Enid Blyton: *Fifth Form at Malory Towers.*

A. It was. The main school building had been left to the religious community by Augustus Hare, a Victorian writer, traveller and self-confessed snob. He filled the big grey stone house with treasures collected from Grand Tours of Europe – stained-glass windows, linen-fold wood panelling, collections of birds' eggs, stuffed owls and stoats; and outside on the wide stone terrace were leaden urns and statues of dogs. The original sandstone statue of Queen Anne stood in the grounds, a copy having been made and put in front of St Paul's Cathedral, where it still stands. The grounds were beautiful: huge sloping lawns and pine trees, massed rhododendrons, soft tennis courts, vegetable gardens, ponds, fields and woods. In the distance you could see the sea.

The house had been added on to again and again: long corridors with small dormitories, rambling annexes with wooden floors upstairs and down, a tiny chapel in what had been a stable, a big new chapel – the nuns' side, which was strictly out of bounds, containing their little cell-like bedrooms and religious libraries. The corridors were gas-lit. Windows were opened wide at night no matter what the weather was like; sometimes you'd wake to a room full of leaves, or flannels frozen on the washstand. You had half a small chest of drawers to put your clothes in and bells started ringing early in the morning to summon you to lessons, chapel or food. My first letter:

> *I have got masses to tell you . . . we have our lights out at a quarter to nine and we get up at seven fifteen. We have two preps each night and five at the weekends. There are forty of us in 4B so we have to be divided into 4B and 4B Parallel. I am a waitress on my table and I have washed up the supper mugs . . . the lessons are jolly easy but I hope I'm not speaking too soon . . . Mary Steele was jolly homesick but she is better now . . .*

This is the same Mary Steele who nearly got a Blue Cross pony when I was at Mickledene.

Q. Do you still see her? Do you keep up with people?

A. I can honestly say she is one of my oldest friends. All my
letters home contain news of my closest gang, Anthea,
Sarah and Mary; and when Mary got married to David
Spry, my little Jamie was her page boy; and I am godmother
to her youngest son, Oliver. After lessons had finished
and the day-girls had gone home, the boarders changed
into home clothes and mucked about – we put on plays,
swapped things, raced about in the garden, listened to
gramophone records and read books. You *never* telephoned
home, unless something was seriously wrong; in fact I
think there were only two telephones in the entire school,
one in the headmistress Sister Barbara's study and one in
the nuns' side.

We saw our parents for two Saturdays a term and for a
short half-term holiday. We were completely contained
within the school walls. On special occasions we would be
taken down to Hastings to listen to a concert or watch a
play, but otherwise our lives ended at the stone wall under
the gloomy laurel bushes, where a streetlight shone dimly
on to the waxy leaves. The outside world ceased to exist,
and all our energies were focused on the strangely intimate
community existence of 70 girls aged between 11 and 18
living in close proximity – that is to say, sometimes sleeping
with seven others in a not very big room for three months
at a time. *Big Brother* would hold no fears or attractions for
a boarding-school girl.

The Sisters of the Community of the Holy Family were
extremely tolerant of our wayward behaviour, but if I
remember rightly we were in any case, by today's standards,
paragons of courtesy and virtue. We always stood up when
a nun or lay teacher came into the room, always stood still
and flattened ourselves against the wall when a senior girl

passed by. We always wore our chapel veils to chapel three times a day: the bell would go, chapel veils were pulled hurriedly out of a pocket or desk, and tied over the hair as we raced up the winding path to the big glass doors, slowing to a reverent walk into a pew – the lovely smell of incense hanging in the air from the last time, or gusting from a newly-lit censer swinging vigorously from a nun's hand.

There were Quiet Days, and retreats and visiting missions, sung Eucharists and catechism classes, and the bells would ring the midday Angelus while we were sitting in our classrooms. We started each day of school with a lesson on religion, Old Testament or New Testament, and I got to know it all pretty well, off by heart, and all the services. I don't go to church services now because they've changed; all the language is different. I don't want the Church to change: I want the Church *not* to change – that's the whole point of religion, its changeless timelessness. Then you feel you're in a long line of people over the centuries all saying and singing the same things . . .

Q. In Latin? I don't think you sang in Latin.

A. The Book of Common Prayer, that's the one I knew. I know it was all originally in Latin or Greek or even Aramaic. (We heard the Lord's Prayer said in Aramaic in Syria, and now Mel Gibson uses Aramaic in his film *The Passion of the Christ*.) I just like to think that I'm at a service that the excellent Reverend Francis Kilvert would have recognized. I love reading his diaries of the 19th century. Anyway, in case this all sounds a bit priggish I should add that we used to laugh till we cried in chapel, in lessons, at mealtimes, anywhere. We were a very normal group of normal girls in what I see now as an exceptional educative system. We weren't stressed (wouldn't have ever considered suicide), we complained about the food, got bored, got on with it. It was an extremely happy time.

Later, the school gradually closed down: first there were no more boarders, then no day-girls; then the dwindling community of nuns moved out to an abbey in West Malling, and Augustus Hare's house and grounds were sold. The chapel has been demolished, the nuns' side too – but the house and school have been divided and converted, and new homes have been built in the gardens where our classrooms were, on top of the school vegetable garden and on the paths to the games field. Everything must change. The nuns' graveyard has been protected, where the thin iron crosses look east across the fields under the apple trees and wild flowers; the libraries are now re-homed in a beautiful old building in St Leonards; the wooden crucifix from the chapel hangs on its wall. I bet they didn't pull down Malory Towers.

Not going to drama school – not even trying to get into one after I had been turned down by RADA – was a serious error of judgement. Now, 40 years later, the pendulum has swung the other way, and casting directors often stipulate that they don't want to audition young people who have been to stage school; but in 1964 it was the only way into the profession, the only way to obtain a coveted Equity card without which you were not allowed to work. I had drifted into modelling, which gave me nail varnish, looking grown-up, travelling and good money: sometimes I earned £100 a week – all of which I frittered away on living. I saved nothing. Nobody did then: no one I knew had a pension plan or a savings account in a building society. We earned it and burned it. No one dreamed of owning a house: we rented flats and shared rooms, and many people squatted and skived their way through the sixties. Flashes of fear leapt up sometimes from your empty purse; but you'd get by, largely supported by kind and probably despairing parents.

But modelling was a good friend and a kind master to me; and for all that it was despised by the acting world, I learned about lenses and lights and composition, which stood me in good stead for a film career, as drama schools usually focused only on stage work. Confidence at auditions was largely bluffed, as was experience. So many films were being made, and television plays, and so much theatre work done, that you could fake a list of things you were in that were about to be released; nobody bothered to check up on you. Little fish in a big pond: as long as you could acquit yourself in the small parts you were offered, you could drift about in the aquarium for years.

The step from modelling to acting was made easier by Richard Johnson, a leading actor I met at a drinks party. 'I don't know how to get into films,' I said. He looked at me keenly, then said, 'I'll get you a part in something I'm filming at the moment; if it's a talking part, you'll get your Equity card.' The film was *Some Girls Do*, in which he starred with Daliah Lavi, and the line I was given was 'Yes, Mr Robinson.' Just those three words, and suddenly I was a bona fide screen actress with experience – and an agent, Terence Plunket-Greene; and the aquarium began to empty into the sea, and I had grown from a minnow to a small tench in a few days. Telescoping your life with hindsight over-reduces the long and exciting journey into a few significant snapshots. The truth is I was in several films, plays and television shows, some parts big, most small, for about nine years. Pay was poor, but life was sweet – and having a small baby to look after made choosing jobs very easy: I just took anything that was offered to me.

Each job inched me forward: a short part in *Coronation Street*, a Dracula film, *General Hospital*; but the biggest lurch in my acting life was being given the part of Purdey in *The New Avengers*. We, as a family – that is Jamie and I – were to be honest stony broke, and I had gone back to modelling for a catalogue, doing photographs in Italy. Three times I was sent for to audition for the part at Pinewood Studios, to do screen tests and rehearse action sequences; and when my heart was at its lowest, after the long journey back to Amalfi to complete the catalogue shoot, I was called to the telephone: 'Sit down, you've got the job.'

I was sharing a room with the model Sandra Soames: it was about six in the evening; we were both lying on our beds. Outside, the Mediterranean sky was pearly pink in the evening light, the sea was soft grey-blue and my life had changed. (I copied Sandra's haircut for Purdey: I asked her who had done it – a neat glossy bob with a heavy fringe – and she said it was a young hairdresser called John Frieda.)

For the next two years of my life I worked as I have never done before or since. The show had been reshaped: now Steed would have two partners, a man and a woman. Gareth Hunt was Gambit; we would assist the iconic John Steed, languidly and inimitably played by Patrick Macnee, saving the world and keeping Britain's reputation in tip-top condition. Gareth and I were trained to within an inch of our lives in stamina, kick-boxing, karate and screen fighting. I had extra ballet lessons, as Purdey had been a dancer.

The publicity machine chewed into our lunch hours and days off, as did searching for costumes and learning lines for several episodes at the same time. We filmed flat out, all the time, every day, and it was the best training I could have had: in two years we made the equivalent of 13 feature films. I loved it completely, with all my heart. After 26 episodes, the producers started work on their next project, *The Professionals*; and the New Avengers put aside the umbrella and bowler hat, the gun and the high kicks, and walked off arm-in-arm into the sunset.

Within a year I was back at work on something utterly different, still for television but this time made entirely inside a studio. It was *Sapphire and Steel*. Taxi drivers still say to me, 'You know that *Sapphire and Steel*? It really scared me.' In a way it was a forerunner of *The X-Files*: extraterrestrial people who could manipulate time and energy, bent on undoing old wrongs and sorting out ghosts. The storylines, the product of P. J. Hammond's fertile pen, were highly imaginative: the spectre of a young soldier killed after the ceasefire; figures disappearing from Victorian photographs and emerging in real life but in black and white; an injustice to be put right in a rich man's family in the thirties. David McCallum was perfect in the part of Steel ('Software and Steam' was the show's nickname). He has 'heart-throb' tattooed on his features; after working so closely with him for two years I would have added 'brainbox'. He and P.J. and our director Sean O'Riordan would huddle together working on the scripts to make them even more gripping and terrifying. As Sapphire, I had to wear vivid-blue contact lenses. (A small boy approached me at a cinema and said, 'I know how you do that with your eyes: double glazing!') With a lens covering your eyeball you don't need to blink so often, and I was able to stare into very bright lights for minutes at a time while they adjusted the blue of my irises from azure to turquoise and back. It was a very technical show, with much use of blue screen and back projection: as different as could be from the car chases, fights, floods and bombs of *The New Avengers* filmed all over Britain, and France and Canada too.

From *Sapphire and Steel* I learned the techniques of television acting, how to use your face to tell a story. McCallum always insisted that if you had to portray a sudden idea coming into your mind, or a realization that something vital was about to happen, you must *always* glance up – just for a split second: up. You can't use all the tricks all the actors use, but some you snitch and keep in your bag, like Michael Caine's not blinking, and just about anything Walter Matthau, Judi Dench and Sean Penn do. Steal and copy and make it your own; but remember you can only alter something that already exists.

Q. Who do you copy?

A. Everyone. Let's go next door.

Drawing Room

This is the drawing room. As you can see it's very tidy apart from having quite a lot of things in it.

Q. It actually looks rather cluttered.

A. When Stephen and I got married we realized we had an enormous number of books, none of which we wanted to give away. So, yes, there are books on three of the four walls and gorgeous pictures filling in the gaps . . .

Q. And some over-large furniture.

A. There are no curtains, just white-painted wooden shutters and floorboards painted white with rugs on them. I love light coming up from the ground, so when we bought this huge five-storey house we took out all the fitted carpets and painted the boards white, all the way up the stairs, everywhere nice and white underfoot.

Q. Not very practical. Also I can see that you didn't sand the floors first, so the old thick paint on each side of the stair runners leaves a sort of groove in the middle like a trench and it's all started to chip quite badly.

A. I do feel that floors are for walking on and one shouldn't be too precious about them. Also, my schoolfriend Anthea Stilwell, who is after all an artist, said she liked the way you could see the colour of the old original boards through the paint.

Q. And these three? They look new.

A. I put those boards in myself: got the timber from the local yard, measured it up, hammered them in and painted them white. This is a small kitchen dresser, painted dusty green; and filling the shelves above the cupboard are poetry books. Poetry is my box of chocolates. I don't eat many chocolates, particularly not as comfort food, but for escaping the world in a matter of seconds I read poetry. We were well taught from an early age. The schools I went to expected us to learn poems as homework, and I've never regretted anything I learned by heart when I was young. One of my earliest obsessions was with valleys; the word itself still thrills me. Songs like 'Down yonder green valley where streamlets meander' and 'Early one morning just as the sun was rising / I heard a maiden singing in the valley below', and even later songs, 'The sun always shines down in my rainbow valley' and the Sutherland Brothers' great classic 'The wind blows up the valley, the light shines down the alley' – or the other way round, actually – these are like opening a door into a secret world. The valley of the shadow of death . . . hair-raising words, three nouns linked together to paint a terrifying glimpse which will appear differently in every mind that encounters them. In my travels I've seen some spectacular valleys, in Hunza and Bhutan, Ethiopia and Austria. None, however, remains as clearly in my mind as the extraordinary location chosen for the filming of *On Her Majesty's Secret Service*.

Like a great circus coming to town, the Bond film rumbled majestically into Switzerland and up the narrow valley south of Interlaken to Mürren, where it settled for a few months in 1968. Bond films mean Bond girls, and I was chosen to be one ('cast' being the wrong word here as we didn't have characters; only our costumes distinguished the English girl from the German girl). Our part of the story was confined to one location: wicked Blofeld's mountain lair, where he was indoctrinating us with the secrets of germ warfare. Blofeld was Telly Savalas with his earlobes Sellotaped back, and Bond was George Lazenby, an Australian model plucked from a chocolate commercial who was expected to keep his head above water acting opposite the RSC's Diana Rigg.

Mürren is an astonishing little village perched high above a wide gorge in the Bernese Oberland. We arrived by train from Interlaken and took the funicular, grinding up nearly sheer mountain walls past the thin veils of the Lauterbrunnen waterfalls. As we rose out of the valley, it became apparent that we were face to face with the Eiger, Mönch and Jungfrau, so close we could almost lean out and touch them in the gold September afternoon. We changed trains and went sideways, along a perilous track through thick pine forests, with the valley darkening far below though the sun was still bright on the high hills. The first and last view of Mürren was the Palace Hotel, a gaunt grey monster right on the edge of the cliff, with no sign of life or gaiety.

There are no cars in Mürren and in those days I think there were no wheeled vehicles at all. The village had somehow been roped off from the outside world. The film company treated it like an extended sound stage at Pinewood, and paid it handsomely. But if Mürren seemed remote it was nothing to Piz Gloria, the restaurant on the peak of the Schilthorn that was being used as Blofeld's domain. Only accessible, it seemed, by cable car, it was controlled by tight security: I think we had to show passes (well *we* didn't: we were Bond girls – our false eyelashes were our identity badges). The little cable car, crammed with gaffers and sparks and cans of film, would speed up to the first stop, Birg, and then on, far over rocky valleys and chamois to the precipitous notch where we dismounted. At 10,000 feet we had to walk slowly at first in case we fainted from the thin air.

Blofeld's hideaway was opulently furnished and thickly carpeted. The Piz Gloria was ringed by range after range of mountains; the view was unparalleled, perfect – too perfect: it looked like a painted backcloth. A props man was given the task of enticing birds to fly around to show it was real, to give it 'location value'. The revolving top of the circular building was like a huge lighthouse.

Apart from eating and reading, there was not much you could do silently except write or sew. Someone showed me how to crochet, and I bought wool at the Wollstübli Gertsch in the village to make a blanket for my year-old son. Soon the little blanket grew; Wollstübli would crack its knuckles as it saw me coming, and by the time the film was over the blanket had to have its own suitcase.

Friday was our day off. Sometimes we would take a cable car to Stechelberg to reach the valley. It had – still has – the most hair-raising drop from top to bottom, almost sheer, one thin cable . . . an apocalyptic vision of the earth rushing to meet you. Interlaken, as October gave way to November, glimmered with fuggy coffee houses and shops selling chocolate hearts, wooden angels and fine gold bracelets. Often we would leave the town under a gloomy leaden sky, rattle along beside the narrow river to Lauterbrunnen and rise through the cloud to find that there was still sunshine on the Palace Hotel.

My bedroom overlooked the mountain, and once I saw the spectre of a young climber sitting on my bed undoing his boots. He turned to look at me and vanished. We wrote letters home and saved our allowance money to make occasional telephone calls. Sometimes we walked in the mountains, on paths marked '*Allmendhubel 1½ Stunde: Pletschenalp 3 Stunde*'. The stuntmen and Olympic skiers arrived, the former summoning champagne by helicopter and raising Cain at night, the latter walking like gods with muscle-bound legs, and faces sunburnt from the glaciers where the second unit was filming.

Every Wednesday was film night: one of the Palace Hotel's huge rooms was filled with chairs, a screen was erected and we would shuffle in like prisoners to be entertained. The first snows came before we left, projecting a pale unearthly light on to the great ceilings and cornices of the drawing and reading rooms. I stared and stared at the Eiger–Mönch–Jungfrau configuration, burning their contours into my mind, and was homesick for them the minute we left – in a flurry of suitcases and snowflakes on a dark December morning.

I haven't got many keepsakes from the Bond film: one poster (without my name on of course – part far too small) and a little carved wooden bear I brought back for Jamie; he was only a baby, and had started to walk in my absence, so I missed his first stumbling steps. Very recently

I mentioned this to Jane Horrocks, and told her how guilty and sad I felt not to have been with him at my parents' house when he first stood. Jane has two small children of her own: it was an overwhelming comfort when she said she didn't think it mattered a bit, and *he* couldn't remember it, and far more important things had happened when I *had* been there. As my dear friend and mentor Robert Robinson used to say when directing us at the Dundee Rep, 'If you forget your lines, or do something wrong, forgive yourself at once.'

Q. Do you forget your lines?

A. I used to have a photographic memory. I had only to glance at a page for it to be transferred, literally like a photograph, into my brain. I could turn the pages in my mind, look at illustrations, read lists. For acting it was wonderful. If someone did skip a line or in some cases a page, I could turn the script through to where they'd got to, and scan the missing bit to see if it had any vital information which would have to be worked into the next bit of dialogue. 'Your Aunt Gloria, whom I know you visited last week, probably gave you news of the family . . . perhaps she told you that Doreen was arriving tomorrow at teatime.' But when I was in my early thirties I had a dose of viral meningitis which rapidly broke my learning mechanism down. The photographs disappeared, and now I learn like most others do, covering the page with my hand and linking words and consonants to give me a clue to the next speech.

I've only gone wrong – 'dried' – once in my life and that was on stage in *The Letter*. It was hot and I hadn't eaten that day, nor drunk enough liquid: my sugar levels were low. My character had a two-page speech describing how she had to shoot a man she knew, because he was molesting her – she was lying, but her audience on stage and in the theatre didn't know that then. My brain had always dealt with this long speech fairly easily as there was a geography to her narrative: he came up to me here, I went to the window, he walked behind the sofa and so on. Just as I started, I felt as though I had had a slight stroke: my arms below the elbow and my legs below the knee started to tingle, and blood seemed to be running from my head in a rustling white sound which was almost deafening. Trying to stay upright and in character was all I could do; I swam off the text, and unable to use my photographic fail-safe device I droned on for minutes, making up a story which was utter rubbish. Like a drowning person, I finally recognized a sentence, and hauling myself up on to it I managed to stop speaking on the right line. I love actors very much; I was on stage with three giants – Tim Pigott Smith, Charles Edwards and Neil Stacey. They couldn't save me because the story I was describing had only happened to me; the looks of sympathy and waves of goodwill helped me to survive it, and a cup of tea in the interval with four spoonfuls of sugar put my energy level back on course. After that, I took in bottles of Lucozade every night. The strange thing is that when you are in the eye of the storm you can often remain completely calm; when the focus is on someone or something you can't help, you tend to feel the stress far more acutely.

I went to Kenya in my capacity as Trustee of the Born Free Foundation, to be part of a project that involved chasing and capturing six wild Rothschild giraffe, keeping them in a compound for a few days, driving them for an hour or two to another location and releasing them, to start a new breeding herd. It was just utterly thrilling and terrifying: giraffes are extremely sensitive and can easily die of shock after a seemingly triumphant relocation. The turmoil in my chest made me nearly ill with concern for several days; but the operation was a complete success and already new babies have arrived, strengthening the chances of survival for that endangered species.

I had been to Kenya before; and also I'd been lucky enough to camp in tents, and wash in canvas shower cubicles and eat round a fire. But I'd never been further north in East Africa, except when our troop-ships, in another aeon, another lifetime, crawled up the Red Sea to the Suez Canal, giving us glimpses of the Middle East's deserts and mountains, crossed by occasional camel trains and herds of goats. The Horn of Africa with its terrifying legacy of starvation became familiar only through news reportage. When Comic Relief asked me to do a short film for their appeal for Eritrea, a small country which was just emerging from a pulverizing 30-year war against its neighbour Ethiopia, I said yes in a heartbeat. The going would be tough, the journey long as we made our way from the capital, Asmara, up country through Keren, Afabet and Nacfa to Rora Habab on the high plateau, due east from Khartoum far across the border in Sudan. This is my diary: usual school exercise book, written in pencil and Biro, with drawings throughout. Would you like to hear it? I jotted it all down as I went, after each day was over, by candlelight.

Q. I have settled comfortably in this gigantic chair. Please begin.

46

A. There is always something new out of Africa: *Semper aliquid novi ex Africa* – Pliny.

30 November 1992

Asmara Airport. People clap as we touch down. Cool – 11°C – but very bright and clear blue sky. Ululations from women waiting to greet people off the plane. Rich Eritreans are searched thoroughly; one couple had to open all five huge bulging suitcases. Buy postcards. Delay over luggage. We hear the airstrip in Nacfa is flooded – unheard of – our onward flight is delayed. We will go into Asmara. Airport is small, humble building with signs handwritten in perfect English. Buy poster celebrating Eritrea's freedom; Zeremariam – Zere for short – translates:

> *Hallelujah, Hallelujah, let those who died rest in peace. The mighty forces could not resist our brave men.*
> *They believe in the numbers of the soldiers and weaponry but we have faith in God and our heroic Children.*
> *The Eritrean is like a black lion and protects his country.*
> *Hallelujah, Hallelujah.*
> *Thanks to her Children Eritrea's suffering and troubles have ended. May those who died for the cause rest in Peace.*
> *A 30-year-long dream has been realized.*

The income from this poster will be given to the war wounded and the orphans and the reconstruction of the country.

Picture of tiger and Saracen shields. Faces are beautiful; Arabic and Asmaric are official languages. Terrifically old script. In Asmara over hotel door: 'Welcome to independent Free Eritrea'; lunch in hotel – vegetable soup, spaghetti, white fish from the Red Sea. Beer. Italian influence – Mussolini colonized Eritrea; the British liberated it during Second World War under Bill Slim and handed Eritrea to Ethiopia and Haile Selassie to keep it tidy. Sally and I walk in Asmara – down National Street – many churches and some mosques. Boy in excellent English directs us back to hotel. He lost three cousins in the war but 'all was for our country'. We can't fly north so three Ladas arrive and we stash everything in and drive off. I travel with Will and Zere. Soon the country becomes hilly and mountainous. Practically no trees or even scrub – what trees there are are imported eucalyptus which flourish and grow quickly, good for firewood. Raining lightly.

Pass glossy herds of goat and fat-tailed sheep and fit cows and gleaming donkeys. Later, creamy camels laden with brushwood, straw or sacks. Road is littered with burnt-out tanks, unexploded shells, wrecked vehicles from the war. People see the rain as a gift from heaven to celebrate peace. Road ruined by wartime tanks and soon turns to caramel powder sand. Stunning views. Doves have maroon eye patches and plum-coloured iridescent wings. Pass children and girls and women of exceptional beauty. Pure Arab to pure Negro.

We descend from Asmara at 7,000 feet to lower valleys – more trees, mango and citrus, rocky riverbeds. Huge mountainous escarpment leads steeply down to Red Sea on our right. Evening comes, sky and earth go peach red, crimson; flocks of sheep going home. Arrive Keren – lovely clean little town, quite Italianate, unlike marvellous mud-brick straw-thatched houses in small villages. Into Keren hotel. First-, second- or third-class bedrooms. No first available: I choose third – clean nice room, two beds, candle, window on to wide street, bougainvillaea. Drink at bar across road, eat supper – spaghetti, eggs, meat, local wine, water, good coffee; for eight people costs £2 a head. Beds for the night are £1 each. No hot water, wash under tap. Zere's family live here. Kitten in bougainvillaea meows again and again. Very lame hunchback slowly crosses the wide street. Up tomorrow early – 5.30 to leave at 6. Have started on vodka. At supper the white wine was whisky-coloured – undrinkable. The red wine was OK. Red – four months old; white – badly corked and six years old.

1 December

Set off very early. Woken by muezzin call just before dawn. Get up by candlelight. Keren looking sublime. Strong coffee and orange – climb on to wire tower to take pictures. Set off for Afabet, scene of a pivotal battle in the war when the rebel forces overthrew the Russians. Drive through spectacular mountains – unmade roads, rocks and sand. Camels everywhere – man with three pretty wives on top, one of them with child, one with two tiny baby goats, and gold ornament in her nose. Nomads everywhere – pastoralists is their name. Their yurts (dwellings) are cloths and skin thrown over skeletal wooden frames and look like armadillos crouching by identical boulders. Stop to take photographs and do first shot in grim steep valley filled with rusting tanks and armoured cars; two pastoralists under a tree tell Zere that they witnessed the slaughter – 18,000 men. There are makeshift cemeteries – mounds of stone sometimes marked with prayer flags on sticks. The Eritreans camped out in pickets and had eagle's-eye view of road; Will, Zere and I push on leaving the others to do more shots. Drive on up hugely steep and unsuitable roads – past old army redouts dug into the hills now filled with people and goats. Valleys full of fat-trunked gnarled baobabs, thorn trees, blue thistles, lovely white lilies and yellow daisies which no animal eats. Afabet was full of ex-soldiers, several still with Kalashnikovs on their shoulders. Nacfa hardly exists – bombed almost to extinction except for the minaret of the mosque which still stands and is being kept as a memorial. People lived and held fast here, schools and makeshift hospitals underground, sandal and sanitary towel factories. The freedom-fighter girls are hellish tough and smile for no one. They and the boys have distinctive Afro haircuts – chaps very friendly, also old women, children, men, everyone friendly but freedom girls, who wear trousers and scowls. During the war, women soldiers were not permitted to guard prisoners as they shot them dead directly.

We start to track down Tsegai Isak, Dept of Agriculture. People a bit vague as to where he is. We drove over *nullahs* (dry riverbeds) (with some water – rain here recently, hence shut airstrip) into mountain hideaway. There under prickly pears three Massey Ferguson tractors and small huts camouflaged in the hilly rocks. Eventually after a phenomenal amount of toing and froing we all assemble in what had been a flourishing market-place – now a dusty *padang* (square) with goats' feet underfoot and goatskins around drying on twigs; *chai* (tea) stalls. Debate about pressing on to Rora Habab as it's getting towards evening and the hills have vanished in black rainy clouds – we sit and drink excellent very sweet peppermint tea in cloth-slung shelter. Light dies.

We sit and talk as our new tougher vehicles (two Toyota pick-ups, one short-based Land-Rover and a deadly Lada Riva) hurtle round the village collecting petrol from the militia. We decide to stay in Nacfa, and repair to the original ministry dwellings and unload all over again into the guest house. We will sleep four to a room on sweet-smelling straw mats. We brew up spag. and tomato sauce, drink wine, vodka and discover unbelievably a TV set and video. There is an electric light bulb – but it's crouching under cacti for rest-room facilities. Wash up in shampoo and eked-out boiled water. Put plates at window to dry. We will rise before dawn for two-and-half-hour last-haul drive to Rora Habab. One driver (to be avoided) did 180-degree skid for no reason. All play deafening heavy-metal music on cassettes in vehicles.

The veranda at the guest house has wooden slats arranged vertically to make windows, with four fat supports which are gleaming shell cases which have notches to support overhead beams.

2 December

Dark wakening after a fitful night. Most of us wake up every half-hour. My borrowed sleeping-bag is ultra efficient – have to unzip and sleep ajar. In our dormitory Mark feeling pains – fed him Fybogel; Zere, Will, Bill sleeping on my anorak, and me. Breakfast is powdered coffee and an orange. Load up vehicles and set off. I go with Gerry in deadly Lada. Much of the journey is made up riverbeds – incredibly tough country.

Half an hour on we pass young boys drilling on earthen parade ground in the hills for national service. Fresh, lovely flowers. Exquisite land quickly gives way to rocky mountain valleys. Remote: stone dwelling and tiny vegetable patches built into scabby thorny hills. We climb and climb, over boulders and hellish rutted dirt tracks. Our Lada boils as we climb and we decant into other vehicles. We are giving a lift to three Eritreans who ride shotgun with Russian rifles. Huge vistas of wrinkled velvet hills – ghastly rocky shaly road, precipitous drops; we really go mad at one desperate corner. Soon we go over last ridge and are on the plateau of Rora Habab.

It is Registration Day – there will be a referendum about the future of the country in April 1993 (foregone conclusion EPLF – Eritrean People's Liberation Front – will win; it is essential, however, to be accepted politically and diplomatically world-wide). People have come from miles around – nomads as well – to answer a complicated form and have Polaroid picture and thumbprint if you can't write. Because EPLF was very active in rural areas, and Rora Habab was a huge centre during the war, the news network about the important day is 100 per cent effective. Rora Habab was bombed dreadfully – it is a high vast alpine land. People had to work their fields and herds by night or at dawn or dusk. During daylight hours everyone stayed hidden. For 30 years of war and seven of drought they hung on, dutifully planting crops and trees, building reservoirs, making hundreds of miles of terracing, setting up health and education centres with aid from Comic Relief and other charities. No rain. Just when they started to despair – all crops and herds dead, people starving – the war ended and at once rain came and the first harvest was the best in living memory.

We are in a guest house – very primitive: two rooms and small cookhouse behind. We film a farmer and wife and friends harvesting wheat – four sweet, small children – lunch was a Bounty and an orange and water. Whacked at the end of day. Try to sort out sleeping arrangements, five in 10 × 10 room. Supper ready – rice, tomatoes, onions and chickpeas – excellent. We make a fire on the little veranda and watch stupendous sunset behind colossal hills stretching for miles and miles over Africa. Sleep – Gerry, Fraser on the floor, Sally and I on a kind of enlarged mantelpiece. V. uncomfortable. Forgot to mention – Banana à la Rora Habab: take half-bottle bourbon, toss into blackened saucepan, add one hand of bananas and two teaspoons honey; dash of flat mineral water – leave for seven minutes on medium bonfire. Stir with teaspoon attached to a stick. Tilt into flame occasionally to ignite. Eat from aluminium cup. When Sally gave the farmer Osman's children some Sainsbury's bull's-eyes they just held them like trophies.

3 December

We all seemed to have been awake all night – but overslept and finally got up at 6.00. Rapid breakfast – the usual coffee, orange and biscuit – and off to film. Stop across the plateau on our way to meet Satel, the woman whom we are going to interview. Flawless mountains. Do a piece to camera about dead trees and

drought. Splendid man, Musa Omar Ali, in white cloth-
ing with sword, stops on road and is filmed. I find a
basking lizard with turquoise hands, feet and tail and
photograph him. A small bird, like large black wren with
white cap, sings stupendously from tippy-top of tree on
top of hill.

Get to Satel's place and walk down lugging equipment
to film interview. She is very beautiful and has fluent
account of life during the war and drought. Her brother
was killed, and bomber planes strafed the valleys round
her small farm. Boys – one aged nine guarded the goats,
and the eight-year-old walked for four hours every day
to school. After the interview I gave her presents – pens,
balloons, balls, Biros, scissors, sewing kit. She said next
time I came she would have an apron ready for me.
Walk back in hellish heat to trucks. Average speed on
roads here 7 mph. Return for lunch (biscuits, oranges,
tea and bananas) and film three pieces to camera. Sudden
cloud rushes over hill making it seem like Mull of Kin-
tyre. Film village elder and give him shirt, scissors and
bag, give administrator a shirt. Elder says they are poor
people but when we return we will have their present
for us. Administrator says it's the thought that counts.

Do last piece to camera in cornfield with sheaf and
photographs. Our drivers laze like Brueghel peasants on
corn-sheaves. Back for sunset drink – red ribbons of sky;
prepared supper – potatoes, tomatoes, garlic, wine, rice
– best food. Zere says we can visit the schoolmaster
tonight to give presents. Last night (and tonight) we fed
the drivers, walking over the rocks in the moonlight to
smoky stone rooms with a tin saucepan of rice and beans
and tomatoes. They've learnt my name: 'Joanna!' –

'*Shakram! Salaam aleikum!*' Satel was truly thrilled with her presents.

4 December

Woke Sally at 1.30 a.m. thinking it was time to get up – but it was the chaps carousing the night away. Woke again and got up at 4.30 a.m. to pack and leave – covered with flea bites – packing in dust and dark and loading trucks in pitch darkness; saw two shooting stars. Pleiades had slipped down to horizon in west, Orion's Belt just above, fading as dawn came up. Everyone feeling frail. Drive off and see sunrise from top of escarpment. Begin a hellish journey downhill, but it has rained and new flowers and birds are out. Two hoopoes, and beaky toucan-like chaps.

At Nacfa no plane. Much toing and froing and we are somehow crammed into three cars: two Toyotas and a Lada. See goat with twins born two minutes before. Drive off on second leg to Ad Chrum, take more snaps of tanks. Bash on to Afabet, get stuck in riverbed, jolted witless. Will, Brian, Gerry riding shotgun like refugees. Bash on to Keren, drink cappuccinos that are just sweet hot milk and eat fresh bread. It's 4.30 and evening approaches. Have seen sword dancing and wedding procession – market day everywhere. As we go up the ghastly road a truck has gone over the edge – no one hurt, great delay. Darkness. Road closed to let more trucks down. Zere's jeep gets a puncture. Our driver is nearly dead with tiredness and Sal and I quiz him on his life to keep him awake and on the roads, which are worse than you could dream of. Arrive Amba Soira hotel at 8.45 p.m., eat good supper, have hot baths, shake

dust from shoes etc. Home tomorrow. Dogs barking in
Asmara night – cold under a thin mist. Must pack and
leave at 7.30 a.m.

Q. Have you been back to get the apron from Satel?

A. No. I think about her a lot – her little empty mud-floored
hut with almost nothing in it, but as neat and clean as could
be. Her boys will be grown-up. I don't know how to go
back.

Q. Just go. All these things, all these regrets, and you set your
mouth in that self-pitying letterbox shape and say you can't
. . . why not?

A. Life just gets hold of you and you find you're being galloped
off in another direction. If I had to describe my character,
at the top of the list I would write 'willing to learn'. I
would have to add 'rather reactive as opposed to proactive'
which means that I usually do what other people suggest
rather than thinking up things myself. If nobody ever asked
me to do anything again I would be found here, in exactly
this position, covered with dust, waiting for my next
orders. This is partly complacency, partly idleness, mostly
aimlessness. I have no ambition, except to do what I do
better. Someone I hardly knew once suggested that it
would bring me great benefits if I were to sit down and
write a letter of love and admiration to myself and post it
in a self-addressed envelope. When it arrived, he assured
me, I would gain confidence, regard myself highly and be
able to get on. I took fright before I even wrote 'Dear
Jo . . .': I couldn't think of a word to say. I write many

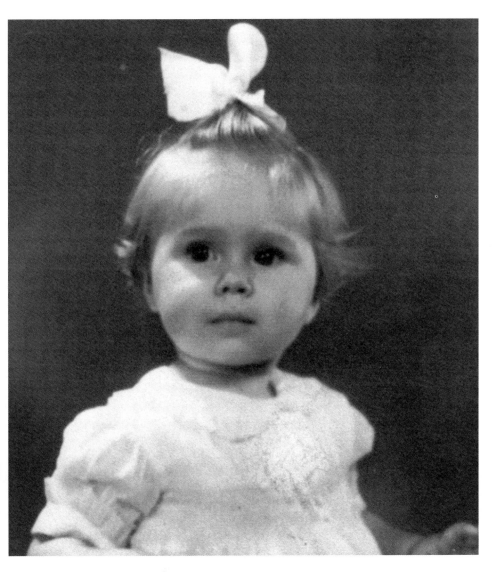

In India aged one.

I was an eternally cheerful child.

On board troop-ship with cousins (left to right): Ayah, Reay, Ælene, Maybe, me.

The Weir women (left to right, back row): Beatrice, Joan Mary, Great-Aunt Dagmar, Maybe. (Left to right, front): Jo, Thyra Weir (seated), Ælene. Taken by Uncle Ivor in Count Lodge Farm. A *thangka* from Tibet hangs behind Maybe.

Mummy on trek, 1942.

Daddy on Juhu Beach, India.

Daddy just before my parents got
married in Srinagar, 1941.

Mummy aged 20 in India.

Aged 11. The picture 'Hooter' ordered.

With Mickledene schoolfriends.
In the back row, Mary Steele
and I are in the centre.

Mickledene School:
our classrooms were in
the oast houses.

School House from Playing Field, Mickledene.

Sarah, Anthea, me and Mary on the terrace steps at St Mary's.

With Anthea and
Sarah and statue of
Queen Anne.

In Carmel,
summer term.
Anthea and Sarah.

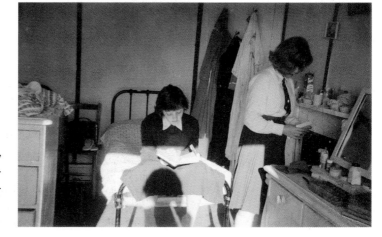

With Ælene and
Maybe during school
holidays, 1957.

Being insufferable
at school, 1960.

letters every week, so it wasn't for not knowing how; it was just, for me, a shocking proposition. Why? 'Keep going, old stick' was about all I could muster, and that was hardly worth the price of a stamp. It is as though I'm standing in a market-place with nothing much left to sell on the stall, smiling at everyone, buffing my nails, just being there. Something always comes along, and suddenly you find you have embarked on a new adventure, never at all what you would have expected to happen. Sometimes it's to do with acting; many times it's not.

Christopher Dowling of the Imperial War Museum asked me to write a book to accompany their forthcoming exhibition Forces Sweethearts in 1993. In fact he had asked Jilly Cooper, but she couldn't fit it in as she was so busy and lived far out of London. She sweetly suggested me – and wrote a foreword for the book. (I've known Jilly since I appeared in her sitcom *It's Awfully Bad for Your Eyes, Darling* . . . for the BBC in 1971. In those days, as the credits rolled a voice intoned, 'Joanna Lumley is also appearing in *Don't Just Lie There, Say Something* at the Garrick Theatre, London.')

The exhibition and book were to be about wartime romance from the First World War to the Gulf. A space was cleared for me in one of the museum's offices: my desk was next to that of the distinguished historian Malcolm Brown. Letters were coming in daily from all over the country and abroad following our appeal for contributions from the public, and Penny Ritchie Calder, Head of Exhibitions, had already assembled a mass of suitable material for me to consider. Documents that belong to the museum are not allowed to leave the building, but I was allowed to make photocopies to take home, where I did most of the writing at night.

One story from the archives in particular stood out, showing the kind of love and loss experienced in the First World War. The love of Will Martin and Emily Chitticks was told in letters, dating from before their engagement until Will's death in France in 1917 when Emily was 20 years old. I wrote to ask the donor for permission to use the correspondence and received this charming letter in reply:

> *Dear Miss Lumley,*
>
> *I am replying to your letter addressed to my late husband, Don Williams. What a wonderful idea – the exhibition and your book. Perhaps I should explain that we were not related to Miss Chitticks or Will Martin. My husband, as Deputy Housing Manager of Brentwood Urban District Council at the time, had the task of removing the effects of Miss Chitticks from her council bungalow. Her only relative, a niece, apparently had no interest in her papers. Don, who had a keen sense of history, couldn't bring himself to destroy them, and several years later offered them to the Imperial War Museum. (I had, by then, shed tears over them many times.)*
>
> *Perhaps, now, their inclusion in your book will afford this young couple a kind of immortality otherwise denied them.*
>
> *My best wishes to the project, and my thanks to you for writing. Don died in 1985 – please don't feel that your letter reopened a recent wound.*
>
> *Yours sincerely, Helena Williams*

So Will and Emily came home with me. The photocopied material was spread out over the dining-room table, with all the other letters, poems and photographs, for the difficult task of selecting the most suitable for the book. The nights were long and quiet and completely absorbing. I was aware of people standing behind me in the darkness, out of the pool of light on the table, just behind my chair.

Q. Ghosts?

A. I don't know. It just didn't feel as though I was alone. Some presences stayed longer than others and seemed to be more tangibly in the room, rather than in my head.

Q. But you do admit to having a vivid imagination, and a willingness to embrace the paranormal?

A. Yes – but the nature of the writing, quite often where I seemed to be a third person, between the writer and the recipient, and the fact that the love and death – and sometimes betrayal – were so intense, meant that the reson- ances really got to me. The disturbing factor in the Will and Emily story was a little note she had written on 6 June 1917, just over a month after Will had been killed by sniper fire and her letters returned marked 'Killed in Action'. The note, found by Don Williams with the letters, read as follows:

> Sacred to the memory of my Darling Sweetheart Will, the only boy I love with my whole heart and soul, who loved me so well he gave his all, his life for me. When I die, I wish all his letters to be buried with me as my heart and love are buried in his grave in France.

But this note and the letters were found *after* Emily had been buried, still single, aged 76; and now the letters belonged to the Imperial War Museum and could not be released, as is the custom. The book *Forces Sweethearts* was published in 1993; the exhibition, and therefore the book, was a huge success. But nagging in the back of my mind was a small voice saying that somehow I must fulfil Emily's wish. So the kind museum allowed me to photocopy all the letters – 75 of Will's and 23 of Emily's. I brought them home, trimmed them so they looked the same size and shape as the originals and tied them up with a blue satin ribbon.

Finding out where Emily was buried was made easy by the kindness and efficiency of Brentwood Borough Council and the Cemeteries Administration. Mrs Gladys Warren and I talked on the telephone and arranged to meet, with Helena Williams, at noon on 28 June 1993 to bury the letters in Brentwood Cemetery. I remember the day as being a bit grey. We met in the car-park; we had all dressed smartly and I felt very jittery with a beating heart. We were led to the grave, which had no headstone: number J3, in common ground. Nearby, but a little way off, stood the grave-digger. The freshly-turned earth showed where he had made a small place for the interment. I said a few words and put the package of letters into the ground. My throat was so constricted I could hardly speak. I'd brought along a basket of silk flowers which we put on Emily's grave; and then we all went off to a nearby pub and had a drink and talked and talked.

Q. Did you cry? Don't you always cry at funerals?

A. We all cried a bit. It had been very moving; we, as strangers, remembering other strangers, rather like Remembrance Day at the Cenotaph. Gladys wrote to me afterwards:

The basket of flowers has been placed in the Chapel with a brief outline of the story. I have enclosed a copy and trust it will meet with your approval. This and the little card you placed in the basket have been laminated. Mrs Williams returned to the offices with us, and several staff had a quick glance through your book which Mrs Williams luckily had with her. A huge interest was shown, and tears were shed . . .

The story of Will and Emily still haunts me, but the lovers don't any more. After this tying up of loose threads and making an end to it, they stopped coming to the dining room at dead of night, even though I listened out for them.

Q. Do you like writing?

A. It's a very good feeling to have completed a book, an article or even a short foreword to a book. The process itself, as anyone will tell you, can be fairly agonizing – as much as anything, finding the voice you will use. Often it should be your own; sometimes slightly less personal and more formal. Obviously, doing a book like this, or describing a journey or event you have been involved in yourself, you must sound like the person other people recognize. Winston Churchill's advice about painting – don't be afraid of the blank canvas, show it who's master, splash the stuff on – is very valuable. You can think yourself into a deep hole and come to the conclusion that there's no point in even starting. It's much easier to write about something that has actually happened recently, particularly if you keep diaries. I always take an exercise book with me on journeys; even things you think you will never forget can fade away or get crowded out by more recent memories. I've done two books for the BBC inspired by two documentaries I made for them: *Girl Friday* was the first.

Q. Desert-island stuff?

A. Exactly. It was the first programme of its kind in a way, and it seemed sensible to us all that it had to be a fairly tough assignment to be worth watching or writing about. I wasn't allowed to take anything that could make life easier: no music or books, no toothbrush or soap, no camera (except a video camcorder to record my end-of-day thoughts), very few clothes, no towel, no sunglasses, no hand cream, no alcohol or tobacco. No sleeping bag or tent: I had to construct an A-frame bed from poles and, when the rains came down, sleep in a cave filled with volcanic razor-blade rocks. Fires were made from kindling and driftwood – which I prepared carefully with my two sharp knives – and lit with my flint-striker. In fact, I lived like an animal; as the days went by I found I could see in the dark, know when the tide was turning, predict to a second when the rain would fall. In such a short time I had found all my old unused instincts, which mankind must have had for ever but hardly uses in the developed world.

Without radio or television my mind roamed freely, and half-remembered poems and songs bubbled up in my brain. I was never bored – hungry, tired, despairing, ecstatic, inventive, but never bored. The lasting achievement I keep in this drawer of the tallboy – there! My bra shoes, made by stitching my bra to the insoles of my trainers, to protect my feet from the slashing rocks inside my cave. I love them and would like them to be buried with me . . .

Q. . . . don't *you* start . . .

A. . . . or actually I shall leave them to a museum. Or my family. Or perhaps they can just stay in the drawer. Here's the coconut-shell ladle I made; here is the big shell I used as my dish and the little shell I used as my spoon; and here's my shell necklace on green army twine.

Q. Can I just poke about in this drawer a bit . . . sewing baskets, bits of Indian silk, old 1930s jet decorations, a tin with a girl holding a rabbit on it, containing hundreds of buttons – do you do any needlework? Or, as they asked Princess Anne when she became engaged to Captain Mark Phillips, will you darn your husband's socks?

A. To mend a rip in a jersey is very satisfying. I am good at mending, bad at making. But good at bra shoes! And sewing roses on hats! Very good at fiddling about. It was an easy pleasure, a mad rush but wonderful, to write up my diary from the island into a book. I worked night and day for three weeks as they wanted it done almost straight away. I wish it wasn't out of print.

Q. May I sit down on this white-covered sofa? Near this over-large white coffee table which looks like a normal kitchen table with the legs sawn off?

A. It is. But even though there is a lot of ivory-white there are colourful cushions, and glorious paintings and of course the books, and objects of every kind – dishes, sets of scales, a bronze model of a bear, a photograph of Stevie as a little boy in a wooden frame, statues, a wooden toy duck, a large swan and a Sarawak hat. These two pictures are done in pastels, both of *dzong*s, or monasteries, in Bhutan. My mother's mother, Thyra Laetitia Alexandra Weir, did them when she went with my grandfather on his diplomatic journeys. The wooden trunk under the window, covered with books – look what is stencilled on its side: WEIR. Rope handles. It went on the back of a yak across Bhutan in the 1930s with my grandfather, Colonel Leslie Weir, who was the Political Officer in Sikkim at the time. His duties were many, in his roles as administrator, ambassador and adviser. He had been invited (in the most friendly terms) to visit the King of Bhutan, and it was decided that he should present the King with the insignia of the KCIE – Knight Commander of the Most Excellent Order of the Indian Empire. The journey they made, with over a hundred pack animals alone, was in midwinter and would take two months – luckily for us, much of it was recorded on flickery black and white film and in stunning photographs.

My cousin Maybe and I took the idea of a documentary to Harry and Laura Marshall of Icon Films, and the BBC commissioned us to follow in the footsteps of our grandparents – and I would write a book about it: *In the Kingdom of the Thunder Dragon*. It was for both Maybe and me an unforgettable time – incredibly moving, fairly tough (but nothing like the hardships of climate the earlier travellers had to endure) and, as luck would have it, in the nick of time. Without my wanting to sound too gloomy, the fact that Bhutan now receives television programmes means it will be dragged into the wider world. Seventy-five years ago it was shrouded in mystery, its doors and borders closed to almost all foreigners, a country veiled in secrecy, known only to itself. When we went in 1997, a few noblemen had video recorders, but the children we met everywhere were as different as can be from the young in the West: there seemed to be energy, courtesy, curiosity, good humour, high spirits – fit little bodies, used to hard physical work and walking miles every day, bright faces which looked straight into your own. I've painted them as saints, and I don't mean to. I just think it would be better if our children didn't watch so much television. Stop looking at screens, start looking at faces. That's my slogan.

Q. And a very un-catchy one it is too, if I may say. You sound very passionate about these expeditions. Here's a pile of folders marked 'India', 'Hunza', 'Kenya', with notes and diaries and drawings inside. You must be pleased to have written two travel books.

A. I am in love with travelling and with books – also with travel books: books to read whilst travelling and books as secret personal journeys. Ever since in childhood I hacked in desperation with my Bowie knife to try to save Injun Joe from his ghastly bat-fed death, or listened to the wind blowing in the fir trees as I lay on my straw bed with Heidi, I have known that I could travel everywhere in the world, skip through centuries, experience glory and terror all in my own head, all through books. Everyone reading this reads books, so there's no need to over-egg the custard; but struggle with me along a sustained metaphor of books as travel. They are at the same time travel agent, courier, packhorse and adviser. First the dust jacket, titled, beckoning you inwards, advertising its wares with alluring designs, stark or twiddly lettering, vivid or subtle colouring . . . come on in! See what I've got inside! Then upon opening it you meet the sleeve notes, summarizing the contents, a wish-you-were-here to tempt you. Is there a photograph of the writer (your guide and dragoman)? Yes; and look – he/she's got a dog, a pearl necklace, a thick jersey, a wryly humorous expression; this will be a trusty companion. Chapter One! We have lift-off. Now the journey itself has begun.

Turning my face into the sun as the path leads steeply upwards, I take a short walk (Eric Newby) towards precipitous places clinging to the handrails of humour. The view is over vast open plains of Africa or Tartary (Wilfred Thesiger and Peter Fleming), deserts which seem to have no end; through Central Europe and the Baltic States to the lip of Asia (Patrick Leigh Fermor, Fitzroy Maclean), taking the eastern approach between the woods and the water. Now the mountains loom ahead, impossibly high, probably Himalayan, causing us to lean on our sticks, holding our hammering hearts as we survey that undiscovered land from the roof of the world (Eric Shipton and Peter Hopkirk); but below us, in Caribbean heat and rain, the Malayan monsoon gathers and breaks (V.S. Naipaul and W. Somerset Maugham, not travel writers as such but what the heck), banana leaves and Mr Biswas dripping in the sunset of a rubber plantation. And rattling past in solitary splendour on an ill-lit train comes Colin Thubron, who has learnt the language and can translate for you as you go. They are your friends and you, a complete stranger, are theirs. They wrote their books for you. It doesn't matter if you lose your way and turn back a few pages because the jeep will still be waiting, with its engine running, for you to drive on or pitch your camp for the night.

What were the earliest travel books I read? The Bible, I suppose, with huge journeys but not many of the geographical descriptions I crave: the odd mention of a hill or plain, sea or cave. And then Caesar's *Gallic Wars*, a Roman general fighting his way through France – but his main concerns were with army formations and how to storm a castle. Early explorers are the heroes of this genre, their logs and diaries revealing the splendours and hardships of an undiscovered world.

There is no shadow of doubt in my mind that books as cut-price travel are the best value for money in history (apart from a box of matches: when you think of the little box with its cleverly fitting drawer, striking pad, separate matches beautifully laid side by side, a motto, joke or exhortation – well, one totters with gratitude). No traveller is complete without a book, and no journey is so slight or so immense that it cannot provide a decent basis for some delicious observations. One of my most treasured travel books, published in 1876, is *The Indian Alps and How We Crossed Them* by Nina Mazuchelli, an insanely daring and ill-prepared expedition in the eastern Himalayas. On the gold-embossed cover her name doesn't appear, just 'by a Lady Pioneer'. The book is spotted, browned but not shaved, silked or made-up; slightly rubbed, but the joints are not cracked; not washed or guarded, but not sophisticated: in fact, rather like me.

I can remember sitting aged four cross-legged on the polished wooden floor of the school hall, saying 'A says a, B says ber, C says . . .', and my sister's class passing the back of the hall. I raised my eyes at her in silent resignation to show how bored I was by such childishness, for I could already read.

Ælene, my sister aged six and for ever two years older than me, could not only read but did so all the time. She read every day and every night, whenever we had rests, at meals and on the long sea voyages to and from the Far East. She read anything and everything, like a beetle boring through wood, like – well, a bookworm. I occupied myself by driving her mad while she batted me away like a tsetse fly. Oh, I read a bit too; but I was still with Enid Blyton's *Sea of Adventure* when she was well into Dickens. Kipling's *Just So Stories*, written for reading aloud, were wonderful to listen to, but somewhat creepy as well. There is a strange world outside the nursery door, and even kind Rupert Bear knew the value of hair-raising villains and risk of death by drowning. Tea after these adventures seemed a just reward for the Nutwood pals.

Little by little, I began reading for pleasure. Ælene, now with Thackeray and Jane Austen, had left me far behind, and I dawdled happily through Andrew Lang's Fairy books and *The Golden Treasury* towards Farjeon, Walter de la Mare and C. S. Lewis's Narnia books. Richmal Crompton's *William* was waiting. Wanting to be a boy, I identified with Jennings and Darbyshire in Anthony Buckeridge's school stories.

I suppose the real change came during English O level when our set book was *Pride and Prejudice* – prep was to read a chapter at a time. I read it as a duty, grumbling under my breath, slamming the book shut after each session. When I had thus plodded through it, I thought I might just have a look at it again. The second time I flew through it, gulping it down, ashamed of my appalling misjudgement of Austen's text. Leslie Charteris's 'Saint' books were on our bedside tables by then, and Agatha Christie was everywhere. I was so taken by the plot of *Ten Little Indians* that I read it straight through, aloud, to my dormitory, by torchlight, finishing at half-past three in the morning. They blearily agreed it was brilliant.

Sleep and reading are linked tightly together: reading in bed, or sitting reading on a child's bed; nodding off at your own voice, with a sharp little whisper prompting, 'You've read that page twice, you've skipped some.' At rest, after lunch at first school, we lay on our backs (were hands allowed behind heads?), legs uncrossed, in sardine-like rows while a gentle, adenoidal young mistress read *Heidi* to us. What thrills me as much as anything is this: give or take an inch or two, a line or two, material on the cover, the kind of typeface used, most books are the same. They stand fairly evenly side by side. If they are wrapped up as presents, you grope the package and think, 'Ah, a book.' And yet, within this unchanging discipline – roughly 36 lines to a page, words divided by paragraphs and chapter headings, credits at the front, glossaries at the back – from this seemingly unimaginative and conservative set-up, springs all that is thought and discovered and created and dreaded and lauded and imagined. All you have to be able to do is read. There are books in every room of the house.

Kitchen

We're just going to go down to the kitchen, past the garden door and the downstairs lavatory.

Q. Lots more pictures and drawings even in there – studies in pencil of a bird's head, a map of part of Scotland, trees; a chalk drawing of a wooden chair with a tiny child's shoe on it . . .

A. . . . and there are more here, going down steeply. Careful, there's no banister. We'll put a rail of some sort for when we get older or we'll have to crawl. Circus people, given to me by Betty Jackson; two Edward Lear sketches of Albania; and this is the childhood wall – all pencil or ink drawings, the greatest number of which are Edward Ardizzone's enchanting cross-hatched illustrations for R. L. Stevenson's book of poetry for children, *Home from Sea*. There are drawings of children by Jehan Daly and a study of penknives, and this watercolour of my two great-great uncles looking at a birdcage when they were eight or nine. This is the drawing John Ward did of Jamie when he was twelve – he drew him in his lovely cluttered studio in Kent and you can see familiar landmarks that turn up in many of John's paintings: a classical bust with a straw hat slung on, a low day-bed and, by chance, this beautiful birdcage, at which Jamie is staring intently while the canaries hop and peck inside. He's a wonderful model – perhaps because I trained him when he was very small, perhaps because he has the right quality of stillness. I used to pay him 10 pence an hour to sit for me. When he was in hospital waiting to have his wisdom teeth dug out from his dear little jaw I sat and drew him while he read; I drew him watching the television, holding toys, submerged under safari hats. He's a photographer now like his father; his early skills as a child model, exploited for pennies by his stingy mother, are paying dividends now he's the other side of the lens, or pencil. He never complained about sitting still for so long even though he was longing to rush off to play football.

The darkest times for me and him were when I was in a play. My leaving for the theatre always coincided with bedtime when he was little: just as he started on a long interesting story about something that happened that day in school (he was at the excellent Fox School in Notting Hill Gate) I would start to leave, dragging my feet, going as slowly as I could, desperate to hear his news, terrified of being late for the 'half', the 35-minute call before the curtain goes up. 'Please don't go, Mummy, please don't go!' It was agony. But whichever au pair was with me at the time was there to soothe him and read a story. I wonder if all parents have an abiding sense of guilt that we have somehow done it all wrong, even with the most loving intentions. Most of us, I suspect, just do the best we can and muddle through – and are forgiven by our children who can't remember these gloomy episodes with anything like the clarity of our tortured adult recollections. Lovely wall of childhood drawings; none of mine is good enough to hang here between Christian Birmingham and Stanley Spencer.

Q. It's rather a dark place to hang all these works.

A. Look, there's not an enormous amount of wall space left anywhere. Pictures are nice rammed together, and people hoping to have a handrail can stop and pretend they were looking – and as they go slowly by, they do love to see them at such close quarters and soon forget the vertigo. Past a coatrack of wrought iron, supporting many coats and fleeces and hats . . . and here is the kitchen.

When we moved here 12 or more years ago the owners had the house in peak condition – everything fixed and in good working order, so no need to rewire or repoint or do plumbing – nothing needed doing, it looked so lovely. So why change the kitchen? It seemed to me, who started off with a second-hand cooker rented from the gas board, that this was just utterly gorgeous, with an oven with a light and a separate hob and so on. Honestly, you couldn't ask for more – why get new stuff when this works? What makes people throw out their completely functioning appliances and buy stuff that wouldn't look out of place in Gordon Ramsay's kitchen? You can cook for 20 on these gas rings.

Q. No need to snap. Horses for courses. What a nice checked oilcloth on the table.

A. We both love cooking but, as is the way with many men, Stevie is better at it than I am. He has the patience to follow a recipe exactly and therefore everything he cooks tastes different, whereas mine tends to taste the same. Same old favourite spices, same structure of a meal. But I cut recipes out of magazines and newspapers, and I cook meat and fish for other people. I love curries and poppadums and chapattis. And coconut cream, cumin seeds and garam masala. I'm drooling now. I wish we were sitting down now to a huge table full of curry, rice, pickles . . . and also Turkish delight.

Q. You're not fat; but you're not thin, either. In *AbFab* you're always saying, 'I'm thin and I'm gorgeous' – and you *were* a bit thinner then weren't you?

A. Whenever I work I lose weight, because you're fairly nervous and rushing about and you're also aware of the deadly camera's podgy embrace. I can skip lunch if I'm out of the house. If I'm at home, I have to eat nuts and raisins and great blocks of cheese. I *have* to. But there are two ways of dealing with this weight thing: 1) have a set of clothes that are *at least* a size larger than the size you normally take and wear those; 2) try dieting.

The Toast Diet: for breakfast, one piece of toast with marmalade; for lunch, one piece of toast with Marmite and watercress; for supper, one piece of toast with honey, or, if preferred, marmalade, or Marmite. This knocks pounds off and is surprisingly pleasant to eat. The whole point of dieting, losing weight, staying thin, is to lose interest in food altogether, and eat only as a means of getting fuel into yourself. It takes a long time to retrain your taste buds and to lose the craving for delicious chocolates and nice salty chips. The firmest and surest way is to start the day with porridge, eaten without milk or sugar, maybe just a little salt. Some people like this (I do) but it is, to be frank, a bit of a slog morning after morning and eventually you just chaw it down like stuffing coal into a boiler. Eat fruit and vegetables, but never when they are in peak condition. Apples must have gone soft, bananas black, celery extremely bendy, carrots pliable, and lettuce should have the texture of wet hankies. These things are not bad for you, but they're no fun and you won't call for more. Think poor; think scavenger. Eat some cheese, but only when it has gone so hard that you have to grate it off the rind. Eat the rind. Try to be grateful for all sorts of sad combinations: velvet-soft grapes with wrinkled skins on a piece of bread with margarine and salt; some avocado, black bit cut out; three peanuts; cottage cheese scrapings with blue fur excluded. In fact, live like a pauper. Always keep long-life food in the cupboard: oats, rice, dates, tins of marrowfat peas which you can rip open and devour when a feeling of despair comes over you.

What do you eat in public when dieting? Accept everything on to your plate, or if in a restaurant order some rather ambitiously large dish, a T-bone steak or, for vegetarians, a lasagne (made usually with a grim apology for a filling so you're half-way there); then cut it about like mad, say how nice it is, eat one mouthful and say you're completely full. Order pudding; same trick. You will give the impression of loving life and being a glutton whilst actually getting thinner. People will say, 'Oh, you're so lucky – you eat like a horse but stay so thin,' and you can smile kindly, patting some bony excrescence, perhaps a knee or even the area of a hip bone, and say, 'I know, it's awful.' I have used this method with smoking cigarettes. In the acting world, where the world used to be blue with smoke, most people have given up the weed. Only villains or 'characters' like Patsy in *AbFab* are allowed to smoke on film; actors often try to work it into their character's make-up, just to get a daily fix of nicotine. In real life, I smoke, but not very often. In coffee breaks on film sets, particularly with American actors present, I get out my packet of cigarettes with a guilty rush, saying, 'Oh Lord, I'm behind: my doctor said I *have* to have a smoke every two hours at least to get over this abdominal complication' (I have none) – 'What a bore'; then I light up and puff away with a lugubrious expression. There is a clamour to find out my benevolent doctor's name, which of course I don't give because he doesn't exist.

Ten years ago I was cast away on the desert island Tsarabanjina, in the Mitsio Archipelago, off the north-west coast of Madagascar. I say 'cast away', but as it was filmed as *Girl Friday* I obviously had a small crew with me, who stayed off the island in a well-equipped diving boat moored a mile offshore. There had been expectations of an island dripping with guavas, mangoes, coconuts and bananas, but in the event a late monsoon had destroyed anything edible – the fallen coconuts had turned rancid, and the bananas had never been pollinated so had no fruit in them: in short, slim pickings.

I had been equipped with a pound of rice, three veg-etable stock cubes, one orange and four tea-bags – to be used, squeezed out and used again. My cooking vessel was an already rusty catering-size baked-bean tin, empty but with a home-made wire handle. Every day I collected and prepared firewood, started a flame with my flint-striker, got the water to boil (also collected and then purified), cooked a tiny handful of rice flavoured with half a stock cube, and ate it with a shell out of a shell dish. This palaver was so tiring and so disgusting that eating became a duty, not a pleasure. Of course I got thinner – and after I returned to civilization I only wanted to eat lettuce and things that crunched. But the crew often sneaked me a special treat which I would find after they'd left the island for the night: a mango or an apple, unexpected and delicious beyond description. I got used to being very appreciative of each small mouthful. So, part of dieting is being grateful for every single thing one eats – yes, even the 78th spoonful of porridge.

The School Diet: give up sugar, bread and potatoes. That's it. People only said they were 'going on a diet' when they had inexplicably been chosen as one of a relay team for sports day. Nobody ever seemed to talk about fatness or thinness, no one knew or cared what their weight was. If you couldn't do up your skirt, you knew you had grown thicker and then you would either do 20 toe-touches a day or use a hula-hoop (or cut out bread, potatoes and sugar). Girls with slim waists and good figures ('she's got a terrific bust') were admired, but I can't remember anyone trying to change their weight or shape. Fat girls were called 'Fatty', I suppose . . . or were they? No, I don't think they were. Our nicknames didn't reflect the person's appearance, but were usually a play on their name, or a fantastically unimaginative suffix, i.e. Warman-bug, Hambone (for Hammond), Bowles (for Bewley) and so on. The actor Simon Williams – who of course wasn't at school with me – calls me Jo-bags, Ruby Wax calls me Lum or Lummers, Jennifer Saunders calls me Jack (as does Ben Elton – only them), and a lot of people whom I've known for ages call me Jo-Jo. But I digress.

The Modelling Diet (circa 1966): grapefruit and steak. Breakfast: half a grapefruit. Lunch: half a grapefruit and a grilled steak. Supper: ditto. Its only similarity with the Atkins Diet was the bad-breath factor. Also the idea of a good acidic start to the day was propounded. PLJ – pure lemon juice – mixed with hot water was considered a marvellous way to clear out your filthy system and scour out your tubes ready for more steak. Constipation was a shadowy attendant. There was a rash of pill-fed diets, amphetamines jittering and burning up every waking hour, and injections, which I don't remember how – or even if – were supposed to take off seven pounds in as many days. I was always hungry as a model, and still rather spotty, but eventually managed to remain at about eight and a half stone for two or three years, with the occasional absolute fatness (or normality) returning.

Luckily, the kind of mid-grade work I did only required you to be a size 10; but even when I looked, for me, pretty emaciated, my face was still a puppy-fat moon. My hands never became nice skeletal claws. I can only remember one girl with anorexia and we all clucked and tut-tutted with anxiety about her as we squished our dear little teenagers' bottoms into Bri-Nylon slacks and pencil skirts. Bosoms were 'out', unfashionable: cleavage was something very vulgar, for men's magazines or glamour models. Legs were very in, and puffy lips with faintly gormless expressions, and straight hair and toes pointed inwards like the dimwit youngest daughter. Exercise was absolutely out: the athletic look for girls, with locker-room muscles and pool-slicked hair, had yet to arrive. I remember eating Limmits biscuits, waxy digestive circles with a sandwich of orange-flavoured cream inside. There was a savoury filling too; one of each with a cup of instant coffee made a good model's lunch, as the biscuits seemed to inflate as you ate them leaving no pangs of hunger.

Q. But you are a vegetarian now. When did you stop eating meat?

A. Half-way through a rare steak in the sixties. It suddenly looked like flesh, it looked like my arm. Up till that moment I had somehow never really associated meat with animals. It struck me that I could live just as well without any animals having to lose their lives for me, and so I stopped eating them. Since then, in all the long years since then, I've learnt more and more about meat production; how much of Africa is planted with maize and wheat which is then shipped back to Europe to feed factory-farmed animals for our tables while African babies starve. It's been estimated that if every person on earth ate as much meat as an American, we would need four whole planets to provide enough animal foodstuff to keep us going. We eat five times more meat than we did 50 years ago (in the West, that is – but now meat-eating is catching on in China and South America too; soon the whole world will be smacking its lips for a bigger Mac). It would seem to be better to eat less meat: our health would improve, animals wouldn't have to be reared in intolerably cruel conditions, and the poor farmers of the developing world would be able to feed their own families and countries. And water! Two thousand litres to produce a kilo of soya beans, but 100,000 litres to produce a kilo of beef. It can't be right for us to ignore these facts. What would change things? A health scare of colossal proportions, and possibly some financial intervention by the subsidy of organic food.

Q. Could you lighten up a bit? I know the effect of these gloomy speculations, and they are absolute killers as far as entertainment goes. Lighten up! What is it the Epicureans say? 'Eat, drink and be merry, for tomorrow we die.'

A. You can't lighten up about everything. I truly hate the cruelty and indifference with which we treat farm animals; we can't change the world's attitude but we must make sure we do the best we possibly can in our own country.

Q. Favourite foods?

A. Peanuts, avocados, basmati rice, mangoes, dried apricots, Emmenthal cheese, radishes, marmalade, toast, runner beans . . .

Q. Let's leave it there. You may have lost a large section of your audience.

A. But please think about what I said: that a man in Africa is growing grain, which is shipped to Europe to feed cattle, which are then slaughtered for our tables, whilst the African watches his family starve. Please remember that sequence of events and eat less meat.

Q. I have given up eating meat altogether.

A. I love this kitchen – the big double doors lead out on to the garden; there is a little terrace where we eat out when it's hot enough, and on the wall above the sink is a huge board where I put up pictures and photographs and post-cards. There's a poster of a man singing on a terrace in Italy, with the lights twinkling on Lake Garda behind him, and there is a birthday card showing a man and a woman in Edwardian dress poring over a map, planning where their next journey will take them.

And here is the cottage in Scotland. We went to stay with friends of ours in Dumfriesshire – my mother's god-daughter Hilary Reid, who's married to Michael Weir. Michael had been Our Man in Egypt for many years, and is an Arabist of distinction. We'd only ever driven through the Borders before, on our way to the Western Isles; but that short stay showed us what is called Undiscovered Scotland, great bare rolling hills, deep glens and rushing rivers. It was wintertime; they drove us up a valley lane which wound on and on and would eventually come to an abrupt halt in a forest. Off the road on a high hill we saw a little ruined cottage, which had been empty for 50 years and was beginning to crumble back into the land. The next day in a light blizzard we walked up the hill; there was only a faint cart-track across the snowy grass, leading up and up. The wind blew mightily, but when we got up there in the freezing gale I suddenly felt completely warm and safe. We creaked open the door and saw the utter devastation – no floors or ceilings, bits of lath and plaster fallen on the floor, the glassless windows rattling their frames at us. Two barn owls flew out, low over our heads. The byre attached to the cottage was used by the tenant farmer, John Fawcett, as a lambing pen and feed store. It was, however, the phenomenal view down the valley that stole my heart conclusively.

We bought that gorgeous place, and with astonishing speed and competence, under the dangerously demanding eye of Pat Lorimer, our architect, a road was built (only a farm road, nothing spivvy needed or wanted) and electricity and telephone wires buried underground as they made their invisible way up to the little house – which didn't even have running water. Two springs were tapped on the hill above the north-west side of the property, and crystal-clear sweet water was harnessed to rush into every tap and tank. We had an owl-house built into the roof above the kitchen; the stone walls, or dykes as they're called up there, were rebuilt; trees were planted – Scots pine, rowan, oak, ash, beech, willow, in fact all the trees that grow in the valley and in the deep gorges where the streams tumble by.

The byre was transformed into a music room with a big open fireplace and vaulted roof; windows look out to north, south, east and west. The old kitchen has been made into a cosy little study, with a wood-burning stove and a desk for me to do my letters. The walls are soft red, 'fox-red': there are old French candle-holders on the walls, with candles which we light when the power cuts come, i.e. quite often. There's a soft old sofa, a dresser filled with books and a television set. All the windows on the ground floor are shuttered for warmth. We put in a bathroom under the stairs, with a huge bath to soak away the stiffness from hillwalking and a window so we can watch the sheep on the hill. Our bedroom, which when I first saw it was like a damp bombsite, is changed beyond recognition with rugs, a tiny Victorian fireplace and a big iron bed. Upstairs all the ceilings slope inwards as we are right up under the roof: two bedrooms with iron bedsteads, wood painted soft green, bare floors with rugs and views down and beyond the valley. The smallest lavatory known to man is tucked under the eaves, with a hand-basin, for our guests to limbo into when it's too dark to come downstairs.

The new bit of the cottage already looks as though it has been there for a century: a single-storey addition butting into the hill, giving the cottage an L-shape. This is the kitchen and dining room, windows all along the south side where, outside, a small terrace made of wood gives us a place to sit and listen to Stephen playing the piano, or to eat or sunbathe or just to sit and stare. One thing we'll never change: the old original door to the cottage, massively weathered to a faded pinky-brown with its great iron hook to secure it. This was where I stood when I first looked in through the blizzard, and when I knew it would be our home.

In winter there is thick snow, and gale-force winds: in summer, often boiling heat and storms and rainbows. There are no midges, there's no standing water. Everything rushes and dashes and bubbles underground. The fields around have black-faced sheep and Luing cattle whose coats are coppery red. The owls have taken up residence in their new home, as have an active family of stoats who run about the roof space in high heels and shin down the drainpipes. Buzzards wheel overhead, larks sing all day in the long summer light. At night it is as quiet as black velvet, and because no extraneous light is visible the stars are as bright as diamonds.

The rough land round the cottage is seeded with wild flowers – viper's bugloss, daisies, poppies, mallow – and we've built a stone circle where we can burn the docks and nettles, and sit round the bonfire with a glass of Drumlanrig whisky given to us by the Duke of Buccleuch, whose land this is. (All around Drumlanrig Castle, four miles away, are signs saying 'Welcome' – welcome to the woods, pathways, welcome to the lake – he is the kindest landowner imaginable.) About a mile over the hills live the Weirs, our dear friends. Without them we wouldn't have this. We're for ever in their debt.

Q. Let's go there now! Let's drop everything and run away to Scotland!

A. Don't think I haven't thought of that. We could leave the rest of the book as blank pages, and be like Meg Merrilees whose house was out of doors, plaiting rush baskets and wearing a great cloak. 'Old Meg, she was a gypsy . . .'

Q. Don't do that now. People can look it up in poetry books if they want to.

A. And here's a thing: I love very much the song 'The Ash Grove', and from the cottage, looking down the green valley, we can see an ash grove, 'where streamlets meander . . . when twilight is fading I pensively rove/Or at the bright noontide in solitude wander/beneath the dark shades of the lonely ash grove . . .'

Q. Don't go on: it gets terribly sad and morbid, with a love lost for ever – and I think there may even be a grave involved.

A. I wouldn't mind being buried up there. No! Not buried! Cast to the viewless winds! 'Washed by the rivers, blest by the suns of home.'

Q. Why say all this in the kitchen?

A. I spend a lot of time in here when Stephen is away. On my own, I am as tidy and niminy-piminy neat as a teeny little mouse. The fridge becomes completely empty; everything looks tidy and quiet and dull. I daydream over the papers and watch the television which sits between the coffee and the wholemeal flour. Television is a wonderful friend; so is the wireless, which is usually tuned to Radio 3 or 4. You can talk back and say goodnight and answer the questions on quiz shows or *University Challenge*.

Q. Really. *University Challenge*.

A. Amazingly, yes. And sometimes when I don't know the answer I hear it in my head in advance and it's right; a kind of precognition. I don't like watching myself on television, though, or listening to my voice (except for my reading of *Pride and Prejudice* which made me laugh out loud). But after a reasonable period of time, say five or ten years, I can watch shows I've been in with great interest and pleasure.

I've watched the bit of *AbFab* when Eddie and Pats are very old and still clinging to Saffy like barnacles, in a house next door. We had immensely elaborate prosthetic make-up, which Jennifer and Dawn use constantly in their shows but I'd never had done. It's an alarming experience: your hair is pinned back under a very close-fitting plastic cap, taped tightly with Sellotape; you are smothered with Vaseline and a cool, quick-setting liquid rubber is dripped down over your head, gradually filling your ears and weighing heavily on your eyelids. You breathe through a straw; just the rasping breath you draw is all you hear in your heavy black world, which lasts for about 15 minutes. It's far worse than going into a scanning machine, as your senses are utterly stopped: you feel as though you are being buried alive.

When the rubber's peeled off the technicians have a perfect cast of your whole head, upon which they can model the wrinkles and jowls and eyebags. Then when the day itself comes these feather-light prosthetics are glued, centimetre by centimetre, to your face and neck so you can move and speak normally but look horrendous. We had dowagers' humps as well, and prosthetic ancient hands, bald wigs, droopy bosoms made of sacks of sand and thickening padding round our waists. False teeth, liver spots, bad make-up as if done with a trembling hand completed the look. Patsy wore popsocks with a skirt. We weren't mocking old people; we *were* old people: this is how I will look when I'm very old.

We set off round the corridors of the BBC Television Centre, hardly able to contain ourselves we were laughing so hard. On the bus ride out to the location we stopped at a traffic light and I doddered and waved at the car beside us. I could follow their lips: 'Oh, look, it's Joanna Lumley.' When we came to shoot the scene our director, Bob Spiers, was getting fairly tetchy as we had already taken up too much time. His impatience only made it worse – and when Patsy's pants fell down and Edina whizzed them off her and threw them into a bush I thought I would actually die of laughter. We couldn't do the scene again as we were, by that time, fit for rags. I still laugh at that scene quite hugely; I think I always will.

Here on the board is a photograph of Edina with a brush

in her mouth, painting Patsy in the South of France in the first series. Jennifer is very good at painting and at riding, gardening, organizing – she is a demon at crossword puzzles and is in fact the polar opposite of Edina with . . . and here's the trick . . . with *all her tendencies*. These are arranged in no order: these photographs are of my mother in Norway, Stephen's parents, George and Irene in New Zealand, Daddy in France at a wayside café . . . my cousin Maybe grinning on a boat, Stevie conducting in Albania and Jamie and Tessa getting married. How absolutely touching and lovely – look at my son! And look at that gorgeous slim Tessa with dark tangly curls, in a stunning white dress.

And here's Alice! Our first grandchild, quite unbelievably delicious; her name is Alice Daisy Claydon Lumley, which is perfect as it brings Jamie's father Michael's name back into the equation. I was unmarried when I had Jamie so he has my maiden name. Michael and his wife, Rita, and his mother, Joan – we're all part of the same family now, along with all the Barlows and all my family. That's how kith and kin works. It's very different from the old days, when they had specially small humble birth certificates to show clearly that the child was born out of wedlock. But the clerk in Canterbury was charming: he liked the names I'd chosen – James Æneas Sebastian – and he said, 'I'll do it in my very best writing,' which he did, God bless him. Heigh-ho! I wonder if they've changed all that now. I called him Sebastian after the saint of that name, who was tortured by hateful arrows: I thought it would protect him from the barbs of unkindness in life.

Q. What are you afraid of?

A. Drowning. Being sick. Wearing polo necks. Going mad. Being trapped. Being boring. Heights. Losing my temper. Being trapped with a bore. Chopping through my shins with an axe. On the desert island I was given two knives: one like a large penknife with a foldaway blade, and the other a big sharp sheath knife which belonged to CSM Paddy Shields of the Irish Guards – he lent it to me on pain of death that I wouldn't damage it and would sharpen it properly on a carborundum. As I got dimmer and slower on the island, from lack of food and sleep, my mind would race like a hamster in a wheel and when I tried to hack into a coconut, holding it steady with my left hand, I could almost hear the scrunch of Paddy's knife as it severed my wrist. In the event I didn't even scratch myself; but I could imagine the pitiful stump and the awful finality of your own hand lying there in the sand. Any time I have to chop logs or use a chainsaw the spectre of severance looms.

Q. Is that what's called a dumb waiter behind those cupboard doors?

A. Yes, and it works; when my study upstairs was a dining room, it would have been used to trundle the food upstairs, like a miniature lift operated by a rope. Above it is a picture of Patsy, the only one in the house. It's an enlarged Polaroid of Pats with her voddy bottle and a cigarette, having a swig on the roof on the 67th floor of a skyscraper in New York. Behind her is Central Park. She is wearing dark glasses, a lovely oyster-pink suit by Betty Jackson and a chain neck-lace. Hair: immaculate if big. She holds the bottle to her lips and is turned slightly away from us. The Polaroid was taken by Jan Sewell for a record of make-up for continuity.

I remember that day: we'd already had a hell of a time. An English tabloid newspaper got wind of the fact that we'd be doing some helicopter shots in NY so they sent a reporter out to do a 'spoiler', with a camera. They threatened that unless we let them photograph us – interrupting an already hectic schedule – they would hire their own helicopter and make sure our filming was ruined. So we had to comply, or lose our sensational shot of Edina rising up like a Valkyrie in a chopper past the roof where Patsy stands. The irony is that the picture he took was taken up by fanzines or fanmags or whatever they're called and now I sign dozens weekly . . .

Q. Weekly?

A. Monthly – OK, yearly. Anyway I now sign dozens yearly of the spoiler's blackmail snap. But this one by Jan is inviolable. There is a blur of greeny blue, like ectoplasm, across it and in one corner the light got in or the film was damaged and what looks like a child's drawing of the sun hangs in the sky. It was about 112 degrees and my vertigo had never been so sorely tested. When I first got out on to the roof I had to go down on my hands and knees, staring like a statue; then after quarter of an hour I could move about like a robot, still staring straight ahead. In two hours' time I was leaning against the waist-high parapet, laughing and putting on lipstick and leaning over to look down the dreadful chasm to the tiny street below. Jennifer had her own terrors to contend with. She's pretty hopeless at flying at the best of times, but shooting about in a helicopter dangerously close to buildings, victim of every updraught, angling and climbing, she looked absolutely paralysed with

Very first modelling photograph. Hairstyle eerily pre-dates Purdey by twelve years.

Me at 19. Very horrible hairstyle worn by no one before or since.

(*right*) Me at 18. Test shots for my photographic book.

(*far right*) Hair and demeanour much inspired by Sue Lloyd in *The Ipcress File*.

Feathery shots for
modelling book.

Royal Hospital Gardens in the 1960s, Chelsea.

In Jean Muir with Biba shoes, 1970.

My favourite Biba boots.

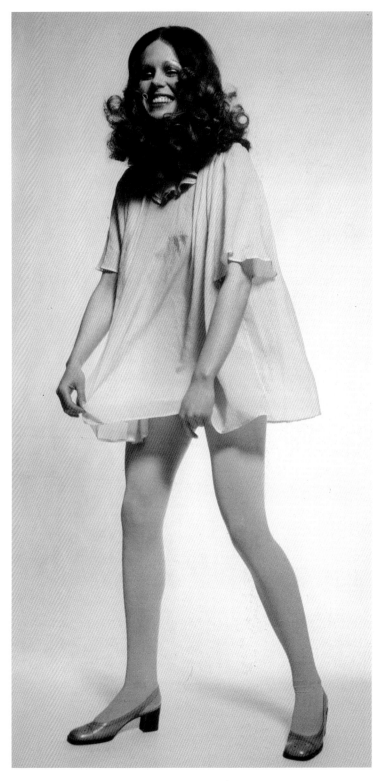

The way we were, apparently.

white fear. But when in all the din 'Action' was called, there she was waving, yelling, laughing . . . I tell you, actors will do almost anything if there is a camera turning. She couldn't blame anyone else: she wrote the scene. (She also addressed the tabloid man in very vivid language – I hope he remembers what her advice to him was.)

Next to this colour photograph of Alice at six months is a tiny black and white polyphoto from 1947 of me when I was a little older than her: to my eyes, the nose and mouth are almost identical. I've pinned it very close to her, hoping her youth and innocence will somehow leach through my own baby face into my present-day being. She's next to the picture of my father, who never saw her; and he in turn is protected by a dragon drawn by Ælene, a picture of Jamie looking handsome at the Parsonage, and a carved wooden angel.

Q. And a laundry ticket.

A. I'm quite superstitious about photographs. When people send me pictures of their children, whether I know them or not I keep them on my desk for a year so that my remembrance of them will form a sort of Colgate ring of confidence round them. If ever I throw away a photograph of a person, or even a group of people, I kiss it first. I also don't like statues to be lonely, so next to the terracotta mother holding her baby aloft is a terracotta goat. And the Egyptian cat in the bedroom has the carved wooden woman from Madagascar; and statues all get hats – except for the bust of a lonely pale young man by Christie Brown in my study, who has got some necklaces on.

On an easel on my desk, leaning against a seascape by

Harold Speed, are my school teddy bear and a doll I bought in Tenterden only about eight years ago. She's very like my sister's wonderful velvet-limbed doll, Fairy – which I loved and adored, but I never had one of my own. Now I have. She's dressed rather stridently in orange and wears badges and pins of charities I support. But that's upstairs; down here in the kitchen on this little shelf are the figures of the Virgin Mary holding the Christ Child; a wooden clown who arrived one day 30 years ago from out of the blue; a lead figure of Her Majesty the Queen, mounted on her horse Winston, at the Trooping the Colour – only her saluting arm has dropped off; and an original metal puppet of Muffin the Mule, dangling by his strings. They are all happy together there, and they protect the kitchen with their virtue and good humour, and, in Her Majesty's case, sheer bravery.

It is something to do with household gods; in the ancient Roman religions the deity or spirit presiding over a thing or place was a *numen*, from which we get the word *numinous*, which means divine, mysterious, awe-inspiring, arousing spiritual or religious emotions. Now, almost everything I see, every day, somehow seems to fall into the category of the numinous: people I pass in the street, trees, a chair, light coming through a door, a bird flying . . . they all have their being, all are equally important in some way.

Here's another lovely talisman, a severely bent teaspoon. I was at a reception in 1997 held at the RAC Club in Pall Mall. It was a glittering occasion filled with sports stars, actors and politicians. Uri Geller was there; Selina Scott introduced us. I told him how once I had been waiting to do a voice-over in Soho, sitting in the green room with a cup of coffee watching afternoon television while the studio completed the job before mine. (From my model-ling days I have always been a stickler for time-keeping: if you arrived even a few minutes late for a session, half an hour of your pay was docked. As I was earning 4½ guineas an hour for editorial work and 5½ guineas for advertising, this was a severe blow to my income: having been late once, I never was again.) The next programme announced its guests for the afternoon chat show, one of whom was Uri Geller. 'Uri Geller!' I thought. 'I wonder if he'll do something with keys and watches.' At that moment the clients arrived, the studio was free and I went off to do my voice-over. Afterwards I went back to my car, parked outside on a meter, and found that my car keys had bent so badly that I couldn't even open the door, and I had to call out the AA. No one could bend the keys back to their original shape.

When I'd finished telling him this story, Uri immedi-ately called a club servant over and asked him to bring a teaspoon. Holding it upside down by the bowl, he very gently stroked the back of the stem with his forefinger. In seconds the handle bent upwards and stayed there. By now a small group had gathered round him; he beckoned them nearer to a brass door handle – 'to give more energy' – and rubbed again: it continued to bend, into its present position. No energy or stress was used and the handle was quite cool. Uri gave the spoon to me and said, 'This will bring you good luck.' I saw it all with my own eyes from very close range and find it extremely hard to explain away. Treasured spoon! I am aglimmer with good luck.

Q. What would you pack for a picnic lunch? (These are the

questions I have written down as I sense that food doesn't come first in your kitchen or your life.)

A. Hard-boiled eggs, free-range of course. I boil them with the flaky outer skins of a couple of onions and they come out the most beautiful amber-brown. Then I write on them with a thick gold Pentel, 'Hard Boiled Egg' – sometimes I put the person's name as well. Sandwiches, which have never been equalled as food to be packed and moved around. Salt and pepper in little twists of paper. Cold sausages, if you like, vegetable samosas, packets of crisps. Cherry tomatoes. Hearts of lettuce, maybe a spicy rice salad. Bananas, chocolate bars, tangerines, apples. Sandwich fillings can be anything you want: mashed avocado, cottage cheese and peanuts, Marmite and watercress, strawberry jam. You could get some little pork pies, but it's getting hard to find out if the pigs are reared outdoors. (In supermarkets I always ask where the outdoor-reared bacon is; it's criminally expensive, no wonder people go on buying cheap imported pork meat from pigs reared in conditions that are outlawed in Britain.)

I don't think picnics should have too many things on offer, though. Sometimes one cheese sandwich and an apple is enough. Always pack a dampened J cloth in a plastic bag, always take extra carrier bags to tie the rubbish into neatly. Thermos flasks are exciting because the coffee or tea never tastes quite right. Bottles of tap water, with a few drops of elderflower cordial sprinkled in. A tablecloth to spread on the ground. Umbrellas to keep off the rain or sun. A camera, because picnics are worth recording. And if you drink alcohol, a bottle or two of wine and a corkscrew, or some tins of Guinness, and maybe a teeny little quarter-bottle of Scotch as a backstop for when you can't find your way back to the car and when you do it's got stuck in a swamp and the wind and rain are lashing in horizontally under your hood – a nice little nip of whisky could cheer you up, I believe. Less is more on these occasions: half a capful makes you feel you've been in the pub for four hours.

Of course, it's possible to have far more elaborate picnics, with folding tables and chairs, tablecloths and napkins of linen, food in china dishes, sometimes even candlesticks – but these are enormously high-maintenance and require such a lot of fussing about that you can find you've lost your appetite by the time it's all set out. I prefer a dashing mountain stream, tomato sandwiches, a groundsheet or coat spread on a rock and above all a view. The problem with eating picnics when you're dressed up to the nines at Glyndebourne, Garsington or the Grange Opera is that you invariably get mayonnaise on your front and can't get to the ladies' room in time to see that you have watercress in your teeth. So it's ho! for the stale chapatti and the handful of raisins . . .

Q. It's getting grimmer and grimmer. Are these vitamin pills beside the toaster?

A. Ever since they first came out in this country – about 12 years ago – I've taken Imedeen tablets, two every morning. Although it doesn't say clearly on the box exactly what they are I believe them to be made of bits of fish that we throw away, the bones and scales, that sort of thing. This is evidence that I am a bit fraudulent as a vegetarian – I don't really eat fish very often, and here I am daily gobbling up pills made entirely of marine substances. They come from Scandinavia and are advertised as effective in reducing wrinkles and lines on your face. I can't prove how effective they are because I haven't got a parallel me who *hasn't* been taking the tablets, a sort of Dorian Gray version which would show what I'd be like without them. But they seem to make sense: when humans were less pernickety they would have eaten their fish whole; in fact, I can remember a French boy when I was 10 called Alain who ate the whole kipper – head, bones, the lot. If he's still alive today and hasn't choked to death on a fish-bone I bet he has a wonderfully smooth face.

And here are two sets of scales – one heaped with fresh lemons, which usually has a wooden duck sitting on them as though it were hatching them, and this huge glorious set of street trader's scales: a big brass scoop, enamel stand and heavy weight. There are more scales upstairs, an Edwardian post-office set and a chemist's balance – I'd started collecting scales long before I knew that my son Jamie would be born a Libra. How easy it is to drift into collecting things! I adore jugs – they're above your head on that shelf; and birds; and things in threes: three tin cyclists, three lead racehorses, three solemn little plaster girls in white dresses holding candles for their first communion. I got the last in a Paris flea market in the sixties – I've always been a mad collector of junk.

At school it started with swapping: my set of jacks, one missing, for a tennis ball which was still impressively hairy but bounced like an apple; three crayons, in yellow, pink and a reluctant burnt umber, for a little wooden donkey on a pedestal whose base, when depressed, caused the donkey's legs to give way – only some of the elastic had perished; a bra, all cotton, 32A, for 'Bama Lama Bama Loo' by Little Richard. Particularly strapped for cash one summer term, Mary and I emptied out our desks and top drawers and arranged the – well, frankly, the detritus, the gubbins, on a tray, priced it and trotted round the corridors selling the stuff. We displayed half-eaten erasers, broken pencils, lids off lost jars, bottles with no tops, Italian stamps, elastic bands, three sheets of crumpled airmail paper – nothing was too shabby or dingy for our sales push. In an hour we had sold every last gewgaw and were the richer by £1. 0s. 2d. As our whole term's pocket-money was one pound we were in a frenzy of wealth and excitement.

Even today, when I have virtuously loaded up a cardboard box to take down to the Trinity Hospice Shop, there is in my heart an understanding that this is only to make way for more stuff which will be acquired every time I pass a junk shop. Things! I love 'em! Even on the desert island when I had nothing and nowhere to put anything, I collected shells off the beach, smooth bits of wood, shiny nuts from the trees. When we were filming *The Cat's Meow* in Kyparissi in Greece, a tiny village whose waterfront was doubling as California in the 1920s, even in remote Kyparissi I managed to collect smooth pebbles from the beach and write on them 'Kyparissi The Cat's Meow' and then the actor's name, 'Kirsten' or 'Ed' or 'Jennifer'.

Kirsten Dunst played Marion Davies, the young actress adored by Ed Herrmann's William Randolph Hearst; Jennifer Tilly was Louella Parsons, the first and most lethal of gossip columnists; they were all so terrific – such fun and so hard-working. Quite a lot of the cast were English, speaking with American accents, and the servants were local Greek actors pretending to be Hispanic; and we were all miles from anywhere on a bucking boat moored off a small wooden jetty with hot jazz playing on deck and intrigue boiling up. Kirsten was being wooed by the *Spider-man* producers – she was fairly sanguine about it all, having been in movies all her young life. Apart from the beach pebbles, there was nothing to bring back from Kyparissi: we left too early in the morning to secure the purchase of litres of freshly pressed olive oil.

Mediterranean cooking comes equal first with Indian cuisine for me. Thick, dark-green extra-virgin olive oil, home-made bread or pitta, olives, tomatoes, garlic, and, if you eat fish, something grilled over charcoal: these things cannot fail to please. Sea salt and coarsely-ground black pepper, herbs by the kilo, fresh lemons and limes, local honey, bowls of just-picked cherries, dripping peaches and sun-warmed figs . . . I *am* interested in food: just not in terrifically complicated recipes. Anything that says 'Leave to marinate for 48 hours, turning every hour, with 12 bay leaves and the jus of a sweated-coriander coulis . . .' gets the page flicked over pretty quickly.

My mother used to make the best marmalade I'd ever eaten – chunky and quite bitter. My father, like chaps of his generation, just didn't cook at all. He could do boiled eggs for his breakfast, which he had hours before any of us woke as he was always up at five. He and I did a long train trip across Europe to visit Vienna, a place he had read about with the passion of a historian. The journey was awful: no food or drink at all, the heating had broken down and we had chattering teeth as we approached Austria in a November whirlwind of snow. But there the tea rooms, with golden lights and newspapers on sticks, hot chocolate, immensely rich teacakes and ice-creams, delighted him.

'How civilized,' he would murmur, 'how very civilized . . . perhaps just one more slice.' For many years afterwards he would reminisce about the Viennese food, and in particular a delicious feast of wild boar he had at the Hotel Sacher after the opera (*The Flying Dutchman* – 'How *splendid!*').

Food is always a reward in children's stories. Reading what Enid Blyton's children chanced upon in cheerful hospitable farmhouses in Cornwall made up for the school's tinned spaghetti and cold pilchards. There the tables always 'groaned' under slabs of fruitcake, jugs of thick cream, brown eggs, sides of ham (and, regrettably, 'tongue', which sounded vile) and home-made apple tarts, with strawberry jam and shortcake and cider to wash it down. Come next door – it's the dining room.

Dining Room

It's rather dark in this little bit of corridor between the kitchen and the dining room. We're under street level and the rooms are only lit properly by daylight in the morning in the dining room, which faces east, and in the evening in the kitchen as it faces west. But before we turn the lights on let me give you a tip for the darkness. You can see almost anything in the darkness as long as you don't look at it directly. Look away from it slightly and your peripheral vision will see it quite clearly. I learned that on the island, where eventually I could see like a cat at night-time. If you project that idea on to any problem in life it also works. Don't look too hard or too directly at the worry: look beyond it, and if possible imagine an even more testing or exciting scenario ahead. That way, the problem that was keeping you awake at night will diminish by comparison.

The other thing to do with problems is to examine them minutely and run past them a series of what if? tests. What if your dress is wrong – will you lose friends? No. What if you fall over as you walk up the aisle – will you be left there on your back? No: people will help you up. What if you lose your job? The chances are you'll get another one. For scaring events, always imagine a pleasant treat at the other end. Noël Coward used to have a pint of Guinness in his dressing room: half a pint for the interval, and the rest to look forward to after the second half of the play. The other thing to remember is that the busier you are, the less time you have to fret over things. Now, out of the darkness and into this room which is painted quite a seriously bright yellow: not exactly a mistake, but I wouldn't like David Mlinaric to see it. I'll repaint it directly I finish this. I did it this colour to look OK – it seemed to be an OK dining-room colour which I first saw in a large country house. Down here I must admit it looks rather unforgiving . . .

Q. . . . but to be honest we can't see very much of it owing to the number of pictures, dressers and screens – not to mention the enormously elaborate overmantel.

A. This delicious piece of carved wood came from a dealer in Kent when we lived in the Parsonage. It had once stood over double doors in a grand house, with its swagged laurel wreaths, berries, carved ribbons, tulips and roses. We fixed it up here and married it to the small fireplace by rather cunning wooden panelling so the whole thing looks as though it was meant to be. We have a B-movie flame fire which I put on when I'm working – old habits die hard, and even though I have now got a study of my own, I still do my writing down here. The cupboards are filled with files of letters and articles, and with boxes and suitcases of cuttings and photographs and slides, but when the doors are shut fast on their wealth of contents it looks fairly reasonable, and by candlelight positively ravishing.

I've written every book at this table: first at the Parsonage; then – attended by ghosts – down here. Strangely enough this is a room for dreaming. Through the windows you can see the balustrades and the pavement beyond – people can see in, which I rather like; they can see my table covered with papers, boxes, pens, and always some flowers. There are pale, very thin muslin curtains, which it may amaze you to hear I made myself – and this time I didn't even bother to hem them. If people we've invited to dinner see there are no hems, are they going to leave in a hurry? I think not. They might think, 'Poor Stephen, being married to her,' but again I think not. Their eyes will instead be savouring these paintings and trying to work out where the draught comes from. We love entertaining, Stevie and I. We've both got special talents, i.e. getting out the wine, doing the table, cooking the food, lighting the candles. Some of these are not so much talents as pleasures.

We've eaten at fabulous houses and palaces and cottages and flats in our time: the best thing you can do as a host is not to flap or be overambitious. Patrick Lichfield's sister, Lady Elizabeth Anson, is the driving force behind Party Planners, which caters for society fixtures every day of the year. I've known Lizzie for almost as long as I've known Patrick, which is a full 35 years. The way things are done at Shugborough, Patrick's beautiful house in Staffordshire, and the way Lizzie does things in her London house have influenced me hugely. At one dinner party there were immensely tall thin glass vases with veritable branches of blossom fanning out overhead, so that when you were sitting down you could see easily across the table between the slender glass stems and above your head was a canopy of flowers. I loved that idea and now have a mass of tall glass vases into which I stack bamboo fronds cut from the garden. I like little things to look at on the table between

salt and pepper pots and candlesticks: a tiny wooden rock-
ing horse, a snow dome of New York city, a Gurkha piper
made of silver, my three leaden racehorses and the two
silver gryphons my dear tall thin ex-husband Jeremy Lloyd
gave me when we were married.

Q. Do you still see him?

A. From time to time, although we talk quite often on the
telephone. His name is on that list you're holding, of
people I'm not going to be writing about – it's quite a long
list, all nearest and dearest: one day they'll have a book of
their own. I'm trying to write a different sort of book here,
where respect for privacy is all. Except, of course, when I
want to tell you about someone for a reason.

Q. I am holding no such list.

A. Let me try to describe a banquet I attended at St James's
Palace. Prince Charles had invited a spectacular array of
people who support the Prince's Trust to dinner: rock
stars, politicians, broadcasters, actors, writers, comedians,
business people; every name well known, hugely famous,
all of them thronging about in what I think is a throne
room, with massive portraits and richly decorated ceilings
and doors. The dinner itself was at a colossal curved table
in the next-door gallery which seemed half a mile long,
and on the table were trees, literally trees, underplanted
with narcissi and orchids in bloom, on a dark-red velvet
cloth. The whole huge room was ablaze with candles,
twinkling on the glasses and glittering on the silver knives
and forks. It was like a film set, or . . . well, a palace. All

these ideas can be adapted in miniature in your own dear home – they won't be anything like as grand but they don't have to be.

I suddenly remember the hat designer David Shilling's small house off the Marylebone Road. There were great swathes of cloth draped from a door frame behind a statue, a fire burning in the otherwise bare room lit by candles – it looked sensational. Cloth and candles; not too close together or the whole thing will go up and you'll be fried to a crisp. Candles, actually, are what it's all about. So if you have nothing else on your table, light up the candles – which can be in saucers – and if you can't stretch to flowers put out some leaves, a bit of ivy or some buddleia which grows wild in London on building sites. Unfortunately, I haven't got round to getting a set of chairs, so there's a hotchpotch of designs; some of them are actually old school chairs from the art room. They're not a success, sitting-wise: as soon as I've painted this room less yellow, the seating requirements will be attended to.

Q. You've had 12 years to get some decent chairs.

A. But time runs away! Look, let's open these cupboards – this is my extended form of diaries, I suppose. I keep all my appointment diaries, which record where I was supposed to be, what play or film I was working on, which year I went to which countries, but all the substance of these happy events is stored away in the form of cast lists, programmes, letters, journals and a thousand thousand photographs. I found yesterday a book I'd been planning 18 years ago – the whole story worked out, page upon page of it. It was a complete surprise: I'd forgotten I'd ever done it. All those years ago when Stevie and I had just got married and were living in Wimbledon we were, to be frank, a bit strapped for cash. In a very short time we found we couldn't afford the house we'd bought on a colossal bridging loan, and had to sell up and go to the country where property was cheaper and you could hear the owls at night. I thought then I'd try to write a novel: now it seems rather over-romanticized and would be suitable only for turning into a children's television drama-saga. And here in this file is my proud link with Pete Goss, the former Royal Marine turned *Boy's Own* hero.

Pete had asked me to officiate at the naming ceremony of his boat the *Aqua Quorum*, which he and Adrian Thompson had designed for the famous 24,000-mile round-the-world yacht race, the Vendée Globe. At Lucy Fleming's suggestion he first wrote to me in October 1994; two years later in St Katharine's Dock in London under the shadow of Tower Bridge she was named, and I had the chance to see at close quarters the little craft that would take Pete on his solo trip in the famous race. To be honest, I was completely shocked: it seemed to have nothing *in* it, no downstairs or cabin, just a kind of hollowed-out pod. The mast reached up to the sky and below her hull was an immensely long hydraulic swing keel to counterbalance the hugely high sails. It was a racing vessel stripped bare of anything but essentials, utterly beautiful – and it looked about as safe as a hairnet.

The trip itself is best read about in Pete's own thrilling book *Close to the Wind* – the story of the preparations, the building of the boat, the struggle for sponsorship and the race itself. What we didn't know, as we all crowded round Pete and his wife Tracey and their adorable children, raising glasses to him and the *Aqua Quorum*'s success, was that he would very nearly lose his own life whilst rescuing another competitor. In summary, half-way through the race he received an SOS in the Southern Ocean to say that a fellow competitor Raphael Dinelli's yacht had capsized and sunk and Dinelli was lost in the water. In the teeth of a terrifying storm, Pete turned round, and sailing 160 miles into the heart of the tempest, his own little yacht blown flat, his elbow injured, he reached and rescued Dinelli as mountainous seas obscured them both from the RAAF plane above. Do read the book! It's mesmerically exciting.

Pete gave one of the best lectures I've ever heard at the Royal Geographical Society, and the French government recognized his bravery by awarding him the Légion d'Honneur. Our country honoured him too, with an MBE. It's funny, that: we have the George Cross specially for acts of conspicuous bravery and we gave him an MBE. He's far too modest to think anything except that it's marvellous, but I remember there was an underground murmuring of displeasure from the Royal Yacht Squadron and professional sailors everywhere, who know what the sea is and recognize the true extent of his heroism. Look: I've kept the InMarSat messages he sent me on the trip – BT Inter Marine Satellite letters on fax paper:

Dear Joanna, just rounded Cape Horn 17.15 hrs gmt 10th Feb 1997. Amazing – I passed three miles to the south so had a great view. Half an hour beforehand the sun came out, I had 15 knots from the west so it was perfect. Not only that but an Australian tour ship was just south of us so we had a chat and they took a picture. What more could you ask – sunshine, Cape Horn, champagne and company. Just great. I could burst with the sense of pride and achievement I feel at the moment. One of my deepest emotions on rounding the Horn is one of gratitude to all those who have helped me do this; it really is a team effort and I just wish you could all be here to share the moment – magic. As a special member of the team might I suggest you get some champers down as well – thanks so much for all your help and I look forward to taking you for that sail when I return. Hope all's well with you – cheers, Pete.

Q. You should copy that out on to proper paper – that fax paper is already fading fast. Look at all these fading yellow pages of faxed messages, the ink growing paler as we look. You should get a machine with real paper, not thin shiny stuff on rolls. How else will you keep these letters from everyone? From your mother, look, and from Jennifer, and here's a whole box of faxes from Stephen when he was at the other end of the earth for months on end and convenient moments for telephone calls were impossible to time.

A. As you get older you realize you can't keep everything and nothing lasts for ever – I've got all these darling letters and they'll fade and go the way of all flesh (well, obviously not flesh) and only memories will remain. Strangely enough, that was one of the things I noticed at the Imperial War Museum: a postcard from 1914 still exists with a message clearly legible – 'I love you dear and will be at Waterloo at four-fifteen' – but today's equally simple text messages are gone for ever, leaving future historians with a bit of a hole in their research. We will be recorded in the 21st century on film and videotape, audio tapes even, in photographs – but not so much in the written word. I wonder if this is good or bad. I love to see handwriting: it tells you about the person, and also can reveal how their spirits are and whether their health is good. I love the human hand underlining a word for emphasis, altering spelling, doing a little drawing to illustrate how the bonnet ties under the dog's chin when he's dressed as a baby. You don't get that on email. Listen! Do you hear that deep rumbling sound?

Q. I've been hearing that since I first came into the house.

A. That's the Northern Line as it travels far below us on its way from the Oval to Stockwell. It stops at night, but in the daytime it roars quietly along and the glasses in the kitchen cupboards jingle and hum. On the back of this cupboard door I've copied out two of my favourite John Betjeman poems, 'Youth and Age on Beaulieu River, Hants' and 'Business Girls': 'Morning trains through Camden cutting/shake the Crescent and the Square'. That's how it is in this city: planes overhead, cars, buses, fire engines and ambulances, trains like mechanical moles muffled by yards of earth, police sirens screaming day and night in empty streets.

Betjeman's daughter Candida Lycett Green asked me and Kenneth Cranham to read a few of the great man's poems when, after his death, he was officially received into Poets' Corner in Westminster Abbey. It's odd to stand on the same steps in front of the high altar where so many kings and queens have been crowned, and face out down the vast echoey nave, with rood screen, choir stalls, tombs, banners, effigies, all watching you quietly, another tiny mote of dust caught in a sunbeam, turning and sparkling for a second, then gone, down to the dusty stone floor. I was puffed up like a duvet with pride; and I met Patrick Leigh Fermor in completely human form, although I had half-expected him to be a demigod; it was all very wonderful. (I think I sounded dismissive earlier about going to church – I adore going to churches, chapels and cathedrals but I prefer it when there are no services going on. I often go into the Brompton Oratory to sit and be quiet because there's sometimes a whiff of incense lingering in the air – and I love to wander round and think about things, which quite honestly you can't do when you're reading recently-composed responses off a sheet of paper or trying to follow a brand-new hymn. I was brought up as a Christian but I love to be in temples, mosques and synagogues as well.) I do remember that no matter how clearly I tried to enunciate the poems, the words flew out and vanished with a muffled resonance, rendering them fairly incomprehensible despite strategically-placed microphones. Cathedral public-address technique is a devil to master.

It was considered normal at school to read the lesson in chapel if you were a senior girl. Before the hymn ended, you sidled out of your row, stepping over the hand-stitched kneelers which we still called hassocks, up the aisle towards the altar, the genuflection (sometimes a bob, sometimes the full down-to-one-knee curtsey), flipping open the Bible on the lectern to the right page and facing the school with the steely eyes of a bored politician. Prefects were immensely important people: they were the Cabinet. Difficult fourth-formers seemed as dangerous and subversive as the Soho underworld, new girls just like tiny malleable constituents, beefy fifth-formers a kind of crack para regiment. The nuns were the government, the lay staff the Civil Service, and the Head Girl was the elected Prime

Minister – though not chosen by the school, who would always have gone for the popular games captain. Matches played against other schools were minor skirmishes against neighbouring countries ('Look, you lot, we've got to smash Hollington Park today').

Our ceremonies were as traditional and ancient as the hills (since before the First World War, in any case): sports day on Ascension Day, Rogationtide, when we followed the cross round the school gardens blessing the vegetables and going purple with suppressed laughter; the carol service, when the loveliness of the carols and readings touched our stony hearts; the school play (me as Aaron in *The Firstborn*, me as Jo March in *Little Women* and, as I got spottier and hairier, me as Petruchio and even me as 'king with beard holding frankincense', when Ælene was Mary and I think Jocelyn Ayerst was Joseph). There was a special service on the first day of Lent ('What have you given up?' 'Peanut butter' – 'Oh I say, hard cheese'): early communion when our foreheads were marked with the priest's finger dipped in ash and you didn't wash it off till the evening – and for one day you looked a bit holy and could wear a martyred expression and not cut round the heads of film stars in magazines leaving their ears as huge as Mr Spock's and laugh so much you thought you would be sick.

There were the GCE exams when every classroom suddenly looked as horrifying as an abattoir, with desks the regulation four feet apart and a blackboard propped outside on an easel: 'Silence: exam in progress 2.30–4.30'. There was the end of school, the last day of term – the Michaelmas term with all our Christmas cards (Gordon Fraser 2½d each) taken down and packed into trunks along with hand-made clay models of angels as presents for parents; scarves round necks, velour hats crammed on, big tweed overcoats worn buttoned up if you were a new bug but left rakishly open like Clark Gable if you were an old lag. 'One more day of starvation/Then we go to the station/ Back to civilization/I want to go home.' The end of the Lent Term, Easter egg from crimson-cheeked pashite in the blazer pocket, lacrosse stick over the shoulder as next term it was tennis and swimming; the girls who went by train from Warrior's Square to Charing Cross the next day watching from upstairs windows; the nuns smiling at everyone, probably secretly looking forward to the silence for their holy retreat before Easter. And then the end of the Summer term ('Anyone want this racket cover?' 'Fains I!') and the girls who were leaving looking for the last time at Utopia, Singleheart and Pilgrim's Progress, the school common rooms.

All the rooms had names: either from the Greek alphabet – Kappa, Pi, Mu, Sigma – or biblical names – Hebron, Beulah, Salem – or St Pega, St Crispin, Miss Kennedy's Lawn and Edgeworth. The huge gardens are now gone for ever; then they were filled with shadowy paths, thickets of bamboo, plants we called American rhubarb, chestnuts, magnolia and rhododendrons of every size and colour. There were huge beech trees, a big black yew on the front lawn, Scots pines and maple trees; and wild garlic, anemones and bluebells carpeted the woods in spring. 'Lord dismiss us with thy blessing/Those who here will meet no more . . .' Ahead of us was a world we really knew nothing about, filled with Boys and the unbearably frightening idea of getting a job. We were extremely unsophisticated, had been taught to think the best of everyone we met; we came from a place where it was a punishable offence not to wear the school beret at the bus stop.

Q. Is this an avalanche of nostalgia?

A. I'm trying to work out what it is. I think it's this: we were innocent, which means 'unacquainted with evil' in my OED. Today we seem to know every kind of horror and despair; we've seen the pictures and read the articles. Today we have lost people we love, or witnessed or endured pain – but then we knew nothing of these things, and our hearts were untroubled by anything greater than working out how not to eat the leathery liver on your plate, or how to scam your way round handing in your chemistry prep late. Nostalgia is sometimes just trying to remember what it was like before our backs were bent with the stone-filled rucksack of experience. You can't un-know things: you can't blot out images from your mind. So sometimes you put on Buddy Holly and remember the Saturday-night dance in the school gym, with the stack of 45s and all that standing by the wall bars, hoping that some senior girl would ask you for a jive, in your sugar-stiffened petticoat and back-combed hair. Across the Atlantic, the Bay of Pigs was brewing up and the nuns said special prayers for a peaceful resolution (and the prayers must have worked – result!) but we only worried about whether our cardigan went with our skirt, and when the village shop would develop the film of us on the cow-shed roof.

I have turned into a school prefect now – I have volunteered to attend to all duties and requests and I do what I can, and I never do a wrong thing; but, much as I love my life, I sometimes think I'd like to skip classes and smoke cigarettes in the duck-house again. Patsy is the other person I could have been, if I hadn't turned out to be me. Patsy is a figure of nostalgia, doing everything we daren't do because of our obligations to our families and society. Edina is her decadent bedrock, a parent figure who pays for everything, sorts out trips, manages to keep a house and car. When Patsy went to America to try working on an American magazine (leaving home, leaving school) she couldn't cut it and had to be rescued. Edina and Patsy just want to have fun – but Eddie is split: she has a conscience which is Saffy, ever-present, critical and finally responsible for them both. That is a wise-after-the-event analysis. I don't think Jennifer wrote it with such beady introspection.

This dark-red carpet under the dining-room table is Tibetan. Several years ago I got a letter out of the blue from a Mrs Margaret Wood in Somerset: she had heard me mention my grandmother Thyra Weir in an interview; could this be the same person who lived near her in Kenya in the early 1950s? I wrote back and told her it must have been. My grandparents retired to Kenya when they left India, and built a house in Karen, where Karen Blixen lived. When my grandfather Leslie Weir died, he was buried in Nairobi and Granny Weir moved to South Africa, leaving with Margaret Wood several things she couldn't fit into her luggage – one of which was this carpet. Margaret asked me down to Somerset where she gave me the carpet and a shiny Tibetan jug: back to the family, she said. She has gone on now to the great hereafter; but I'm so grateful and touched that she hunted me down. She told me that her own house in the Ngong Hills had been used as Karen Blixen's home in the film *Out of Africa*.

And the portrait above the fireplace has a similar provenance: a woman wrote to say that she wondered whether the subject, Major General Sir James Rutherford Lumley, was a forebear of mine and whether I would like to buy it. I did so: on the back in copperplate writing is inscribed 'A present for my little son William Brownrigg Lumley the Second on his birthday 8th of January 1868, this likeness of his Grandfather, and may he become as great good and fortunate a man. W. B. Lumley'. The old man had died in Ferozepore in India in 1846. He was Colonel of the 9th Regiment of Native Infantry, and Adjutant General of the Army, and had been the Senior Officer in the Bengal Army for many years. My own father's name was James Rutherford Lumley; it was lovely to have his great–great-grandfather back home again.

I love reading about anybody's life, the more different from mine the better. That's why books like *Angela's Ashes* rush up the bestseller list: we are all so curious about other people's lives. The most depressing thing about the present-day insistence that children should read only books relevant to their own circumstances is the narrow vision of the world they're offered. (I want to read Jung Chang's *Wild Swans* and about the three generations of Chinese women; I want to read about Emily Dickinson, about what happened in *A Day in the Life of Ivan Denisovich*, and of Nelson Mandela's time on Robben Island.) So although the school I've described has gone for ever it is part of me, part of my life. My family's time in India, on both sides of parents, goes back for more than 200 years and I am inescapably a product of that existence.

Incidentally, when I was in South Africa in 1995 I met Tokyo Sexwale – pronounced 'sek-wah-lay' – and his wife, Judy, in Cape Town. Tokyo had been incarcerated on Robben Island with Mandela; as their long prison sentence continued they were permitted to watch television from time to time. *The New Avengers*, being funded by French money, was one of the very few English-speaking programmes that were sold to South Africa, as sanctions by Britain and others were still rigorously enforced. Tokyo told me that after one episode, in which Purdey had escaped from the clutches of evil by the skin of her teeth, Mandela had remarked, 'If Purdey can get out of that, we can get out of this.' That, actually, is the greatest shock of being in our business: the realization that sometimes even world-famous figures see your shows and have opinions on them. Terrific! Yet hard to believe that while I was demonstrating outside South Africa House in Trafalgar Square, holding a placard saying 'Free Nelson Mandela', he was listening to Laurie Johnson's signature tune '*Baaaa – buh buh berba baah!*' and watching what the Italians called the *Infallibile Tre* setting the world to rights.

Let's go upstairs.

Stairs

Early in 1981 I was asked down to Pinewood Studios to meet Blake Edwards. Although Peter Sellers was no longer alive, Blake had decided to make two more Pink Panther films: one, *Trail of the Pink Panther*, in which Clouseau had disappeared and a French journalist was given the task of trying to track him down by interviewing all those who had known him; and a second, *Curse of the Pink Panther*, in which a colossally inept American detective tried to discover where Clouseau actually was (in a health spa, having had radical plastic surgery which had caused him to turn into Roger Moore). My meeting was about playing Countess Chandra, raven-haired Euro-aristo of dubious morals who ran the Health Spa Clinic. I dressed up mightily for the interview, even wearing a green hat, I remember, with culottes and green stockings. Blake was suave, surrounded by a group of film heavies, all wearing dark glasses. I liked him at once although it was all fairly terrifying. I think I read a short scene; he invited me to stay for lunch but I couldn't; he gave me the script to take away with me. The script was very good – I think I would have taken the part even if it hadn't been. A few days later I got a letter from Blake:

Dear Joanna,

 I am glad you think it's terrific and very funny and I want you to read every steaming page of it because Chandra does have a bigger part. In fact, she occupies most of the last thirty pages, seducing the hero, looking beautiful and being funny. Would you like her to be foreign? Be my guest. No, I did not mean for you to look at the grandmother's role. I don't believe there are more than one or two grandmothers in the whole world with your legs. No, you don't have to send the script back. I'm sorry, too, that you didn't stay for lunch, but for me it's just another one of life's little tragedies.

 Lovely meeting you.

 Blake.

Blake gave me the part of Chandra; and he also gave me the bigger part of the French journalist in the first film, *Trail*. The two films were to be shot back-to-back, that is to say at the same time, as many of the cast would be in both – David Niven, Graham Stark, Capucine, Herbert Lom, Burt Kwouk. We filmed during spring and summer of 1982, flying to and fro across Europe, changing locations unexpectedly, spending money like an exploding fire hydrant. The absence of Peter Sellers was clearly a draw-back, but Blake hurdled that one easily by using clips from previous Panther films. He and Julie Andrews hated smoking so I gave up at once (and put on about a stone in three days).

 Julie often visited the set, incredibly slim and lithe and . . . well . . . familiar. I'd first seen her on stage as Eliza Doolittle in *My Fair Lady* with Rex Harrison, Wilfrid Hyde White and Stanley Holloway, when I was 10. I'd seen *The Sound of Music* and *Mary Poppins* and here she was walking about in blue jeans with cropped hair being kind to everyone. Huge star – as Sellers had also been a huge star and as David Niven still was, despite the onset of motor neurone disease. I loved Niven, fell for his charm and humour and wrote to him after the film had finished to tell him how things were going. During filming, the on-set doctor had prescribed for him a cocktail of very strong drugs which were withdrawn as soon as his part was over. His life was impossibly difficult: I lunched at his beautiful house in Cap Ferrat during the shoot, and his lovely but alcoholic wife, Hjördis, came downstairs very late and ate nothing. His health deteriorated steadily, but not his gorgeous courage and sense of fun. In that respect he was very like his cousin Patrick Macnee, who now lived in Palm Springs – although they adored each other their paths seldom crossed any more. When I got back to London I found a letter waiting for me, painstakingly written out in longhand with childish clarity:

St-Jean-Cap-Ferrat, 12 August '82
Darling 'Lovely Lum',
  This dull reply to your long funny newsy and altogether lovely letter will also be short I'm afraid. (I've clocked the effort, with marking ink pen and clawed fingers, and it is already STOP! . . . 8 mins 23 secs!!) Why don't you write a book? If I can do it, you can – and there are so few fun things to read these days. PLEASE DO. After you left I was very sad. It was a bonanza seeing you even briefly. 'H' fell apart completely during the family visit which was a draining Hell for me (and them) but for the last month, after finally getting really ill from under nourishment and liver trouble, she has taken a 100% turn for the better and is right back to what I bought when I

first saw it in the window – How I pray it may last, because selfishly it helps me so enormously with my own dreary problem. She looks – and is – her old self as though she has never been away. My problem I'm attacking tooth and claw. Thrice weekly floods of vitamins in the vein, strange pills and if poss: lots of rest. There are some odd side effects – Ten days ago suddenly while snorkelling off our rocks (I've done it almost daily for forty years all over the world) – I panicked! No reason – just instant claustrophobia inside the mask – spasm of the upper chest muscles and not able to get one sniff of air!! Quite terrifying!! *And v. hard to make it back to land. However, starting again in the pool: taking a few strokes holding the mask on, then trying with the flippers, graduating to 'in depth' goggling of a few minutes' duration. I have at last conquered the bastard and have just come back from 1/2 an hour round the furthest rocks and I peed my disdain at the place it had happened! Both girls are home now – Fiona flushed with success having sailed through her Baccalaureate – not bad for a Limey! It's lovely for me but 'rest' has to be insisted on. I do notice very slight improvements but it's going to be* long *and the frustration of not being able to speak properly makes one* immediately *speak even worse! I now eat alone; it's better for all and I don't choke when spoken to. A huge kiss then. Always looking for the miracle cure, I come to London occasionally. Be an angel and leave your number at the Connaught – I could always watch* you *eat! I do miss Pat Macnee.*

Much love then, Niv.

When you've finished filming you're only half-way to the film being released. It has to be edited, have music added – and be promoted. My allotted targets were New York, Chicago, Los Angeles, Toronto, Paris, Nice and Madrid.

The days are pretty much the same: rank upon rank of showbiz interviews, photo-shoots, chat shows, which start straight after breakfast and go right on up to midnight. You quickly learn a few succinct and amusing lines to say which can be quoted easily, you declare your love for everyone involved with the movie, you busk together some kind of a future even if you're utterly out of work. 'Any future plans?' 'Have you got two hours?!! No, I'm kidding! There are a couple of *good* things coming right up but I haven't signed yet so I can't talk about them. Then I'm trying to make a TV series and a Broadway show work at the same time, but I think I'm going to have to ditch one or the other . . .' And on and so on – bare-faced lies, usually. I hardly ever know what's coming up next.

Q. But you wish you did. You wish your diary was crammed with overlapping film schedules like Nicole Kidman's . . .

A. Oh don't be so stupid. I love the way work turns up. Lots of it has to be rejected because it's not what I want to do at that moment, but I'd be stifled and claustrophobic if I knew what I'd be doing this time next year. The great thing is to have confidence and enjoy things. I psyched myself up to enjoy promoting the Pink Panthers and I loved every second of it – First Class flights, swish hotels, bouquets of flowers, ironed clothes, limousines . . . they really do it well. When we'd done America and Canada I was dusted down and sent off to do the European tour. My first date was Madrid, where the films are called *Pantera Rosa*. I don't speak any Spanish, alas: I struggled with futile incompetence and they quickly appointed a charming Finnish girl to be my interpreter. We rattled through the interviews in great style. There was a popular programme on Spanish television at that time called *Bla Bla Bla*, on which I was a guest. To save time the presenter would ask the question in Spanish and I, having memorized the content of his inquisition in English, would answer in English and Anneli would translate them off-screen simultaneously back into Spanish. The only hazard was trying to remember what his questions were to be and to know when he had finished asking them. I had to open the programme by saying 'Blablabla!' as amusingly as possible, three times.

The late-night news decided to make a short film of me roaming disconsolately through the hotel, saying how much I missed Clouseau but that he would never be forgotten. I rashly agreed to say it in Spanish. The cameras turned: I travelled up and down a spiral staircase four times, walked round a statue of a naked couple and came to rest in a vast empty ballroom. Here I said my line, which I had rehearsed with Anneli. 'Is berry good,' said the director. 'You must also say "*Buenos noches, España*. That is the end of the late news." Is how we say goodnight. Is berry seemple.' We recorded the rehearsal without any serious loss of understanding, and seven of us went off to a restaurant and to give the last interview of the day.

As midnight approached it was decided that we should watch to see if our Oscar-winning short would in fact be included in the late news, which was apparently watched by every living soul on the Iberian peninsula. By this time a small excited band of paparazzi had collected around us, snapping away madly as we pulled on our coats and stumbled down a dark street to a dingy bar, where a black and white television set hung above the door. It was an eventful programme: train crashes, important political appointments, the Pope. Our faces grew longer: was *Pantera Rosa* in the same league? To crown it all, there was even footage of the King. '*El Rey!*' murmured our press agent glumly, mopping his face with a well-designed hanky. But suddenly there I was! And speaking in Spanish too! '*Buenas noches, España. Ultimas novicias han terminado.*' The bar erupted into cheering, the cameras went mad, the press agent danced on a chair. After all it's not every night that one addresses a nation.

It's always difficult to find something to do that is eye-catching and appropriate for a photo-shoot. By the time we got to Paris I was strolling arm-in-arm with a huge furry Pink Panther in front of the Arc de Triomphe holding up the traffic all down the Champs-Élysées. I posed with champagne glasses in a variety of dresses in the Bar Anglais of the Plaza-Athéné; I was pictured slavering over the jewels in Bulgari, a ritzy shop in the Avenue Montaigne next door to the hotel. As we left we saw a terrific commotion going on 25 yards away at Cartier. There were police cars, cordons, crowds and an air of outrage and excitement. A million pounds worth of jewellery had been stolen, guns had been brandished and the thieves had escaped into the balmy Parisian afternoon. Our disappointment was intense, our press agent almost inconsolable: 'I 'ad harranged that you go to Cartier; then I theenk I don't want you to 'ave to cross ze road, so I am choosing Bulgari.' We had missed the publicity coup to end them all.

That night I was a guest on the Michael Drucker show which went out live to 20 million viewers. We were quite an assorted bunch. First there was a pop singer called Captain Sensible and his three girl singers. They wore

Getting my first film part in *Some Girls Do*.

Publicity shot on the rooftops in Canterbury. My first-ever play in the theatre, 1969.

Me as a Bond Girl in *On Her Majesty's Secret Service*.

Blake Edwards on
The Pink Panther shoot.

With Charlotte Cornwell and Siân Phillips in *Vanilla*.

As Elinor Glyn in *The Cat's Meow*. Directed by Peter Bogdanovich.

Miriam Margolyes as Aunt Sponge, producer Jake Eberts and me as Aunt Spiker
with rat's teeth in *James and the Giant Peach*, San Francisco.

With Gareth and Patrick on *The New Avengers'* first visit to New York, 1975.

Episode One.

With Helen and Terry Wogan at David Frost's 60th birthday party.

With Muhammad Ali on *Wogan*.

Giving Graham Norton a Golden Globe in New York.

Promoting
The Pink Panther.

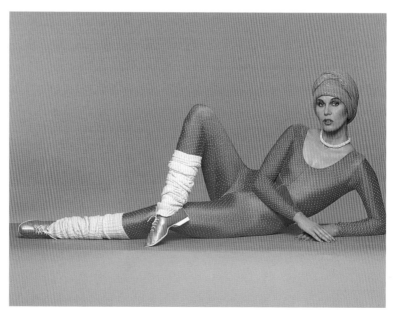

Me and Rich Warwick – we are about to strip off in *The Breaking of Bumbo*.

With Gareth, judging Purdey lookalike competition. Extreme right won.

dense, pill-sized sunglasses and red berets. Some of the act was jumping up and down, and some was Captain Sensible crawling and rolling around on the floor. Their song was very loud ('He said Captain, I said what/He said Captain . . .') and I heard a stage hand mutter, '*Complètement fou.*' Captain Sensible translated into French became Captain Sensitive. Then four dancers, dressed as Pink Panthers, executed a lively interpretation of Henry Mancini's well-known theme tune, marred by the fact that they could only see through their nostrils and had to be led away by the paw. Then I appeared in a borrowed dress, a huge froth of shocking-pink tulle with long black gloves, holding a toy panther and mumbling in French.

Continental – by that I mean non-British European – television is much less cynical, much less prone to tittering in embarrassment about its programmes. Even today in chic Berlin there are daily shows of women in aprons and dirndl skirts singing spinning songs. They love a good variety show, with dogs, and plates whizzing round on sticks and custard pies and a bit of slap and tickle. Captain Sensible and the Pink Panther dancers were just the ticket: I actually thought the Captain Sensible song was rather good, and told him so. He said they were enjoying Paris but that he missed the local chip shop in Croydon.

Here we are.

Bathroom

The bathroom is always quite tidy. I've just done my hair – dyed the roots and given the ends a good snipping and cut a bit of the back where it seemed uneven. As far as I can see, holding a hand mirror and looking over my shoulder, it's fairly straight and, as Gill who cleans for me says, a blind man would like to see it. Why do I do it? Why don't I go regularly to the skilled hairdressers I've known all my grown-up life who are now scorchingly famous – John Frieda, Nicky Clarke, Michael Rasser of Michaeljohn, Daniel Galvin? They could make a flokati rug look good enough for the cover of *Vogue*; they could cut and colour a nail-brush to make you jealous. The thing is, I really love mucking about with hair and make-up myself. I want to do it with my own hands, not because I don't think other people can, but because it gives me great satisfaction.

Jan Sewell, who masterminds the make-up on *Absolutely Fabulous*, lets me do my own face (although Patsy's hair is done by professionals: first it is back-combed up like a clump of elephant grass, then sprayed and cajoled into a Mr Whippy soufflé. In the last series we did, it was less huge and some straightening tongs came into play, but now I have a set of these myself and can look like Björk at a second's notice.) I was taught by Linda Tulley, who did the make-up on *Class Act*, how to mix up hair dye and what percentage of peroxide solution to use. She gave me my first mixing bowl, and a brush to apply the mixture to the roots. The time to do it is when there is a danger of being under bright lights or in a strong wind, when the partings can be flattened and illuminated to show my real hair colour, which is now Arctic stoat.

There have been times when I have attempted highlights at home, involving a plastic cap and a crochet hook. Entailing a grey cellophane head and about 40 thin strands teased through tiny holes this is only undertaken when there is no chance of a husband, or indeed any man, seeing you. Men aren't good at *how* it's done: even when they know your eyelashes are false, or your glossy mane is dyed, or your fingernails are glued on, they are not good at witnessing the art of creation. Either they laugh or say they feel sick, or they ask why. They find hair rollers funny or scary. They are pathetic at tummy-flattening tights, face packs (obviously) and plucking of eyebrows, so I say keep them away from these activities. Men who *are* good at this are hairdressers, who often pause to tell you a good story when they have gripped all your hair so it hangs unflatter-ingly forward, leaving you a fronded crack to peer through while they talk to you from behind, looking at their own handsome faces in the mirror. Nicky Clarke said something nice to me in the Scottish church in Pont Street. We were filming Saffy's wedding in *AbFab* and there was a lot of hanging about in pews. Nicky was appearing as himself ('NickyClarkeNickyClarke') and sitting behind me. Talk turned to hair and I showed him my roots, which I'd dyed the previous week. 'It looks OK,' he said, which I have taken as high praise.

Ever since I first lived in London, staying with my aunt Joan Mary in her huge rambling flat in Earls Court when I was 17, attending the Lucie Clayton modelling school for a month of mornings, wandering about in the afternoons, I knew the city would be my home. First, I only knew my way by tube (about 4*d.* a stop), emerging from the underground at Chalk Farm or Bond Street, not certain how far Green Park was from Knightsbridge. When we shared our girls' flat on the fourth floor in Trebovir Road, four of us in two bedrooms, we could hear from dawn to dusk the announcements from the Earls Court station below us. We bought lamps and chairs from the Portobello Road and Brick Lane, food from an old-fashioned branch of Sainsbury's with sawdust on the tiled floor, and records from W.H. Smith, and put posters up on the walls. Sometimes at weekends we'd catch a tube to Bermondsey, long before it had been tidied up and rebuilt, and walk by the river; or kick footballs round Victoria Park in the East End. We watched the Boat Race from Putney Bridge, bought clothes from Biba in Abingdon Road and skulked about in Soho for poetry-readings and Happenings. The rent was nine pounds a week, and we put one pound each in the kitty for food and household goods. We shared clothes and tights and played 'All You Need Is Love' through the window to the street far below.

At the end of each day's modelling, there was my heavy model's bag to lug up four flights of stairs. In those days models were expected to provide all their own accessories: make-up, shoes, boots, gloves, scarves, tights, white and black polo necks (for coats) and jewellery. Unless you had money, your accessories were the things you wore every day anyway, so they often looked shabby and scuffed.

Standards were not exactly lower, just less demanding. Unless you were to appear in *Queen* or *Vogue*, fashion was pretty much what we made up on the spot: a certain way of adjusting your knee socks, or doing your hair or making up your eyes . . . if it worked, it was in. We carried about our model books as well, filled with what we hoped would be our passport to success: an extended advertising campaign for Pringle knitwear, some good headshots from Supersoft hairspray ads, an editorial on coats photographed by Norman Eales. A lot of it was busking, chancing it, hoping they'd like your new hair-style (cut free on Thursday nights after hours by apprentices at Vidal Sassoon). London was the buzzy centre of innovative designers and cool photographers. (I made Patsy wear her hair as we did when she went to Paris on a fashion shoot – always rushing, we would put our hair into large rollers and tie a scarf over them: this was the signature of the model, this said, 'I am soooo busy and gorgeous I don't have to care what I look like between jobs.') We wore false eyelashes all day, every day; and false fingernails, and hairpieces Kirbigripped on, and brown blusher shading our cheekbones. There was a fashion for wearing men's watches, for dark glasses or granny glasses perched on the end of your nose, and for smoking Gitanes or Gauloise cigarettes. We had big diaries to write our assignments in; at the end of each day at about five o'clock, I'd phone in to Lucie Clayton: 'Hello, darling,' Doreen would say; '10 till one, Sandra Lousada, *Woman's Own*, evening cardigans so take your own dangly earrings; two till five, David Montgomery in Edith Grove, don't you dare be late, it's Bri-Nylon so make sure your hair's looking good.'

Lord! We used to mess about with our hair as models!

In the sixties we were expected to do it ourselves, carrying all our own equipment of hairpieces, full wigs, Carmen rollers, hairspray and pins. We scraped and sprayed and plaited like fury, often looking wildly different but not necessarily nice. We also used scarves a lot – folded into bandanas, tied coquettishly behind our ears or posh-and-glum under the chin. Sometimes we were used as models for a Hair Feature with a great deal of setting lotion and gel. Most of the time we weren't supposed to look like *us* but like cool secretaries, glamorous hostesses, young mums, partying chicks or pale brides. There was an evening look and a day look and you were meant to look as though you had put a lot of thought into how your hair complemented your sequinned off-the-shoulder wool-and-linen cropped kaftan: perhaps with a *diamanté* hair slide and a false plait.

Most magazines had recipes, knitting patterns, an agony aunt, a short story, a letters' page; and our kind of fashion sat easily amongst the editorials and advertisements of the day. I longed so much to join the top-rung divas who did spreads in *Queen* and covers for *Elle*, but there was a puddingy quality about my face which was then rather spotty too, and my beigey-brown hair wasn't up to scratch. Certainly it wasn't a sheet of silky gold, like Celia Hammond's. Celia was the Kate Moss of our day. Nowadays she doesn't give a pin what she looks like, with her arms scarred by wild cats and her hands chapped from tending animals night and day, but you can't get away from that face and how extraordinarily beautiful it was, and still is. Her charity, the Celia Hammond Animal Trust, is one of the organizations I support; it rescues and neuters and re-homes animals – always, like all small charities, with its back against the wall. Shall I put a list of the charities I support and why and what they do?

Q. Not now. Put it at the end of the book. Or not at all.

A. I have invented a few things which I'd like to tell you about. The first thing was called a bear-bag. We were filming *The New Avengers* in Canada and I bought a nice grey toy bear – not a teddy bear, but a real-looking animal about the size of a small cat. It was very nice to hold, very comforting, and had a rather sweet expression. I opened up the back seam, took out some of the kapok stuffing, made a pocket out of a handkerchief and slid this into the bear's back, the opening towards the upside, and then stitched the edges up – so you could slide your hand into the body of the bear and get out your keys or cigarettes or money. It was a success – people liked the idea; so when I got back to England I tracked down some soft-toy manu-facturers, who were based in Alresford, and we had a meeting. It didn't develop any further, sadly, even though I'd thought of having a lead attached to the bear's collar which could clip on to the base of its spine, as it were, making the creature into a portable shoulder bag. Kim Waterfield, a friend of a friend, 'Dandy' Kim Waterfield, the sixties entrepreneur, had thought I should market it as a 'Purdey' bag, but that name belonged to *The New Avengers* and in any case was the name of a superb gun, so the whole idea fizzled out. Ten years later, children round the world were strung about with pandas, cats, chimpanzees and bears as knapsacks and shoulder bags.

Two more quick inventions, one rather more achiev-able than the other: the lip-liner stencil, and rubbish-tip mountains for flat-country enhancement. No, *three* (sorry): batteries powered by car tyres.

1. Every woman who wears lipstick wants her mouth to look nice and an even shape. If your mouth is crooked, and most of ours are, lipstick is only going to exaggerate the irregularities. Think now of the rubber clamp you have to bite on when you're going to have a dental X-ray. Now imagine a much smaller, pleasanter version, and, extruding from the side sticking out of the front of your mouth, a spring-loaded mouth-shape made of firm but slenderly-wrought rubber, like a stencil. You would coat the mouth-shape with a darkish lipstick, clench your front teeth over the rubber clamp, stencil the mouth-shape on to your lips, remove clamp and fill in the outlined mouth space. You could choose your favourite mouth – Joan Crawford, Marilyn Monroe or Angelina Jolie – or have the shape custom-formed to look like you, only more gorgeous.

2. The rubbish-tip idea is in its infancy. It's to cope with the unstoppable flow of plastic which is non-biodegradable, or will only break down over decades. Special collections of all that plastic and polystyrene that we shuck from our supermarket purchases would be taken to the flattest part of the country that is about to be built on providing homes and factories. My heart has often leapt when I'm driving to see what I think is a range of distant mountains behind Sydenham or Ashford – but it always turns out it's only cloud formations. If, however, all our plastic trash were compressed and set, with a bonding agent, it could be moulded over colossal skeletons (like those primitive yurts, the stick-and-skin structures nomads sleep under). Within these huge hill-shaped contrivances

would be channels for electricity, refuse, water and gas. Access would be by tunnels, like in a sophisticated gold mine. The new hills would be moved into place, with viewing days to make sure the new skyline was attractive from all sides, and then earth for trees and gardens would be brought on and rivers and waterfalls could be made – and perhaps a cable car. It would be worth a try, just once.

3. The battery idea came when we were driving up to Scotland past a small wind farm – what if the wind didn't blow? we wondered. The road, however, never seemed to sleep: vehicles move up and down the motorways night and day. If there were a strip across the lanes that housed rollers embedded like cats'-eyes in a sort of rubbery trench, the rollers would be spun by the wheels going over it and the resulting power could be harnessed for lighting. The rollers would be just flush with the road's surface so you wouldn't have a speed-bump situation – and people wouldn't even feel they were going over them. This idea has been scrutinized by my friend the architect Pat Lorimer, but he gave it the thumbs-down, for reasons too complicated for me to understand.

Q. The bathroom is rather lovely, now that I look around it. A free-standing Victorian tub; an open fireplace with what we call B-movie flames; huge painted shutters from Morocco; tiaras, shells and feathers on the little mantel-piece; prints and paintings; and a picture of a nice muscly Michelangelo youth half-looking over his shoulder from the shower. There is also quite a large tree.

A. Long ago, back in the sixties, we used to give, and go to, parties where people just left their front doors open;

and along with real guests there would always be some passer-by (and the occasional thief). There was a shoal mentality: if there was a party and one of the people you knew had met one of the people going to it, you were all perfectly entitled to go along, carrying a bottle of Nicolas wine or a flower, or a tin of spliffs; an incoming shoal of minnows – or sharks. I can see now why politicians writhe around when asked by reporters, 'Did you smoke dope? Did you inhale?' But truly they should all say, 'Yes, I tried it.' Just that. All of them should just admit they knew what it was and probably had a weeny little puff and probably tried to inhale it properly, even if they couldn't manage without coughing. The culture then was not the drug culture it has become. Smoking pot was the adult equivalent of having a gasper behind the bike sheds, and many joints at parties were actually passed around in the lavatories, which made it all seem very thrilling and daring. The prohibition stance seems to me to be mad. I don't smoke dope now – haven't since my son was born over three decades ago – but I did occasionally then. People made hash cookies and we ate them and felt stoned and laughed a lot; but you grow out of it in the end or use it in a controlled manner. Prohibition provokes crime, which means robbery and violence. I would make all drugs, just like all alcohol, legal to people over 18 and sell them in ordinary shops. The government could control the quantity and quality and buy them legitimately from the producing countries, and they could have an accurate register of who was an addict and who needed help. There would be no need for dealers, any more than there are 'dealers' for hard spirits hanging round tube stations.

Q. This sounds shockingly irresponsible. Don't you realize how many young people might die?

A. Don't you realize how many young people today, encouraged by advertising and, by implication, the government, drink themselves into trash every night? Unless you teach children about the dangers of lethal things they *will* die of them: cars, guns, alcohol, drugs, cigarettes . . .

Q. But you smoke!

A. In moderation. I drink in moderation, I would loathe to get drunk. My solution would rest in education and we've discussed this already. Without education, the *very* best our taxed money can buy, we haven't got a single chance left. Would the money the government received from selling drugs be 'dirty' money? No dirtier than cigarette taxes, which they cheerfully use to build hospitals and primary schools. If you stand near a huge sharp knife in a kitchen, you don't feel you *have* to cut your hand off or stab someone. I don't *want* drugs, even though I could easily get them. If people have addictive natures they need to be identified and steered clear of minefields. We can't be run by part-time Puritans.

Q. The tree. (You'll get letters about that, you'll really regret it, raving on about drugs.)

A. Drugs exist. 'War against drugs' is as fatuous as 'War against terrorism', a completely bogus concept uttered to keep the high moral ground and addressing the underlying problem not a jot. (I love Billy Connolly.) Now. This lovely tree, the common *Ficus benjamina*, was given to us as a little plant 12 years ago. I love a tree in a room. When I saw a standard bay tree in Sibylla Edmonstone's grand flat in Ennismore Gardens I thought it was the chicest thing on the planet. It was 1968 and the event was one of the aforementioned parties, but this one was different because the flat was huge and beautiful and not a wacky dive off the North End Road. Sibylla was very beautiful, with long dark hair; she had a title, and a nightclub was called after her. In her white bedroom, at the foot of her huge bed, around which party guests milled trying to look as hip and cool as possible, stood the bay tree, a straight bare stem and a clipped round ball of leaves at face height.

Many years later, saddened by a perpetual leak in my Addison Road flat which dripped monotonously on to the ground at the end of my bed and which the landlord wouldn't fix, I bought a bay tree of my own. It grew and flourished there, nurtured by the London rain funnelled through the gap in the roof, making its way through the roof space and appearing in glistening drops on the ceiling plasterwork. (I would have fixed that tile myself if I could, but it was too high up on the tall sloping roof. On the whole, I like fixing things myself and have a very comprehensive collection of tools for all occasions, which I keep neatly in order, some in their original boxes.)

Q. Why did you just mention Billy Connolly?

A. 'Not a jot' – it's a phrase he used in one of the funniest sketches I've ever seen. The occasion luckily was taped and recorded so it hasn't disappeared. It was *An Audience with Billy Connolly,* and the sketch was about a young raver who had an incontinence problem but wore big incontinence pants under his groovy clothes and went out dancing. I was in the audience at LWT; we laughed so much we were nearly sick. It's silly to call it a sketch – Billy, as we all know, just develops and elaborates themes. Eddie lzzard operates in the same sort of way: they have an idea where they're going and then they just fly unscripted. Eddie did an excellent Charles Chaplin in a film I was also in called *The Cat's Meow* directed by Peter Bogdanovich, but then Eddie's a very good actor, too – as is Peter, as is Billy. I was playing Elinor Glyn, the renowned woman novelist who fell in love with Hollywood and became Chaplin's friend and a lifelong admirer of William Randolph Hearst. Let me open this cupboard for you – there! Towels and so forth up here, but underneath, on this lower shelf, a huge amount of make-up and hair equipment. I did Elinor Glyn's make-up myself. I'd studied photographs of her and read a biography and one of her books. She was a redhead and enhanced her hair colour by rinsing it through with red ink; mine was a wig, of course, but I wanted to use the dark matte red lipsticks and kohl pencils and white powder that they used in those days. I made the eyebrows very different from my own, much darker and slightly plaintive.

For Aunt Spiker in the film of *James and the Giant Peach,* I transformed my mouth by blotting out my biggish lips and drawing the meanest little slash you could imagine, going down to nothing in the middle: a sort of reverse Cupid's bow. This looked very good with the long rat's teeth I'd ordered to wear over my own. Because the camera comes so close, you have to try to alter your face physically as well as thinking your way into the part. The way you look in your own natural-born face can be a deterrent – you might look too good or too bad, too un-handsome or not clever enough. Lucky actors have regular features, which can become canvases for the imprint of the new person they will become. But that's a ridiculous generalization – Meryl Streep's face is very distinctive and yet she absolutely fits every character she plays. She does, however, change her appearance completely each time and she alters the cut of her jib, and the way she *is*. Her *being* changes. We all like a nice Plasticine nose or, in my case, dodgy false teeth, but beware of them in general. As a model and then as an actress you find that much time is spent staring back at yourself in the make-up mirror, and wondering how you can improve or alter your appearance. By holding a finger across your eyebrow you can see what you'd look like without eyebrows; or with a pencil – even a toothbrush – held across your upper lip you can imagine yourself in a moustache.

I look good in a beard, with my hair scraped back. I made a very convincing Prince Charming to Lynsey de Paul's Cinderella in a marvellous version of that pantomime which we did to raise money for the Bobath Centre for cerebral palsy in 1982. The cast list was awesome: it included Henry Cooper, Charlie Drake and Ian McKellen, Su Pollard, Caroline Quentin, Jenny Agutter, Billy Connolly (as a fairy), Ned Sherrin, Helen Mirren . . . It went on and on, with the glamour and glitziness underlined by the writers, each of whom contributed one scene: Alan Ayckbourn, John Cleese, John Fortune, Michael Frayn, John Wells, Jack Rosenthal, more and more. I can't remember being in a one-night-only show that was so lovingly and elaborately prepared. Tudor Davies was in charge. Dressing rooms at the Prince Edward Theatre were crammed, the names on the doors reading things like 'Britt Ekland, Lucy Fleming, Rula Lenska, Patricia Hodge', or 'Gordon Jackson, Lionel Blair, Simon Williams, Roy Kinnear, Peter Bowles'. Ian Ogilvy was my Dandini, the head of a gang of eager courtiers who would form an armchair with their bodies whenever I wanted to sit down. My very short boy's-haircut wig and Ruritanian moustache and clipped beard were unsettlingly convincing. In my scarlet sash and gold epaulettes with knee-high boots and white gloves, I looked a hell of a smoothy.

I'd been bearded before, of course: as a seven-year-old Father Christmas; as Petruchio in the school play; as a really ambitious copy of Henry VIII – cheeks, stomach and all; but Prince Charming was a gorgeous person with more than a hint of my hero Dirk Bogarde. I'd only become an actor because I admired Dirk Bogarde so and felt I looked like him. In interviews I always said I thought he was the bee's knees. Suddenly one day I opened an envelope and out fell a postcard:

France, July 1st, 1983

Dear Miss Lumley,
I have to type this because I really do want you to be able to read it! I have received a number of Happy-Fannie letters recently which have been anxious to let me know that you were on the BBC (with Maria Aitken?) and that you said very many 'really nice things' about me! So insistent have the letters been, and so pleased, that I feel compelled to write and thank you! Forgive me: but in an age when being clobbered is the fashion it is so super to know that someone like you, far away on the

BBC, *bothered to speak kindly of me. But it was reeeely nice*
of you! And thank you very, very sincerely,
   Dirk Bogarde

There is a moment, in all our lives, when something so
utterly exciting and unexpected happens that you feel quite
unreal. The first time I had seen Dirk Bogarde was in the
film of *A Tale of Two Cities*. I was 10; my parents were
together in Malaya, and Ælene and I were staying with my
godmother Diana Reid in Sevenoaks. She and Allan, her
husband, had known my parents in India. Now, in their
house, with ponies and dogs and the children, Hilary and
Martin – who were roughly our ages – we felt we were in
a home from home. (Hilary was to become our link to the
Scottish cottage: we are cross-godmothered, as it were.)
They took us to the theatre in London; we rode every day,
went for walks and, one magical afternoon, went to the
cinema in Sevenoaks. Because I hadn't read my Dickens,
I didn't know what the story would be about. The sight
and sound of the guillotine was to haunt me for years to
come; but what stole my heart and mind was the self-
sacrifice of louche, handsome, bad Sidney Carton (played
by Bogarde). I can remember sitting in my seat at the
end crying and crying as though my own head had been
chopped off . . . Dirk Bogarde, giving up his life so that
Lucy could marry the dull good guy – the pity of it! (Then
came *The Spanish Gardener*, *Song Without End*, *The Singer
Not the Song*, *Doctor at Sea*, Dirk Bogarde the super-
megastar with languid insolence, eyebrow and thinness –
my hero!) His finest work came later in *The Damned*, *The
Night Porter* and *Death in Venice*, but the reason I loved him
was because he had given up his life for someone he loved

in the most appalling circumstances during the French Revolution.

Now I was 37, holding a postcard from a demigod, his own inky signature graceful and decisive, my name at the top written by *him*. He had sat down in France and written out my name. In the way the world turns, I was to get to know him much better, interviewing him for Eddie Shah's newspaper *Today*, travelling from Dundee to be with him on the Russell Harty show ('Let's meet again when I'm over here next time – I'll write well in advance . . . good luck with Hedda Gabler . . .'), but the first cut is the deepest; the very first postcard, in my hand as I write this, is one of my golden possessions. He knew I thought I looked like him ('I do hope you don't look like me now, not even a bit. One turtle on the beach is quite enough to be going on with . . .') and I do.

If you work with people of legendary prominence, if you work with Harold Pinter, for instance, whilst never forgetting that he's now a *dictionary word* for heaven's sake, you get to know and like the person. When I've got three teeth left and my great-grandchildren say, 'Did you really know Pinter?' like 'Did you really know Ibsen?' – I suppose then it will sink in. Death removes people to the Valhalla Hall of Perpetual and Ineradicable Fame – before death, everyone behaves fairly normally. Can you imagine saying, 'Herr Beethoven, could you pack your bags and move out of the upstairs flat because we can't stand you banging away at your music'? But poor Beethoven had to move again and again, more than 50 times (can that be right? When I went to Vienna, I asked to see Beethoven's home and they just laughed and said, '*Bitte!* Which one exactly?') Fame is an interesting hat to wear: some people wearing it are indeed unforgettable; others are simply famous – familiar faces and voices, well-known but not known, a curiosity. A peep show. Most televisual fame merely makes you instantly recognizable, like a zebra. If you see one, you say, 'There's a zebra,' and you might try to feed it a bun or shoot it; most people just want to look at it, and go home and say, 'I saw a zebra in the street and it was fatter than I thought but it looked at me.' Real fame belongs to Julius Caesar, Einstein, Mozart and Dirk Bogarde, who will always be famous to me, because he changed my life. After *A Tale of Two Cities* I knew I *had* to be an actor.

Q. Look at all these mirrors, all along the wall behind the basins, on the cupboard door, on telescopic arms off the walls . . . are you vain? This hugely magnifying one on a stand beside the toothbrushes . . . what's going on?

A. They're all useful. If I'm cutting my hair at the back, I angle this one and look backwards into that one and can see quite well. Sometimes it's difficult remembering how to convert left into right when the image has been reflected twice, and there have been the occasional mishaps and large clumps of hair have fallen in error. The terrifying close-up mirror is essential if your eyesight is getting worse gradually – just normal old-age short-sightedness, nothing sad: just beware of doing make-up without seeing the results clearly. And get good lights, too: sometimes you think you've put on a charming foundation and a little pink blusher when in fact you look like an orange balloon with crimson cheeks.

Q. You're not that fat. Why 'fat' all the time, why 'balloon'? One journalist wrote that you had cheekbones like elbows . . .

A. . . . but he went on to say he thought I was retarded. No, I'm not fat, but cameras in your life all the time make you aware that as they add seven or eight pounds to your appearance you have to keep a bit under your average weight. If you can.

Q. Do you weigh yourself?

A. Never. I just make up weights I'd like to be: everyone believes you as it's not very interesting. Mind you, if I really were nine stone I'd carry around a set of scales and step on them in public and boast like mad.

Q. How much do you weigh?

A. Nine stone two pounds.

Q. May we know your beauty routine? Frankly, it doesn't look to me as though you have one.

A. Teeth: I clean them three times a day – I floss, use Water Pik, electric toothbrush, mouthwash. I made up a mouth-wash of rosewater which tasted dreadful but made me smell like a summer garden, I believe. Face: I've always used Astral cream because I'm not allergic to it and because it's never been tested on animals. I use it to take off my make-up and as a hand cream, moisturizer and, very occasionally, hair-conditioner. I've used Ambre Solaire for all the same reasons but principally as I adore the smell. I'm in love with the smell of Ambre Solaire No. 2, the brown oil in the plastic bottle. It smells of freedom, of leaving school and going on holiday to Italy, of being 17. When I had not much money I used to scrub my face with soap and a soft toothbrush; now I use a tube of gritty stuff, like a gluey pan-scourer. When I was a teenager I had horrible spots: not all over my face, but round my hairline and eyebrows and nose. My mother found some wicked-smelling sulphurous liquid which I had to dab on at night, filling the dormitory with the smell of rotten eggs.

Spots – I never thought they would go. Along with my frizzy hair they were the bane of my young life. My hair is now neither one thing nor the other, sort of smooth at the back underneath and charmlessly wavy round my face. If I just left it, as I did on the desert island when I was Girl Friday, it would be sort of wriggly curls. But then it was full of seawater, as there was no fresh water to rinse it: and contrary to popular advice given in women's magazines, seawater is brilliant for your hair if you leave it in. Your scalp itches and you scratch like a dog but the salt is excellent for the hair and, of course, for a sunburnt skin.

Q. Nails? I can see you don't bother with manicures.

A. I used to bite my nails when I was young and may have weakened them fatally. Sometimes I can get them to grow quite long but I prefer short, end-of-the-finger no-nonsense nails. Once I had nail extensions cemented on for a film part – the evil stepmother in *Ella Enchanted* – but I became panic-stricken at not being able to pull them off, and had to go back to the nail salon after two weeks to have them dissolved. Sometimes after a day of heavy make-up and constricting clothes there is nothing better than to rip everything off, scrub your face, take off nail varnish, scratch your scalp – sometimes I would like to snip my hair off too till I'm like a bald monk. Almost always I cut the labels out of the back of clothes because they scratch. It makes you realize the iconic value of a designer name: unless you can see something's Versace it just looks like a jacket or whatever. Red Rum is the greatest horse of all time until his jockey falls off. Then, mysteriously, he morphs into being a riderless horse, no name, no racing colours to distinguish him. You never hear them say, 'And now, with his rider unseated two fences back, here comes Red Rum, a loose horse, making ground on the outside.'

Q. What do you do with clothes you no longer wear, with labels no longer in them?

A. Give them to friends, charity shops, auctions, or, if they are beyond-belief shabby, put them in the fabric-recycling bin at the dump. Our dump is in the shadow of Battersea Power Station. Some kestrels have nested in the tall chimneys and we sometimes have bird-watchers with binoculars look-ing out for them. I love the way wildlife creeps back into cities. In 'Mowgli's Song against People', Kipling writes:

> I will let loose against you the fleet-footed vines –
> I will call in the Jungle to stamp out your lines!
> The roofs shall fade before it,
> The house beams shall fall;
> And the *Karela*, the bitter *Karela*,
> Shall cover it all!

Here on the mantelpiece I keep pelican feathers I picked up in Kenya. Here is a huge old conch shell, with a little enamel dish tucked inside it with Beethoven's head painted on it, so he can always hear the sea. And here is a Malay bride's headdress, all intricate twisted wires and leaves, and Ellen Terry's tiara of fake emeralds and diamonds made of paste and set in gilded metal. It was worn by Vivien Leigh once, and later owned by Dame Joan Sutherland. I bought it at auction: now it belongs to me, the fourth of four generations of performers, waiting to be handed on to a fifth. I can't be without things like these. They make my mind wander and take away the trivialities of a humdrum life.

Q. Your life is far from humdrum.

A. Yes! But we all need reminding often of how tiny our footprints are before the next wave comes crashing in to obliterate them. Footprints in the sands of time. We are like icebergs, only a small part of us showing and about nine-tenths underwater, made up of hidden thoughts and a completely separate life. I believe that's why we love stories and films and above all music. Even though we can, with the top part of the iceberg, the one-tenth sticking out of the water, discuss them with other people, how we interpret them is surely completely singular. Our imagination, our greatest gift, is utterly different from that of every other soul that has ever lived. Remarkable! Miraculous, even: a daily miracle.

Q. You should get out more.

Bedroom

I had the actor's dream again the other night. I am standing at a large make-up mirror in a tatty dressing room. Beside me is one other actor but there are three reflections in the glass. My face is deathly white and an unseen person's hand is drawing a long red slash over my right eyebrow up to my temple; my eyes are kohl-blacked. Now I am standing in the wings looking on to the stage. The curtain has gone up and the lights are on but the play has not started. It is to be a version of *L'Après-midi d'un faune*. I look down and see that I am in a long pink gauze dress covered with paper flowers. The stage has been designed as a grotto, with butterflies, ferns and a real waterfall. I realize that I am about to make an entrance.

Grabbing the stage manager by the arm, I whisper, 'I can't remember my first line.' She shoots me a scornful glance. 'In the herbal . . .' she prompts in a hiss. I look back at the stage. I have never even seen the ballet; I can't imagine what the play could be about. 'I will have to go on with the book,' I whisper. 'Please get me the book.' She makes an impatient gesture and hurries away on plimsolled feet. The stage is very bright and still; I can hear the audience moving restlessly. Mesmerized, I start to walk out of the shadows, my long skirt clenched up in my shaking hands. Flash! I am bolt upright in bed, awake and trembling, the veins in my neck standing out like guy-ropes. The bedclothes are bunched in my fists and I am soaked in sweat.

There are variations on this dream. Sometimes I am locked out of the stage door in the street, knowing my entrance cue is about to be spoken on stage inside the packed theatre. More often than not I can't even find out what play we're about to perform, let alone what character I'll be playing. I'm always pleading to be allowed to glance, just glance for a second, at the book to give me the roughest idea of the text. The other people in the dream are always hostile and never meet my eye, always busy with something more important.

In dreams, I've woken up naked in Selfridges' window in the morning rush hour. I've stood up to make a speech and all my clothes have fallen off. Everyone has naked dreams; do nudists, I wonder?

Q. This is a big room – long windows all along one side, an open fireplace, wooden blinds, a huge Moroccan painted wood chair, a terracotta bust by Karin Jonzen of a woman contemplating, books on tables and on a shelf behind the bed. The curtains look home-made . . .

A. They are. I've got a sewing machine and I can make simple things like unlined curtains. Because I can't be bothered to be too exact the hems are all slightly different lengths, but that really isn't going to bring down the government. The bed I've had since I was 19. It was made by Waring and Gillow in the 1930s and I bought it in a second-hand shop in Hastings. It is made of carved mahogany which has been bleached; it cost £3. 10s.

Q. Now we'd like a list of all your boyfriends, everyone you've slept with, that sort of thing.

A. You must be out of your mind. I don't believe you just said that.

Q. People can't be expected not to be interested. We have to have some romance in a book like this. Come on! Who was the best kisser?

A. I'll tell you why I'm not going to answer that: it's quite simple, it's invasion of privacy.

Q. What a stuffy prudish answer. Are you a prude, do you think?

A. Probably: I have to admit I never relish having to act out love scenes on camera, particularly if you have to take your clothes off. In the sixties and seventies there was tremendous pressure to take your kit off – usually just the women, sometimes only the top half. The threat was that you weren't a proper actress if you didn't get your tits out. We all did it: I was very afraid of being thought an amateur as I hadn't been to drama school, but I dreaded those scenes. By today's standards they were incredibly mild – quite a lot of lingering shots of shoulders and thighs and rather unconvincing looks of ecstasy. The first one I did was in a film called *The Breaking of Bumbo*, adapted from Andrew Sinclair's best-selling book of that name. Bumbo was played by the darling boy Richard Warwick, who was so funny and good-looking and gay that it made the whole shoot completely bearable.

Love scenes! It's back to this privacy thing: we all are used to people talking, fighting, eating in public, but very few of us watch other people groping each other – in fact the opposite. If you opened a door and saw people thrashing about in bed you'd make your apologies and leave at once. So how other people actually go about it is quite a mystery, confidently solved by actors on celluloid (still quite a lot of lingering thigh/shoulder/bottom shots, I notice – and a nude love scene in almost every film). The crew are very good at being workmanlike when the towelling dressing gowns are dropped. Even if your bare back is all that's on show, that means a bare front too, but the team are very blasé and it's soon over. In *A Perfect Hero* I had to go to bed with Nigel Havers who is a friend, a proper friend. Very odd to take your top off in front of a friend and have to smooch them when you're both married. One should be acting and forgetting all that but it's still quite strange. Albert Finney and I had a love scene in *A Rather English Marriage*. He couldn't have made it easier or more natural – Finney is loved by everyone who comes near him and I think it's because he loves them back. He adores women, and women, me included, adore him. Women were jealous of me for my scene with Albert. Tom Courtenay and Finney were the stars of that film; it had taken ages to get it off the ground as the powers that be couldn't see the value of a story involving two widowers and a middle-aged woman. Angela Lambert wrote the original story and Andrew Davies did the screenplay. It got all sorts of prizes and has been shown and reshown here and all over the world. A lesson here for commissioning editors, I think . . .

Q. . . . which they may well ignore. Do you get attached to people you work with? Do you make real friendships – or isn't there time?

A. I think it must happen in all walks of life. At conventions or exhibitions, on cruises and long train journeys, anywhere where you are all together and making the best of it for a given time. Acting is no different, but perhaps because everything is heightened – there's more money, beauty, danger of failing, extremes of emotion – friendships and love affairs blossom and flourish, wither and perish like a speeded-up film. Yes, real and lasting friendships and marriages are made, but not as often as we'd all like. When the job is over, that particular spell is broken and sometimes you find that in losing the shared discomfort, fame, story, make-up room, whatever, in losing that bedrock of friend-ship, you lose the common ground that drew you together. It doesn't mean that you don't keep the fondest memories; it's just that real deep friendships need time and we don't have that. But you keep a special affection, and the more time goes by, the warmer the memory.

Q. Are we about to hear a warm memory?

A. Yes: my heart jumps every time I think of Wogan. He was already the best living broadcaster . . .

Q. Steady on.

A. . . . on radio and television when I appeared with him in Dublin, doing some charity I think, or car show or presentation; and then we were both on the *Gay Byrne*

Show, a late-night programme of interviews and music. He is so funny and languid and good-natured and hides his intellect very modestly and I thought he was the top. Sometime later I was asked to stand in for him on his thrice-weekly show *Wogan* for the BBC. It was only after I'd accepted that I realized the Great Man Himself wouldn't be there, as he and Helen were probably going to be lolling about in Portugal with some golf-clubs. I'd been a sort of co-presenter with him and Sue Cook on *Children in Need* and I was so very flattered that he'd chosen me to replace him (it was actually more likely that Peter Estall the producer pulled my name out of the hat, but my heart says it was Terry). Anyway, although I had never envisaged myself as an interviewer, I knew that because I love and admire everyone on sight I could probably make a fist of it.

Q. Is a fist good or bad?

A. Good. When I saw the list of people lined up I thought, holy smoke! A studio full of heroes and stars! And I was right. This is how it worked: the researchers would read up all they could on the guest – books, interviews etc. – and see the film or play or read the book that brought the guest to the show . . .

Q. Hang on. Hold it right there. Would you have anyone on the show who *didn't* have something to promote?

A. No, that's the thing that's never explained. Chat shows only want people who are hot, who are in something that comes out this week, caught up in a present-day scandal, singing their newest release. You cannot get on to a chat show without that. On the other side of the coin are the publicists who must get their client on air on a prime-time show, or interviewed in the press to sell the product – whether it's a book, play, film or charity. That's how it works. They will always find a spot for the giants like the late Peter Ustinov, Joan Rivers and Lenny Henry because they can do a show on their own, are huge entertainers and can bring a feel-good factor to a programme which might have some quiet or introspective guests. Researchers then interview the guest, wringing out of them short amusing stories, put together a menu of topics to focus on; you, as the interviewer, try to read and absorb everything about their life and plan how to make them happy on air. I was given a list of questions to ask which were sometimes amended as the cameras were rolling and held up behind the guest ('Ask about kids', 'How much paid', 'Who dating now') and you'd have to try to work them round to that subject. It can be terribly difficult to steer people off a long involved story; the usual allotted time for an interview was seven or eight minutes.

Once or twice I had a whole programme with a very special guest, usually American. One was Mary Tyler Moore. MTM was exceptionally sweet and open; she had had some recent traumas in her life: the death of her son and overcoming alcoholism. I found I couldn't ask her about losing her child, a young man who had re-cently died, but she brought up the subject herself and spoke movingly and at length, which fitted easily into the half-hour show. We had a live link to California to Dick Van Dyke, who had played her husband in *The Dick Van Dyke Show*. It was the strangest thing, sitting in a chair, summoning up these very senior and important figures and asking them questions. Oprah Winfrey was another guest; her programme in the States had not yet been released over here, she was not yet the highest-paid woman in the USA. She was on the show with Denis Healey, and they got on famously (a rather appropriate adverb in this case), talking about poetry amongst other things. The three gods of boxing, Muhammad Ali, Joe Frasier and George Foreman, were guests – Harry Carpenter came on too, as a weedy adoring actress wasn't really weighty enough to handle those colossal icons on her own, but of course they were all so polite, so gentle and helpful. In fact in my whole time in Mighty Wogan's chair there was only one tricky show, and it was my last as well. Spike Milligan and Harry Secombe were invited on to talk about a new book on the Goons and Peter Sellers.

Spike, whom I loved very much, was in one of his difficult and depressive periods. Before the show Harry had warned me it might be a bumpy ride. Spike wanted to come on in a wheelchair, for some reason; then, shortly after we had begun (with Spike being fairly unhelpful), a young man holding a crumpled carrier bag to his chest somehow pushed his way up from the audience, between the cameras and on to the floor in front of our chairs. The programme was going out live; as he unrumpled the bag and put his hand into it I had a vision of a gun, an assassination or something. Everyone seemed paralysed: no one did anything. The man pulled out a T-shirt, not a gun, and tried to make a point about some protest he was involved in. Spike livened up and said he'd prefer to talk about that than answer our boring questions, and with false grins and much joshing we got through it all somehow. At the end, after thanking the audience, and doing the photographs which we did at the end of every show, I went back to Wogan's dressing room and blubbed like a baby. Then I wrote a note to Wogan my hero and packed up my lovely borrowed clothes and left. I remember that the next day I got a huge bunch of flowers from Spike, a most special and treasured man. The great Neddy Seagoon himself, Harry Secombe, has gone now as well, and Michael Bentine too; how odd that I knew all the Goons. Best guests? Frontrunners were Michael Palin, Gyles Brandreth, Douglas Adams and James Coburn (who really only wanted to talk about an elephant sanctuary).

I love interviewing people. The most important trick is to listen to the answers, which sounds simple but isn't if you are in a flap. If you don't concentrate on the person opposite your mind can go into an absolute blank. Patrick Macnee said that when he finds he's drifted off during a conversation and suddenly realizes he's been asked a question, or is expected to say something, he leans forward intently and says, 'Go on.' The person is usually taken aback and elaborates on their last remark, giving you time to find your feet. I've used this tactic but cannot always make it work. Beware of 'closed' questions, where you simply spin off a reel of facts, leaving the guest with nothing more to do than nod and say yes. 'You left school at 14, but your parents had split up, leaving you with an aunt. You were unhappy until you discovered a passion for astronomy when you were walking back from the factory?' 'Yes, that's right.' It's better to draw the guest out, particularly as you know the story from the researchers: 'Why was it that you stayed on to the sixth form? What was it like being left on your own? How did you feel when your parents divorced?' and so on. Closed questions show too much research; but they're really only used to hurry things along. Sometimes people are happier to approach a sensitive subject sideways on, so you can start off by asking if they're good at DIY and work them round to a suitable jumping-off point for discussing why they burnt their mother's car.

One of my greatest regrets is not having been on my own to talk to Dr Anthony Clare, the psychiatrist. It was a recorded programme for the BBC and I was his subject. Afterwards I realized that I wanted to talk and talk about the very innermost thoughts I had; but a braking mechanism came into play because I knew it was to be broadcast, and I didn't dare seem . . .

Q. Vulnerable? Shallow? Average? Cowardly? Thick? Self-obsessed? Two-faced? Dull?

A. All those things. And yet he would have been the very best person to unpack your brain to, having been pre-eminent for a long time in the field of psychiatry and being the author of the fascinating book on depression he wrote with Spike's input. A missed chance; a great man.

Q. You could try to see him again, or someone else if you really wanted to do this. The world is full of help: you only have to ask. There is nothing new under the sun.

A. Doing interviews with people opened my eyes to how swift we are to pigeon-hole people, give them a nickname or tag and then never look further. It's a left-over from schoolyard bullying tactics; sometimes accurate, largely not. Perhaps it goes back far beyond schoolyards: think of Ivan the Terrible, Edward the Confessor, Sweeney Todd the Demon Barber of Fleet Street, Bloody Mary and so on. When Eddie Shah started the independent tabloid *Today*, he asked me to do five full-page interviews with prominent people – I could choose them myself. I chose Sir Robin Day, the Duchess of Norfolk, Jane Asher, Matt Frewer – who had a meteoric rise and fall as Max Headroom – and of course Dirk Bogarde.

Q. You weren't asked to do five, you were asked to do six. You chickened out of the last one.

A. I became obsessed with representing my subject with minuscule accuracy – I couldn't bring myself to paraphrase their words, or make any kind of judgement on them, having suffered myself from being misquoted and, frankly, misinterpreted. The strain of listening to hours of taped interviews, and agonizing about whether to put in that Dirk Bogarde told me he had gouged out a boy's eye on purpose made me grey with nervous strain; so I asked to be released before my contract was up. I also couldn't ever ask about their love lives.

Q. Weren't you interested?

A. No, I don't think I was. Is that strange? When I meet people in my daily life, I never say, 'Who are you shagging, by the way?' I'm sorry to use such slang, but that's what it amounts to. If you know someone very well they may just tell you about the romantic side of their personal life, but I discourage it. Some things are meant to be kept behind closed doors. For the same reason detailed descriptions of food rather bore me: either be there, doing it, having it, eating it, or get a life.

Q. Restaurant columns are fun to read.

A. I know that I'm old-fashioned. I love courtesy and punctuality and, to a certain extent, formal behaviour. We used to have it in this country but it's out of fashion at the moment. It still exists all over the world, though; the Americans are far more polite than we are even though they may wear shell suits. That's why I love old people, being with them and hearing their memories. I think that is why I enjoyed live interviews so much. It's utterly fascinating to enter someone else's world.

In 1984 I was asked to be part of a series called *Women of Our Century* for the BBC. Six famous women were to be interviewed by younger members of the same profession. As an actress I was chosen to interview the legendary Dame Flora Robson, who had retired long before – it turned out to be the last interview she ever gave, as she died that July. I took a train and a film crew to Brighton to interview her; I remember there was a heat wave and that I was very nervous: I was afraid she would demand to talk to someone more skilled, more famous, more theatrical. Of course she did nothing of the kind. She received us with great tranquillity, pointing out that as she went to bed very early she didn't really recognize anyone from television.

The first thing that struck me about her was her voice: low, steady and not at all actressy. Sir Alec Guinness said, 'It is the most beautiful voice of a woman in the theatre of our time.' Emlyn Williams praised 'the beautiful throb of her voice and her impeccable diction'. After the voice, the eyes: light, clear blue and rather remote. Although I had read and reread Kenneth Barrow's book, *Flora*, and was furnished with notes from the conscientious research team, the feeling of low panic never left me until two days later when we went back to London. My fear was that I would do a great disservice to the public if I didn't ask the right questions and, far more serious, that I would bore or annoy my subject. I had reckoned without Dame Flora. Sitting opposite me in her little octagonal drawing room, twisting a hanky in her lap, she was as helpful as a Brownie and as composed as the *Mona Lisa* (and sometimes as enigmatic). Her perfect recall for earlier parts of her life gave way to splendidly impenetrable lapses in memory. ('Did I do that? I don't know . . . I suppose I did.') Relentless social etiquette made it difficult for me to leave long silent moments when she might suddenly have thought of something else to say: as soon as she had answered one question, I would leap in with another, sometimes treading on her toes; but she never became perturbed, although I know from experience that it's the most tiring thing in the world to talk ceaselessly about yourself.

As I sat beside her, between takes, and leafing through her bulging scrapbooks, it became clear that her life had been dedicated pretty equally to acting and charities. She didn't marry Tyrone Guthrie, who proposed several times, because he didn't want children, and she did; so, in her words, she decided to marry her profession. How different our lives seemed! Mine, catch as catch can, darting at things, most of my stuff light-hearted piece-work, hers single-minded and almost cloistered and, except for a spell at the Shredded Wheat factory, non-stop performances, each seeming to eclipse the last in a triumphant parade of God-given talent. How different, too, I thought, the circumstances in which we worked. Fifty years ago even quite young actresses enjoyed a kind of protection that has gone from our lives for ever. Dame Anna Neagle once told me that when she was playing even a very small part she had breakfast in bed, a light lunch prepared by a maid and a rest before the show, and was driven to and from the theatre. It was common to have a faithful dresser, who became a dependable friend and confidante, someone who could shoo away unwanted visitors from the dressing room. Now actresses shop in supermarkets, collect children from school, do the housework and ironing, catch a bus to the theatre (or risk having the car towed away) and rush back before they miss the last underground train.

Perhaps this has stolen away some of the glamour usually associated with show business, and maybe that's no bad thing. Television has introduced a new sort of familiarity. In the cinema, the faces of the stars are many times their actual size, viewed in majestic darkness. If you don't like a film you must tiptoe out apologetically. On the small screen, however, we can be switched off, turned down, leaving us mouthing in silence, or even played in slow motion on video machines. This familiarity brings as many joys as trials. The public sees us as approachable friends or incompetent idiots and hastens to tell us so: the days of the distant stars are drawing to a close.

While we sat and waited for the cameras to reload, Dame Flora knitted socks. She'd been knitting socks for years, sending them out to people she thought might need them. During our visit, the socks she was working on were for Sir Michael Redgrave. 'His poor feet,' she said; 'he might like these.' She talked to me easily and informally like an old friend, but when the camera turned, she withdrew slightly and (quite naturally) her speech became more formal. I never thought I'd meet her, mostly because I didn't dream I would talk to a legend whom I had first seen in *Wuthering Heights* at the Tenterden Embassy cinema when I was 11. She was completely without vanity, maybe because all her life she had been labelled as plain. The part of the programme I wish I had changed came right at the beginning: 'Flora was a plain child' – and at that instant a photograph of her at two years old, in a muffler and woollen hat, appears on screen. Her little face is set in a polite smile with an untroubled gaze. I wish I hadn't said that; but the film was shown on Friday 13 July, six days after she had died, so she never knew. She had the kind of beauty that Helen Mirren and Jenny Agutter have: not run-of-the-mill prettiness but rare, unusual and unforgettable. Flora would have been a star in any era because of her talent; but if she'd been around today she would have scooped up romantic leads as well.

Q. Although you play leading parts, you're not often the lead. Think: *Sapphire and Steel* had David McCallum's name first; in *The New Avengers* you got third billing behind Patrick Macnee and Gareth Hunt. You've acted with Anthony Perkins and Rod Steiger, David Niven, Herbert Lom, Christopher Lee, Peter Cushing, Ben Kingsley . . .

A. Yes, but these are all huge names . . .

Q. . . . and you've never really been up there. There's no chance now of your starring in a film, is there, not now.

A. Long ago I realized I'd prefer to play second fiddle, to the extent that I shied away from work that might put me bang in the spotlight. Not on stage: I played top billing in *Hedda Gabler* and *Private Lives*, in *Blithe Spirit* and *The Letter*, but I'm better as second-in-command.

Q. Patsy.

A. Exactly – except that *Absolutely Fabulous* is a lesson in ensemble playing, I think, which is largely down to Jennifer. Like all the best surprises, the role of Patsy came at me out of the sun. I was doing what I thought was good work, lucky-to-get-it work, in a West End play called *Vanilla*, and standing in for Wogan amongst other things. I was working with cracking people, was happily married, life seemed pretty gorgeous. Then two things happened in quick succession.

First, Ruby Wax, whom I hadn't met, came to see *Vanilla* (in which I played an Imelda Marcos figure with short black hair and a Cuban accent) and came round to my dressing room to ask me to be in her show. Ruby always says whatever is in her mind, which some people find startling. She's hyper-energetic, searingly truthful and quite extraordinarily funny. We invented a parallel life for Joanna Lumley, one where she's hit the skids and her career has collapsed. Ruby (whose on-screen persona is itself a fairground version of her real self) befriends this pathetic wreck and tries to make a come-back possible. Joanna is discovered first in a filthy flat full of empty whisky bottles, dead flowers and cat litter, bitching about other actors. She's found in bed with Niall Buggy – both of them clearly in need of help, Niall in fishnet stockings and Joanna on the verge of a nervous breakdown. On both occasions Ruby breaks into her flat with a camera crew. After Joanna comes out of rehab Ruby tries to get her on to game shows, but JL has lost her grip on reality. Ruby puts her into a Purdey wig and sends her off to the BBC to audition for anything with anyone. Joanna tries to recapture her glory days as an Avenger but is now older, can't kick, can't cut it at all. Ruby hides with a cassette player and plays the *Avengers* theme for JL to perform to. She propositions Des Lynam and follows Richard Wilson into the men's room to beg for work. Later, Ruby has her on her own show as a guest cook but it ends in a shambles. I discovered that I liked doing this kind of insane half-scripted performance more than anything I'd done so far.

Then the second thing happened: the first few scripts for the show *Absolutely Fabulous* were sent to me by Jennifer Saunders. I wish I'd kept them instead of doing what we always do, ripping pages out for rehearsals or to stuff into your pocket while you're filming. The scripts were just extraordinary, unlike anything else on television at the time. Of course I knew Jennifer's work through *Comic Strip* and *French and Saunders* – I remember her character in *Girls on Top*, a morose lumpen girl with dull clothes. I remember seeing her and thinking, 'She's brand-new – I haven't seen this character before, this humour is new.' I also remember seeing the original sketch she did with Dawn, with Jennifer as an embryonic Edina and Dawn as a prototype Saffy. So I accepted the part of Patsy and went to meet Jennifer for the first time at the BBC to do a private read-through with her and the producer, Jon Plowman, a man incapable of being perturbed owing to his immense sense of humour and the fact that he'd worked with all the *Comic Strip* comedians, including Jennifer, before. I struggled to make Patsy come alive, come 'off the page', but when I went home after a nail-biting hour and a half I telephoned my agent, Caroline Renton, and asked her to get me out of it: I felt I wasn't up to it, I didn't understand what Jennifer (who after all wrote it) wanted, I was wrongly cast, they must have thought I had talent, on and on. Caroline said, 'Oh don't be so stupid, it's only a pilot. Just do it.' So I did.

Q. Happy days?

A. Very wonderful and unforgettable days. I'd worked with June Whitfield before at Chichester doing *An Ideal Husband*. Jane Horrocks and Julia Sawalha I had only seen on screen. Bob Spiers directed it and we rehearsed in a building nicknamed the Acton Hilton, a tall seven-storey block, filled with rehearsal rooms for BBC productions. There was a canteen on the top floor with a wide concrete terrace where you could look out towards the airport and smoke cigarettes. Straight actors, singers, comedians, huge stars would all shuffle round to the check-out till with a tray of salad and shepherd's pie and you saw everyone there at one time or another. It's gone now, of course. The BBC sold it off; and for the last two series of *AbFab* we rehearsed in church rooms, boys' clubs, public rooms above a pub; all too small, too noisy, too difficult to park near. At the same time, enormous new staff blocks were being built at White City – for management, not for performers, of the BBC. *Eheu fugaces, Postume, Postume, labuntur anni* and other intense expressions of regret. But when we started doing *AbFab* no shadows were in the sky.

Going to rehearse each day was a joy: we all worked well together, the chemistry was right. We laughed till we cried but we worked very hard: comedy is the hardest thing to get right. 'There is a tide in the affairs of men which, taken at the flood, leads on to fortune.' Jennifer had predicted perfectly our roller-coaster trajectory on the riptide of the moment.

Q. How nautical.

A. I'm trying to say that she had her finger on the pulse of fashion, of women's magazines, of the PR world and the cult of celebrity, and a huge audience was waiting and ready for it. She is very, very clever, acutely observant, inventive, flexible and unbearably funny. All the characters we played – Mother, Saffy, Bubble, Edina and Patsy – began to grow lives of their own: we all took care of our own characters and thought of things they'd like, or do, or dress in. Ruby would come in towards the end of the week's rehearsal and she and Jennifer would think up even funnier lines. We recorded the shows in front of a live audience at the BBC Television Centre; nerves in tatters beforehand, babbling lines to ourselves, perfecting last minute exchanges with each other, hearts banging in terror. Then on to the studio floor, all confidence and energy, and in less than an instant (in fact about three hours), the show was recorded and we'd start the next episode.

The audiences were sensational. At first, they would have been fans of *French and Saunders*, but later as the show became well-known they were *AbFab* devotees, and the recordings had the flavour of a gala night out, particularly as we often had famous guest stars on. The show was glamorous and daring and fairly outrageous: the press loved it and so did the fashionistas. Gay men in New York, arbiters of taste in that city, adored it and very soon it was being shown all round the world whilst retaining a cult following. And yet we did so few episodes, really; and there was a long five-year gap after the third series – and then there were specials and then another series. But each series was only six episodes, a maximum of nine weeks' work. In the interim we all went off to do other jobs, never really knowing if or when *AbFab* would return. Patsy became my best-known public face. The figure of me in Madame Tussaud's, which started off modestly and subtly dressed – in navy-blue Jean Muir – changed her clothes, put her hair up and now wears a scarlet dress. People liked Patsy . . .

Q. Better than Joanna?

A. I think people know the difference because I've been around for a long time doing different things; but old Pats, with her disgusting habits and don't-care attitude, was the one they hoped to meet. Edina and Patsy were good fun to dress up as at fancy-dress parties; gay men could look like Patsy very easily with a huge wig, stockings, cigarette and glass of champagne. Jennifer and I were invited over to New York as guests of the LGBT movement, the Lesbian, Gay, Bisexual, Transgender people, whose sexuality prevents them from having full rights and equality. We were to be honoured at the LGBT Pride award ceremony at City Hall on a sweltering thundery afternoon. For some reason we had convinced ourselves on the flight over that it was a sweet gesture but would probably be a light-hearted affair. Speeches? No, we assured each other, just 'Cheers, sweetie, thanks' would be all they expected. Jennifer dressed with Edina in mind – a US flag scarf tied under a Stetson, white suit, clonky jewellery – and I put my hair up and wore black with false eyelashes, as neither of us is really recognizable as our character when we're not dressed up like them; in particular Jennifer, who wears a wig for Edina.

It turned out to be a huge affair; City Hall was crammed and humid. We sat on chairs facing the crowd, with other recipients beside us. Each citation was read out; each recipient responded with a properly-prepared, quite long and sometimes tearful speech. We were in the grip of terror – we hadn't expected this. During the applause we muttered to each other from the corners of our mouths and I managed to convince Jennifer that she would have to make the speech. She was the writer and main protagonist, it was all on her plate. She only had to stand up and they went wild; she made a good speech, we accepted our certificates from Whoopi Goldberg, I said, 'Cheers, thanks a lot' and we went on to a wild evening of entertainment in a gay bar, where we judged an *AbFab* look-alike contest and were visited by Cyndi Lauper who wasn't sure who we were. Hysteria amongst the seething masses became semi-religious – boys sobbing, 'I *touched* her,' one girl clinging to Jennifer's sleeve, screaming, 'You have healed me.' When we got back to the cool calm luxury of the Four Seasons Hotel, I studied the framed proclamation they gave me. It is actually very moving, in the words they use and the underlying message, half-humorous, half-serious:

Whereas a Great State is only as great as those individuals who perform exemplary service on behalf of their community, whether through unique achievement in professional or other endeavours, or simply through a lifelong commitment to entertaining and enlightening others; and whereas Joanna Lumley plays Patsy, the glamorous best friend and confidante of Edina in *Absolutely Fabulous*, a show that brings joy, laughter and warmth to New Yorkers because of the exemplary vision of the writers, producers, performers and broadcasters; and

Whereas JL's generosity and humanity in her performance have created a character that has great appeal to the Lesbian Gay Bisexual Transgender communities, by warmly portraying these communities on *AbFab* in a positive and affirming way, showing how they add to the texture of life; and

Whereas [several more über-complimentary 'whereas'es] . . .

. . . JL is demonstrating her devotion to the Human Rights of those not afforded equality in today's society by joining us today at City Hall in support of LGBT Pride; and [more 'whereas'es] . . .

Now therefore be it Resolved that I, State Senate Democratic Leader Martin Connor, and the New York State Senate Democratic Conference, recognize that in JL we have an individual committed to entertaining the LGBT community and worthy of our highest respect and esteem . . . and proclaim JL an Honorary New Yorker for Today and Forever.

It's signed and dated, 27 June 2002, in ink at the bottom right of the document; on the bottom left is a crest with 'Excelsior' on a ribbon underneath. They may be given frequently to all sorts of people (certainly far more worthy than we were), but it touched me very much and made me think more deeply about the inequalities of life, and the burden of being different, and ostracized for it. Chad Varah, great visionary who founded the Samaritans, said, in his last sermon at Evensong in St Stephen Walbrook in the City of London, that throughout his long life he had encountered all kinds and conditions of human sexuality. I can see him, moving his old arm in a fan-like gesture from the elbow, like a windscreen-wiper, to show the 180 degrees of difference, starting with full alpha male on one side to utter femininity on the other. In between is every shade and peculiarity and normality, all in different pro-portions of male/female mixture. No one can escape that. (He was furious that night about the reluctance of the Church to appoint a gay bishop.)

We're very lucky in show business (whatever *that* may mean) to be able to be fairly open about our sexuality: everyone expects dancers and actors and hairdressers to be gay even when they're not (and who cares anyway). But it's tougher outside the arts, or in an illiberal faith, very tough to be a gay man or a cross-dresser. In *AbFab*, Edina's ex-husband, played by Chris Malcolm, was gay with a lover in tow. Patsy had an operation in Morocco in the sixties. Something was sewn on. I think she also took hormone pills because she certainly grew a beard and looked rather fab in a Sergeant Pepper-style military coat, with short hair and thick eyebrows. It lasted about a year; then, I think, it withered away and dropped off and she went back to being a woman again, a woman of sorts anyway. I think it was that episode that clinched it for Pats in the US LGBT community; that, and the fact that Edina's son Serge was gay and living in New York. Edina was desperate that Saffy would do something interesting, like becoming a lesbian. In fact, the whole show skittered to and fro over the accepted boundaries of sexuality, which we all thought was funny and now find also had a 'positive and affirming' effect on the LGBT community in America and probably in every country that showed *AbFab*. That's a very good thing. Hoorah for Jennifer, and for putting things that are important in a humorous context.

Q. And you've got a lot of Patsy's clothes.

A. Yes, she dresses better than I do. Would you like to see what we rather grandly call the dressing room? Follow me.

Dressing Room

This is actually a narrow corridor off the bedroom; more of a large cupboard, completely stuffed with clothes, boots, hats, bags, suitcases and an ironing board. Please rest against the wire coat-hangers which I save up and return to the dry cleaners: from here you can see that there is a method . . .

Q. But so many coats! Who could need so many? Even with two of you storing every garment that has ever rested on your shoulders, how can you need this many coats?

A. Many of them are dinner jackets or tail-coats which are for Stevie to conduct in. Some, indeed a great many of these, came from Oxfam shops and cost only a few pounds but are too big or too small. I bought them in case he gets bigger or smaller. Then there are all my coats for my parallel existence: coats to throw round yourself in Connemara, silk velvet evening coats for sweeping into the opera in New York, neatly tailored tweed coats for jumping out of a train at Vienna Hauptbahnhof, slinky jewelled mackintoshes for racing from a nightclub into a taxi in the rain in Paris – and here is a very old Jean Muir navy-blue fine-wool duster coat, patch pockets, to wear with boots and a T-shirt; here is an Indian sari made into a hooded cape with a shocking-pink silk lining . . .

Q. Why 'parallel existence'? Don't you live like this in real life?

A. Sometimes I truly do. Sometimes when Jennifer and I have been over to New York to promote *Absolutely Fabulous* or to give or get prizes, we live a life you only read about. A limousine to the airport; ushered into the Concorde lounge; cosseted on the short and hugely enjoyable flight on the best aeroplane ever made . . . then a stretch limo – or, better, a silent Mercedes – stealthily ushers you to the Four Seasons Hotel in the heart of the city, where you sign in amongst the vast pale gold marble halls. A lift, no! elevator . . .

Q. Of course.

A. . . . hurtles you to suites high above Manhattan – there are flowers and champagne in the rooms; a light agenda has been sketched out, with several gaps marked 'free for shopping'. You are positively nursed through the day, brain empty of any responsibilities; parties thrown in your honour, hairdressers on standby . . . it's a kind of paradise. The feeling you get looking down on that fabulous city, as evening draws in and lights blaze in the skyscrapers, knowing it's not for ever, is another reason why I wanted to be in this entertainment business. There was a photograph advertising cigarettes I saw, long ago in a magazine in Malaya: a couple leaning on a balcony looked down over a glittering city, smoking cigarettes – they were cool, smart, dressed to the nines. They looked confident and amused, completely in control, in his dinner jacket . . .

Sapphire and Steel: McCallum at his brainiest.

The beginning of *AbFab*.

'Lost in France'. First series.

Patsy in Val d'Isère.

Not burnt.

In Marilyn Manson mode.

Me, Zandra, Jennifer, Lulu and Britt.

Rehearsing *AbFab*: Jennifer, Julia, me and June.

With the Bee in the garden.

With Ken Frogbrook: behind, Frogmat deployed as oil-spill protection.

Modelled by Steve Swales for Madame Tussaud's.

Q. . . . white tuxedo . . .

A. . . . white tux and her satin cocktail dress. Fabulous! Those
were the grown-ups I wanted to be, rather like my parents
when they had dressed up to go to a dinner party at King's
House in Kuala Lumpur. And now I walk through crowds
smiling, bejewelled in gorgeous evening clothes, and someone really young may see me and think, 'I want to be in
show business!'

Q. But they must never see this room, with its out-of-date
skirts, and trousers you can't get into, and old-fashioned
shoes . . .

A. . . . which come in useful when I'm doing costume drama!
In television shows like *Nancherrow* and *Class Act* I bring in
my mother's – my *grand*mother's – clothes: scarves, belts,
costume jewellery; and in one case a bolt of cloth of Granny
Weir's which I had made up into 1930s evening pyjamas
for the film *Innocent Lies*. Perhaps I could have succeeded
as an assistant wardrobe mistress. It's the most thrilling
thing to give a familiar family necklace or brooch a part in
a drama, clipped to a tweed coat, suspended on a Fair Isle
knit. It's all a glorified form of dressing up, which with it
carries a wider purpose other than make-believe.

When you're dressed a certain way, you can become
the person the clothes suggest. Confident formal clothes
worn easily suggest authority; what my father used to
call being well turned-out is a courtesy to those you're
amongst. Old trousers and a baggy jersey are just the thing
for washing a car or doing the garden where a nifty little
linen suit would be quite wrong – on the other hand to

turn up like a shocking old defunct scarecrow at something nice like the local fête would be rather insulting to all the people who have made a huge effort to make the day special.

During the late nineties there was a terribly patronizing attitude about clothes you might wear going to the theatre, opera or ballet. The dictum then was that people who hardly ever go to these events don't go simply because they are intimidated by the clothes worn by habitués. *Of course* you have to check out roughly what people are wearing before you go, just as you wouldn't go to a football match in a suit and tie. But most people who want to go out in the evening have some nice clothes, for weddings or anniversaries, or discos, that are just the ticket. I've got a very good black M&S skirt, quite long, which I wear with a variety of tops – sometimes a jersey, sometimes a smart tailored jacket – with boots or high heels, and a bit of a necklace – and opera house here I come! Also the theatres themselves are usually trying to look their best, with chandeliers and carpets and neatly-dressed staff; dress up a bit, I say. Most of not dressing up is fear of looking ridiculous or, worse, over-anxious. Anoraks and jeans and trainers have their place in the world, but not in the evenings. Looking out from behind the curtains by prompt corner before the play starts, it's lovely to see that people in the audience have made an effort, just as you are going to give your all to them for two and a half hours.

Q. Who cares what you wear? Please don't tell me you can't appreciate Berlioz if you're wearing track-suit bottoms.

A. Just make an effort. In every country in the world since time began people have known the power of clothes, jewels, body paint, headdresses – it's as much a part of human nature as it is of lyre-bird nature, peacock nature. Men look wonderful when they're scrubbed up and smarmed a bit and ruffled a bit. I dread a world where we all waddle about in gym clothes or shell suits. Comfort isn't everything.

Q. Do you have many evening dresses? What about those award ceremonies – do you have to get new clothes every time?

A. You know I don't. It's the custom to borrow designer clothes for really huge occasions like the Oscars, but there the fashion houses fight to win a star to wear their dress, even making it up in her size specially for her to try on . . . it's a huge palaver.

Q. Which I think you know nothing of first-hand.

A. No; that's true. I've never been invited to the Oscars. Also there may not be such a scramble to chase me with frocks now that I'm older.

Q. How sad! I'm sure they'd hustle up some vast beaded velvet tent for you to pull on over your non-girlish figure.

A. But that's what I hate about the business at the moment, the idea that you've got to wear almost nothing, like a pole dancer or a lap dancer, to look glamorous.

Q. It's only fashion. The pendulum will swing, just as the mini skirt was followed by the maxi skirt and the Annie Hall look. People take just as much time and care nowadays: beautifully made-up, carefully-prepared hair, lovely high heels and little evening purses – it's a look; it's only fashion.

A. I was rumbled by a newspaper wearing the same long silver evening dress three times over a period of about four years. I got it in a sale: it was by Frank Usher and it had a diaphanous evening coat to match. Outing one: worn as bought. Outing two, I cut the top about a bit, and scissored up the coat to a sort of bolero . . .

Q. Unwise.

A. . . . and outing three I cut the top off completely, cut the coat remnants into halter straps, and wore it with long mauve gloves to meet the Princess of Wales. Luckily the stitching didn't come undone and all eyes were naturally on the Princess anyway, and I was only in a line-up. But an article appeared months later in the press with photographs of the dress getting stranger and stranger. It's gone now. I sent it to Help the Aged.

Q. What do you take with you when you go abroad on trips that are half formal and half camping? Bhutan, for instance. You travelled there with your cousin Maybe to retrace the journey your grandparents made 50 years earlier. You were walking, riding, camping, but also lunching with the Queen Mother and visiting monasteries. What do you *have* to have?

A. Obviously the right clothes for the actual journey: T-shirts in plain colours, comfortable trousers – three pairs – a lightweight hooded mackintosh or long cagoule, two warm jerseys, three pairs of pants, three bras, pyjamas, socks, cotton neck scarves. Remember, layers keep you warm and you can peel them off gradually as the day gets hotter. For the formal part I take a string of pearls or a handsome necklace, a black top and skirt, and always long sleeves. Arms are considered rather vulgar in most of the world, as are thighs; always err on the side of modesty. No gaping cleavages or bare shoulders in the Middle-to-Far East. Don't take too much, don't take things that you're not sure about. Find some good-looking low-heeled shoes in case you're invited to the presidential palace.

Q. Is this likely?

A. It can happen. Pack only one evening bag. Take one pair of easy-care black trousers which can look smart or casual. Try to colour-co-ordinate a few things, in fact try to stick to only four colours, of which three are black, white and khaki.

Q. Good grief. And the fourth?

A. Anything bright – pink, lime green, purple. Purple T-shirt, khaki trousers, sunglasses: perfect daywear. Lime-green T-shirt, black skirt, presidential shoes, pearls: a night to remember.

Q. Trinny and Susannah may have something to say about this.

A. Always remember that nobody really recalls what you wear as long as you look confident. When you have very little with you, you begin to respect your clothes, and you devise ways of keeping them clean and tidy on the trip, like washing them in shampoo and rolling them up to prevent creases. It's a well-known fact that T-shirts, even when worn for a week, will miraculously become clean if you fold them very neatly and keep them for two days.

When I first came up to London in 1964 I took a course at Lucie Clayton, the famous school and modelling agency. We learned how to walk on a cat-walk, put on make-up, sit with our ankles crossed and get in and out of an E-type Jaguar. My first job, which only lasted six weeks, was at a huge department store called Debenham and Freebody in Wigmore Street. My job was not much different from a shop assistant's, except that every now and then I would put on a model suit (mine was the Model Suit Department) and wander round the store doing three-point turns and showing off the clothes. Model suits started at size 12 and I was a 10, so I rolled each skirt over at the waist as if I was concealing a python beneath the jacket and slunk about the counters with heavily made-up eyes. I was poached one day by Lucienne Phillips, an unforgettable French woman who had a chic shop in Knightsbridge: she saw in me something that the designer Jean Muir could use.

So I went to be a house model for Jean Muir, whose brand was then called Jane and Jane. I can't overemphasize the influence Miss Muir, as we called her, had on me. Not just her flawless taste and rigid discipline and perfectionism in dressmaking, but her enthusiasm, broad knowledge, kindness and fearsomeness. She was frightening in the way that Dame Ninette de Valois was frightening to ballet dancers: she expected and demanded the best from everyone. Miss Muir was quite small, with fragile wrists and ankles, ruler-straight hair cut to jaw-length by Michael Rasser and dark reddish-brown lipstick. She preferred to call herself a dressmaker and thought the term 'designer' pretentious. Her clothes had a timeless quality, and over the years I collected them and wore them again and again. I've never thrown them out: there is a huge suitcase full of Jean Muirs in the spare room, all neatly packed away so that one day I can get them out and wear them as retro chic. Not so much of the retro either: many of her patterns could be remade today and look as beautiful as they did then. But she was the only grand label I wore, and that was because of her generosity at the Jean Muir sale every year I could afford them.

The rest of my clothes were from the high street. Biba and Mary Quant lit a fire that has never gone out in London: just to own one thing in Quant's signature colour scheme of rust and black was to have arrived, to be 'in'. Biba moved from its tiny premises in Abingdon Road, where dresses were hung on hatstands draped with feather boas, to Kensington Church Street and finally to the huge building which had been Derry and Toms; and we followed faithfully, with our pale legs and tight-sleeved jerseys, kohl-blacked eyes and suede boots. We hunted through markets for junk jewellery, grandad shirts and army uniforms; we wore nightdresses to nightclubs and huge straw hats in midwinter. Thin scarves from the thirties were round every throat – boys' and girls'; handbags were huge, practically small suitcases; bracelets were worn by the hundred, earrings often plastic and the size of hubcaps.

Hair was hugely important – and huge too. Lace and satin trailed down our hips, greatly buckled belts cinched in layers of waistcoats of chiffon and chenille, our many dangling cross-bedecked necklaces snagging our tights and catching in our granny-type lace mittens. Fabulous! There were shops called The Carrot on Wheels and Granny Takes a Trip, to be succeeded by Mr Freedom, whose platform boots increased the height of many a glam-rock star by several inches.

When we dressed we hoped to stop the traffic – or at least cause a small crash, as I did with gold stockings and lipstick on my eyelids in the Earls Court Road. Men were peacocks, led by Mick Jagger – and, actually, all the music scene. We cut each other's hair, and turned up or took in each other's trousers and skirts. The look was just this side of dressing-up basket – to be toned down when you went abroad, as this was very much a swinging London thing. Or was it? Suddenly appeared The Fool, a group of de-signers from Holland who were as wild and inventive as all get out. Eighteen-inch cigarette-holders waved about, fitted with hand-rolled smokes, possibly containing illegal substances. But still there was no money, not that I could see or get hold of. The Beatles had Rolls-Royces but that only seemed fair. Terence Stamp had a Roller *and* a Mini – but I saw him in the street on foot outside our flat in Trebovir Road; I saw him from above, four storeys below me, immediately recognizable by his sheer coolness and beauty, and I got down those stairs in seven and a half seconds flat, so I could stroll past him and say, 'Oh hi,' as if I knew him. And now I remember that same street, late at night in a summer cloudburst, and me running up and down with *nothing on at all*, no one to see me, just streaking about in the pouring rain because nothing seemed to matter much and I felt like it.

Fashion grew up as we all did. It became important to look rich, and the designers began to sew their labels on the outside to show where our money was going. Newspapers began to take an interest in the clothes celebrities wore, and to comment on the way people looked, and that altered the way people dressed; not wanting to be criticized for their taste, they could arm themselves with the defence of a designer's name: 'Lacroix, sweetie!' – 'Fabulous!'

In my wardrobe now there is a predominance of Betty Jackson, Nicole Farhi, Jasper Conran, Missoni, Bruce Oldfield and Armani, and a colossal knitted cardigan given to me by Christian Lacroix after he had appeared as himself in an episode of *Absolutely Fabulous*. Edina wore Lacroix; Patsy wore mostly Betty Jackson – who in her early career had made clothes for me as Purdey in *The New Avengers*. Most productions allow you to buy the clothes you've worn in the show at half-price. When you see actors wearing luxurious clothes in a dodgy television series you can be sure it's because they have chosen them for a post-screening life in their own wardrobes. ('I know she's on the dole but I feel she would have a really soft leather trench coat'.) Anyway, I loved Jean Muir; and like all her customers, friends and workroom staff I felt when she died that she was irreplaceable, a one-off – herself a fashion icon and, apart from that, a darling friend.

I love hats: look at them, all piled up here, rather dusty it's true but I put different things on them, like flowers, net, taffeta swags and brooches to dress them up for weddings or fête days. They're all a bit out of fashion now; no one seems to wear hats today. They'll come back. I always used to wear a Herbert Johnson man's panama, cream straw with a black petersham ribbon. It was my trade mark, or in the words of the old passports 'special peculiarity'. In the early eighties just as I was due to go abroad I found my passport was out of date, and having only a day in hand I snipped the heads out of my postcard-sized fan photographs and applied for a new one. The picture was of me wearing my panama. After much sucking of teeth the official at Petty France finally allowed me to use the photograph, and for ten years I was the only British subject whose special peculiarity was a permanent hat. I liked the old passports. For a woman, it showed your married name and your maiden name, I think; it also gave your profession, height, eye colour and title (if any, i.e. Mrs, I suppose). Now I have two names and have to have printed on one of the inside pages 'also known as', because airline tickets are often booked unwittingly in my Lumley name and my passport says Barlow. The Scottish system is good: a woman can keep her own name but be titled 'Mrs Hamish MacPherson' (if of course that's her husband's name).

Q. Look at these boots, all with boot-trees in, and shoes in a neat row, some in boxes. It reminds me of that rather touching film about Mrs Thatcher when she was Prime Minister, showing us rails of colour-coded dresses and suits. You take care of your things, don't you. Not very rock'n'roll.

A. Remember I was trained as a house model; I know the importance of hanging and folding things carefully. Also there is a character in clothes (which is why they're so hard to throw out when someone has died). You think, 'Look at that dress, faithful old friend, it deserves better than being a crumpled heap.' 'Dear old jacket, you've served me well – here's a nice wooden hanger.' As I pack up things for charity shops I always say goodbye if I've liked them. But many of one's clothes are just a hideous mistake, an impulse buy, or something that nearly works but actually misses by a mile. I've got rid of tens of black plastic sacks of things that would be better off in a new home. It would be quite nice to leave a note in the pocket saying, 'Cheers, lovely new owner, have a great time in this.'

Years ago my mother used to collect clothes from around her area in Kent to send out to Poland with a Dr Hreherow. Everything for all ages was welcomed, as long as it was in good condition. My mother ironed and folded and sewed on buttons, and the clothes were packed neatly into sacks and bags to be collected by lorry. She was a governor of the village school and she'd asked the children to give clothes they'd grown out of to send to children in Poland who had so little. Poland was suffering severe shortages of all sorts of things, principally medical supplies, but also sewing kits, pens, scissors, soap; almost everything was in short supply. The children were asked to donate one bar of soap each, which they wrapped up. My mother taught them how to write 'with greetings' in Polish – '*pozdrowienia*' – and they'd sign their own name and put a bar of soap into the pockets of the clothes they'd given.

My mother, like all mothers, is the very best. She hates to read anything at all slushy or sentimental about her, so I will just say that she taught me much: about putting other people first, do as you would be done by, nothing lasts for ever, don't kill spiders, prevent bullying, volunteer at once, be polite to everyone, never wash your hands before you eat, what the eye doesn't see, feed the birds, go up mountains, learn a language and pronounce it properly, cheer up, tell them to bugger off, read a book. She sleeps with a Baluchistani dagger under her pillow to maim assailants, and keeps a long yak-hair rope over her headboard to tie them up with when she's finished. This, although true, makes her sound rather tough: she's as gentle as a kitten with little defenceless creatures, especially babies and young children. However, her interest in people is insatiable, almost matching her curiosity about rock strata, the migratory route of the salmon and the weather forecast. My parents were too good to me! I shall snuffle into a hanky for a bit. Let's go down to the garden.

Garden

There are two ways out into the garden: through the kitchen, or from the hallway upstairs through this lovely old door with Victorian coloured glass, red and blue, colouring the daylight as it streams in on to the pictures by the radiator. Look at the radiator! It's huge and very old-fashioned, like the ones at St Mary's. It came from County Hall. When the Greater London Council was disbanded and sent away from County Hall there was a great debate about who should inherit the building. I supported the LSE's bid: it seemed to me to be right to have students in such a grand and central location. After a lot of pencil-gnawing, however, it went into private hands, as a hotel, a restaurant, an aquarium and now a Saatchi art gallery. The Edwardian wooden panelling was listed and so is still in place, but the plumbing was obviously inadequate and out of date. We'd just moved in to this house across the river and I yearned for a radiator or two as a memento of the old County Hall (which I never knew – utterly false sense of nostalgia there). This is one; the other is in our bathroom: both different shapes and weighing about half a ton each.

Reclaiming and salvaging old bits of buildings gives disproportionate amounts of satisfaction – and you find, as years go by, that you exaggerate a) how little you spent and b) how hard it was to track down that particular feature. In my mind, I've reduced the price of these radiators to a few pounds each when in fact they cost 30 times more. 'Coupla quid, this,' you say, nonchalantly banging the incandescent pipes as you pass. But that is a lie: if the tax man asked to see the accounts he'd smirk at how much I coughed up. Like that of all purchases, its actual value evaporates and it becomes indistinguishable from other remembered bargains, until your whole house seems to be knock-down, drag-out, bargain-basement cheap and you feel thrifty and smug about the savings you believe you've made.

Q. Small York-stone terrace, brown Turkey fig tree, lemon tree, standard bays in tubs, bushes of box roughly cut into globes, an iron archway. Two benches from Homebase . . .

A. . . . . assembled by me and Gill, and now nicely weathered to pale grey in the dry sunlight, khaki slime-green in the wet. Gill has been with us since we came to this house 13 years ago. She was born and bred in this part of London and can remember the days when there were local street markets, before the huge retail stores moved in. She knows our house and our habits like the back of her hand. We've become close friends, sharing family news and local gossip, keeping up to date with each other's grandchildren and supporting each other in times of trouble. We've got a lot in common, not least of which is a mid-morning cup of coffee and a cigarette and 10 minutes to chew the fat. She loves gardening too: sometimes we make time to inspect new seedlings or sweep up leaves. She's immensely practical and her advice is always sound. She has also invented a scary cocktail of vinegar and something else which clears the kitchen drains in a matter of seconds.

You will see that the garden isn't very wide – in fact, it's the exact width of the house – but for London it is massive. We have the garden divided into what experts call 'rooms': three rooms. The first section contains a fuchsia bush; a bay tree I planted as a twig, now eighteen feet high and home to nesting blackbirds; a rowan tree whose leaves turn apricot in the autumn; and a rather spiny, spindly, unprepossessing acacia tree which drops barbed twigs on the grass and only has the most meagre amount of blossom. Squirrels like this tree, having easy access from the wall with its surmounted trellis so they can hang upside-down like vampires on the trunk, furiously chirping and rattling at us as they plan the next raid on the tulip bulbs. Wisteria grows at a colossal pace here, loving the London earth. In no time a slender tendril becomes a thigh-thick branch, wresting pipes off the wall and prising the wooden trellis from its moorings. I know it to be at most 20 years old, but people gasp and say, 'A hundred at least!' so triumphantly gnarled is its stature.

I'm not going to do proper names unless I can remember them, but this bright shiny evergreen tree-bush makes a lovely archway under the lilac into the second room. Arum lilies, fatsia japonica grown huge with water leaking from the ponds, mulberry and tradescantia (both brought from far away by the plantsman Tradescant, whose gardens these all were: a nearby street bears his name), tiny frail cyclamen, clematis and roses, balsam and honeysuckle all tumbling and growing through each other. The two ponds are linked by a small waterfall, a slate from which the water trickles down from the upper fishpond to the lower frog-pond.

There's a net over the fishpond except in full summer when the lily leaves give them protective cover from a constant visitor, the tall patient heron who stands gazing yearningly at their flashing gold bodies till I shoo him away.

The frogs only appeared last year for the first time since we've been here. Next door, Felicia has frogspawn and froglets by the thousand, but each blob of jelly that came into our ponds faded and died with not even one tadpole developing. Then suddenly, like the Jets rounding a corner in New York snapping their fingers, looking for action, suddenly there arrived a band of confident frogs who hopped all over the paths and eventually buried themselves for the winter in the squishy pond bed under the marsh marigolds. We put a plank in the corner for their ease of egress, and there's a garden bench here as well so you can sit listening to the water and watching frogs and fish in the shade of the pear tree. Every year we get a blaze of pear blossom followed by the fruit beginning to show; then in September such an abundance of pears comes down that we can give all the neighbours a carrier bagful each and still have pounds left over to make into pear anything. Bottled, pickled, juice extracted, eaten like apples with cheese, stewed in wine: they're excellent. Over the archways – here's another – we grow runner beans which look beautiful when they're growing and flowering, and then there's the delicious satisfaction of picking and eating then whilst they're completely fresh. We grow tomatoes too, and sometimes aubergines. I've thought of turning the whole place into a vegetable allotment, but our garden is a bit too shaded by neighbouring limes and sycamores. Also, I know how much fruit one tomato plant yields –

with a whole garden of produce to eat or distribute I would have to join the farmers' market at Borough Market.

Finally we come to the third part of the garden, the wild bit: bamboo; ceanothus from next door; a walnut tree given to me by my sister when it was six inches high, now eight foot in the air; broom, rosemary, mint, thyme, day lilies, peonies, delphiniums, oleander – I just love the magic of plant names: keen gardeners will notice that the list I give presents a fairly haphazard assortment of flowers and herbs, but then I've left out hundreds. Every summer I wait for the poppies and wild strawberries; every spring for the creamy faces of the camellia, and the early crocuses. This wonderful garden shed – could anything look more charming, more like a lichen-green cricket pavilion? It came from Streatham; a dazzlingly professional team got it installed and painted in a day, I think. Or two days – no, I think it *was* a day, and it's even got windows and an electric light. You could live here, or at least use it as an extra room. Felicity Dahl once took me down the garden at the home she and Roald Dahl shared together, and showed me his writing room in a tiny little shed. He'd made a nest for himself and his painful back with a high-backed chair and cushions. He had a sort of tray to put on his lap to write on, favourite unchanging bits and pieces around on shelves and surfaces, a jar of exactly the right pencils, perfectly sharpened, and the famous silver ball, as heavy as lead, made entirely from wrappings of chocolate bars. It might be difficult to adapt our hut to writing, as the foxes have dug their lair underneath and we might disturb each other. It's comforting to know that as great a writer as Roald Dahl used pencils and paper. It's difficult to explain sometimes to people with a computer-keyboard mentality how easy and pleasant it is to write in the old-fashioned way. Let me draw a parallel: cooking on a stove as opposed to using a microwave.

Q. There's no comparison at all. What about Miles Kington?

A. As cook or writer? He's pretty accomplished in both 'disciplines', to use a bit of Olympic Games terminology.

Q. Well, I don't think he would know what a microwave was – but he writes scorchingly original stuff, day after day, on a keyboard. *He's* mastered technology . . .

A. Only because he's had to. He and Caroline live so far from London that he has to be on-line or whatever to get his pieces in to the *Independent* on time. Anyway, I've seen the room he writes in and I swear there is only just enough space in there for him to insert his own body in front of the keyboard. It's completely full of books and magazines, old newspapers, cuttings and other organic matter which is decidedly non-hi-tech. It doesn't matter how you write as long as you feel comfortable. Jennifer plays video games on her laptop, lethal racing cars or people being beaten to a pulp with a mallet, and I'm always killed at the first bend. It depends what you're used to. Stevie explains endlessly about search engines and cookies but all I can do is arrange my features into an expression of wifely intelligence and hope he doesn't test me later. I have, to be frank, pretty much missed the boat IT-wise; but I know where the jetty is and have seen the high-water mark.

Just beside and behind the hut are two cypress trees. We bought them to put on the balcony outside our bedroom window but they hated it up there. Ever since they've been planted here, they've grown thick and graceful with new yellowy leaves and a sense of well-being. High on top of these roofs I've attached a weather vane, a copper fish from Canterbury, which spins in the wind and can be seen by all the houses whose back gardens conjoin in this area, Tradescant's old stamping ground. Like lots of London gardens, ours presents us almost daily with new bits of broken willow-pattern crockery; you pick it all up and two days later more bits have somehow worked their way to the surface. The human body does it with splinters; the sea does it with stuff lost during shipwrecks – given enough time, it will collect all the things of a kind together and distribute them on the beach. A metal-detective I knew, whose hoard of Roman coins rivalled the British Museum's, told me that on discovering one silver Georgian shoe buckle on the shingle in East Kent he knew he would find the others nearby: and he did, all carefully pushed ashore by the sea who had graded and sorted them first. Coins here, shells there, shoe buckles there. Sit down with me here and I'll tell you about my humble involvement in saving the planet. The product is called Frogmat, named after its inventor, Ken Frogbrook.

Driving home from a performance in Brighton in 1992 of *In Praise of Rattigan* (with Robin Bailey, Keith Barron and Chris Cazenove), I heard a piece on Radio 4 about an invention that interested me so much that I pulled over and wrote down the name of the inventor. Days later I had tracked him down and he told me how the product was conceived. He'd been living on Papa Stour in the Shetlands as a crofter, sub-postmaster and shopkeeper. The idea came to him in the middle of the night, after he'd been cleaning oil off a puffin's wings with a twist of straw, that you could tackle oil pollution with straw, using it like blotting paper. The next day he poured diesel oil into an old tin bath filled with water, and then put some straw down into it, drawing it slowly across – the whole lot adhered: the straw had wiped the water clean. He invented a prototype machine that would produce extruded-straw mattressing, like a thick wide ribbon of padding stapled between netting. This laid across estuaries would mop up any oil spill threatening to drift inland; if spread across mudflats and beaches it would protect the coastline from pollution borne in on the waves, and would give seabirds something to clamber on to to escape the deadly oil. More and more uses were envisaged and tested: for inhibiting and removing algae in reservoirs, lakes and ponds; as embankment stabilization where plants are being established; as walkways at outdoor events like rock concerts and at racecourses, and as a temporary roadway for vehicles; and as a filtration system for farm waste and for sewage treatment.

Ken had by now moved to the Isle of Wight; when I met him and his business partner Peter Taylor on site, I was able to see the machine with my own eyes – about the size of a combine harvester, capable of making 500 metres of Frogmat an hour using only three men. Straw is largely a waste product in this country, and as burning straw was illegal it provided a perfect solution to the problem, whilst at the same time offering a completely green series of applications. I became part of the team, putting my money where my mouth was, and am to this day a director of the company. Like all innovations, it was met with some scepticism, particularly from areas that had become used to depending on chemicals. But everyone who tried it loved it: a machine was shipped out to Western Australia for 'reverse desertification', and photographs show a scrubby empty desert gradually covered in green shoots and young trees. The straw protected the young plants from intense sun and gave them support, whilst gradually biodegrading along with the netting to provide mulch at root level.

We went on *Tomorrow's World* and received letters from all over the country from people wanting to know more about it and wondering if they could invest in it. When an oil disaster threatened the Shetland Islands, Frogmat was raced up there to help with the clean-up: the booms of the traditional methods had burst in the high winds and the islands were in danger of disappearing under a blizzard of polystyrene bobbles. Frogmat, being absorbent, attracted oil towards it when floating on water, acting like a million dipsticks; when it was retrieved, heavy with oil, the mats were burned to provide energy for the local hospital. It outperformed all its costlier rivals. During the foot-and-mouth crisis, Frogmat soaked in disinfectant was laid across roads in the New Forest; at the same time results coming through from the Middle East indicated that oil-soaked mats laid on embankments not only stopped sand blowing across the highways but attracted the growth of the local clover plants, which stabilized the sandbanks with their root system. It could be rigged on sticks to protect crops from the intense sun; it could delay the speed at which potatoes matured underground so you could stagger the harvest. The Army has ordered Frogmat to restore the land damaged by tank tracks; it has been laid on the grass at Grange Opera to stop the ground being ruined and to protect the audience from muddy-feet misery. I myself have wiped an outdoor water tank clean of oil with one swipe of a Frogmat pad; I myself have walked across a mudflat on this magic carpet, dry and safe as the Messiah, where a long pole showed I would otherwise have been up to my neck in viscous mud.

The Prince of Wales was one of the first people we turned to: his unswerving efforts in all things green and ecologically sound made his endorsement all the more important. Prince Michael of Kent, Robin Hanbury-Tenison and Dr David Bellamy were swift and supportive in seeing its enormous environmental capabilities – Robin was interested in its possible deployment in northern Siberia where the world's worst oil pollution occurs. In that region's terrible climatic conditions the Frogmat could be delivered and laid during the hard frozen winter, absorption of oil taking place during the wet soggy summer, and finally the product would be collected and burned as fuel during the next autumn/winter period. But all these things need money. In his letter to Ken, Robin said, '. . . as we all know getting a project off the ground will not be easy. Ever since Joanna first told me about Frogmat I have been convinced that the best and quickest way to make it happen would be for her to make a powerful documentary about what is happening in Siberia and what should be done about it . . .'

A. And did you?

Q. No. I can't tell you how hard it is to get money together for any project – we hadn't even got enough to keep buying and owning all our international patents, let alone to advertise our product in a world hostile to low-tech solutions. So we never made the film, no: despite the fact that, as Robin said, 'the possibilities for a massive clean-up operation based on Frogmat are almost limitless. The ingredients are all there . . .' we were utterly unable to find funding for such a project at that time. Robin's charity, Survival for Tribal Peoples, was particularly concerned for the Khanti people and other reindeer-herders in the region. I can't bear to think of it now: that great wilderness gradually subsumed by an oil slick the size of France, leaking from pipes decaying for decades under the Soviet system; and the people and animals, dependent on the already sparse resources, driven for ever from their land – or destroyed altogether, as oil companies compete for exploration rights to oil and gas reserves. But it's not hopeless even now, even many years later: all it needs is money on a massive scale. We're still here. Frogmat still exists, and hope must spring eternal or it's time to put out the lights.

It was through Ken that Madame Butterfly came into our lives. We had made a short promotional film showing how Frogmat was made and how it worked, and we used the barn and fields owned by Brickfields Horse Country on the Isle of Wight. Phil Legge, who runs Brickfields, has a huge collection of horses: Shires and heavy horses to plough and pull wagons, riding horses and tiny miniature Shetland ponies who run about like hairy dogs between the immense legs of their stable companions. Would we like to own a Shire horse? Yes, of course, at once please. Into vision came a lovely foal called Shelley, all legs and feet with a body that seemed far too small and a tail like a scrubbing brush. We christened her Madame Butterfly.

She grew and grew; and then she grew a bit more and she's now a massive gentle beast standing 18.2 hands and weighing a ton. She lives at Brickfields with her friends, all fantastically docile bruisers, like an equine international rugby team. When Brooke Animal Hospital approached me to be photographed with a horse for their fundraising book, I accepted immediately: Madame Butterfly's mane and tail were plaited with red and green ribbons and she was groomed till she shone. In a black wig and a kimono I led her on to the beach in midwinter, where she responded to the cameras like Helena Christensen, only fretting when she couldn't see her companion Monty, who being older and wiser provided a calming influence. I took down on the train a bag of carrots from Sainsbury's Nine Elms as a humble reward: they chomped them up, their heads the size of motorbikes, cavernous crunching sounds snaffled by soft lips, eyes scanning the horizon for Pinkerton's ship. I don't think she knows I own her; I don't think we do own animals. We pay for them, care for them and keep them (by which reckoning she belongs more to Brickfields than to me). Now she is going to be put in foal, and the father will be a new horse, Spartacus. If we don't keep rare breeds going they will die out. Madame Butterfly, or her baby when it's grown-up, will pull my coffin through the streets of London; but before that we have a lifetime of pleasure to look forward to.

Last summer I saw a dog fox in full daylight when he put his nose round the music-room door, and he had a dreadful patch of mange right across his back and belly; he looked shocking. I asked the vet how to treat mange in wild animals and he said simply feed them good food. Round here the urban foxes exist on old fast-food throw-outs and left-overs, and whatever else they can scavenge. They never seem to trouble the large cat population; in fact the vet said in all his years of treating septic bites only three were from foxes: thousands are from cat fights. The foxes behave rather like cats, leaping up on to walls and running lithely over roofs, and even when I didn't use to feed them they lived – rather miserably – under the hut. Now I put out a dish of dog food every night. I have a special whistle for them and gradually I've moved the dish closer and closer to the house, further and further from this end of the garden, so I can watch them eating. They leave things they don't like – spaghetti shapes and beans – behind in the dish, and yowl and screech like strangled geese. I've seen foxes trotting down Piccadilly, and crossing the road by Harrods, and I once counted 11 in our square by the light of a full moon. Our cat, the Bee, used to watch them from the kitchen window, with no fear but great interest. The Bee has gone now, and we miss him more than words can tell. Writing has become boringly simple without his dear furry body flumping down on to the wet ink as I struggled to write round his soft paws; it was extraordinary what a huge emptiness such a little creature could leave behind.

> I think I could turn and live with animals, they are so placid
>   and self-contain'd,
> I stand and look at them long and long.
> They do not sweat and whine about their condition,
> They do not lie awake in the dark and weep for their sins,
> They do not make me sick discussing their duty to God,
> Not one is dissatisfied, not one is demented with the mania
>   of owning things,

Not one kneels to another, nor to his kind that lived
   thousands of years ago,
Not one is respectable or unhappy over the whole earth.

That's from Walt Whitman's 'Song of Myself'; he was a
poet of numinousness if ever there was one. When we lost
the Bee I realized that over the 18 years he had been with
us we had got to know and love him very well indeed, and
to see that in character he was very different from this or
that cat, who in turn was as different as could be from
another. He was only one cat amongst a million million
cats; but because we got to know him we recognized him
as unique and distinctive. Every animal and bird has the
capability of being recognized as totally unique and different from its fellows – sheep, pigs, chickens, cattle, horses.
If we took the trouble to treat a pig, a single pig, like a
pet dog we would bask in its friendship and boast of its
intelligence.

Once I took a pig to Parliament. At that time farm
animals were classed as 'goods', which meant that in trans-
portation they were only afforded the same status as a tin
of beans. To show that animals are sentient creatures,
Compassion in World Farming and I thought up a ruse: I
would have a piglet on a lead and carry a tin of beans, and
people looking at the photographs could make up their
own minds as to which had feelings. The piglet, called
Babe, was eight weeks old and arrived at the house for a
day-long bonding session with me. In 15 minutes she had
learned to use the dirt tray we had put down. I fed her
some sort of mash from a bowl and she grunted and
squeaked and licked the spoon clean. She fell asleep in front
of the fire, dreaming and twitching her toes, occasionally

waking to see if we were all still there. Her companion was a patient middle-aged border collie dog: Babe thought he was her mother.

The next day a London taxi driven by an understanding cabbie arrived, and Babe and I went across the river to the Houses of Parliament. The press were waiting: as we emerged from the cab there was a blaze of flashbulbs, with the photographers crying, 'Babe! This way, Babe!' and we set off at a great pace across the grassy lawn called Abingdon Green, with Babe's nose rootling up the ground leaving a ploughed field behind us. Because it was a cold January day, we had to keep the photo-shoot short, for Babe's small almost hairless body began to shiver. The photographers were terrific; they got some excellent coverage for us, and the happy end of the story is that European law was amended to classify animals as sentient beings. Babe went back to the farm, spared for ever from slaughter, living out her life in freedom in a large orchard.

> Jog on, jog on the footpath way,
> And merrily hent the stile-a:
> A merry heart goes all the day,
> Your sad tires in a mile-a.

I knew that verse when I was four and we were home on leave from the Far East at Belgar Farm with our friends the Shaws. We had rented their converted oast house to live in; just as in Mickledene School, four miles away, the roundels where hops had been dried were turned into circular rooms, with windows looking out over the orchards of apples, pears and cherries. Here's our little London apple tree, whose fruit is small and hard and very sweet. In the hot summer when I had put the sprinkler on to water the garden with its see-sawing arch of spray, I watched a flock of blue tits sitting on the apple tree waiting for the next twinkling wave of drops to reach their branches: then they fanned their wings open and twittered under the light shower, holding fast with their toes for almost a quarter of an hour, flapping and cheeping and preening. The pear tree was here already, and we planted a cherry which is pretty and grows fruit but is stripped of cherries before we can harvest them, by birds and squirrels. So I have remembered here Belgar Farm, with its ponies and geese, and bonfires in the autumn, and hard frost making the puddles squeak with ice, and summer hedgerows full of dog roses, hawthorn and honeysuckle.

In a city, trees make everything look more beautiful. Shortly after the Princess of Wales died in the Paris car crash, people began to think about a suitable memorial to her. All kinds of things were suggested, ranging from churches and hospitals to schools, playgrounds and statues. I thought a garden bridge planted with trees would be a lovely memorial; I telephoned Sir Terence Conran and he thought it was a good idea too. Then, in no particular order, the following things happened: I walked up and down the Thames in central London on both sides of the river, taking photographs, to find a useful and important place to site it. I thought it should span the river between Gabriel's Wharf on the south bank, very close to the National Theatre, and arrive on the north bank at Arundel Street between Temple underground station and the big ship that's permanently moored there. I wrote out a proposal, describing the project, and met up with Nigel Coates, the designer and architect. Together we approached the Chancellor, Gordon Brown, who was

Chairman of the Diana Memorial Committee. He liked the idea. I wrote to the most important people I could think of to support the project and they all said yes. I've never been able to thank them fully for lending their names, advice and sheer clout. They were, again in no specific order: Jorgen Nissen, Principal Director of Ove Arup and Partners; Bob Ayling, Chief Executive of British Airways; Elliot Bernerd, Chairman of the South Bank Centre; Terence Conran, Chairman of Conran Groups; Norman Rosenthal, Exhibition Secretary of the Royal Academy of Arts; Jocelyn Stevens, Chairman of English Heritage; John Egan, Chairman of MEPC; Nick Wapshott, Editor of the Saturday *Times*; and Robin Wight, Chairman of Arts and Business. We were supported to the hilt by Central London Partnership in the form of Pat Brown; many of our meetings took place in the CLP offices behind the Theatre Royal Haymarket.

Ove Arup provided professional designers and engineers: I still have Angus Low's drawings in a large file marked 'The Bridge'; Greg Haigh accompanied me to the Port of London Authority meeting at St Katharine's Dock where several very useful comments and suggestions were made. I had started running the idea of a garden bridge past anyone I met who would listen: my parents, friends and family, taxi drivers, show folk, shopkeepers . . . everyone was enthusiastic. No one thought it was anything but a wonderful project. I had letters of encouragement and support from the Institute of Structural Engineers, from Fitzpatrick Contractors, who were putting the finishing touches to a large pedestrian bridge in Mile End Park, landscaped with trees and shrubs, and from Woods River Cruises whose sleek boats ply the Thames every day.

Thomas Heatherwick, an artist and designer of incomparable originality and talent, would be happy to work on the bridge; he had already made a small prototype bridge in glass, my favoured material. I went to meet Ian Tuckett of the Coin Street Community Builders, whose mission has been to turn the south bank into a better place to live and work by providing low-cost housing, a new park and a riverside walkway. He liked the modesty of our proposed bridge, and the fact that it would be green and traffic-free.

The Duke of Wellington assured me that the big white ship HQS *Wellington* was not connected with his family: to move her from her anchorage would not ruffle the feathers of the Iron Duke's descendant. Like a stalker, I continued to walk up and down the river, staring from bridges and benches, taking sightlines from all sorts of standpoints to ensure that the bridge with its soft lights and greenery would only enhance every aspect it appeared in. Already I had made plans for the maintenance of the bridge, which would remain open night and day. The team would be called The Bridgilantes: young people recruited in Lambeth and trained in arboriculture would patrol the bridge in pairs to answer questions and make sure the trees and plants weren't harmed; they would keep the winding path and cycle track free from litter and make sure the area around the central café kiosk was clean and attractive. There would be staffed public lavatories at each end, and wheelchair access; there would be flower-sellers offering single blooms, which you could throw over the parapet into the water, to make a wish or to remember someone. Container-grown trees would be changed several times throughout the year – whitebeam in blossom, rowan trees in berry, larch and spruce at Christmastime. Because of a famous old rhyme there would be apple trees:

> Upon Paul's steeple stands a tree
> As full of apples as may be;
> The little boys of London Town
> They run with hooks to pull them down
> And then they run from hedge to hedge
> Until they come to London Bridge.

There would be hot chestnuts for sale in winter . . .

Q. . . . I hoped you'd say that . . .

A. . . . and the café kiosk would sell very simple things like coffee, tea, apple juice and champagne. Westminster Council told me they still had the moulds for the elaborate dolphin gas lampposts that stand along the Embankment; I envisaged them recast in opaque Lalique-type glass – the whole bridge clad in glass, lit with small soft lights from within.

Fountains, fed by water pumped up from the Thames below, would never run dry; benches would offer places to sit and take in the dawn coming up and the sun going down. People would be able to hurry across the bridge to work, grabbing a coffee as they went, or dawdle over as midnight struck, with a glass of champagne to say, 'Will you marry me?' It was to be advertised as the *slowest* way to cross the river; and although tourists would flock to it, it would be used all the time by Londoners on their daily business, going to the theatre, rushing to catch the Eurostar to Paris or reading a book in the April sunlight.

Q. I wish we could go there now! I wish it had been built! What happened?

A. The Government finally approved a memorial water feature, to be built very near the Serpentine, so the whole project was wound down. People said don't give up, but I couldn't see how to go forward. I had set up the Diana Bridge Foundation, with Colin Tweedy of Arts and Business, Pat Brown of CLP and my agent Kate Plumpton as directors; now sadly I dismantled it. Strangely enough I feel this is not at all at an end. The proposed bridge has become real in the minds of those who knew it: its phantom shape crosses the river at twilight, its lamps gleaming and flickering on the trees, dim shapes of people leaning on the parapets; I can smell the fresh coffee; and apart from the great river sliding underneath there's no noise of trains or cars, maybe just the cry of starlings as they wheel round and round before settling in for the night.

For the 18 years that Jamie and I lived in Addison Road we were in a top-floor flat facing due east. There was a large communal garden downstairs, but to use it meant packing up and leaving as if we were going for a day at the seaside, it was so far below and out of easy reach. We didn't have mobile phones, so the answering machine had to be switched on (always one's ears, like bats' radar systems, were tuned in for a call from the agent with news of an audition or – far less often – an actual offer of work). The door was double-locked, baskets with extra jerseys, books, balls, tanks, bits of food and an umbrella were loaded on to our arms (and I should add the au pair girl's arms) and off we went, down three flights, past Mrs Battine and Miss Harvey, both in their eighties, past our beloved friends the

Me with shell ring, coconut and Paddy's knife on Tsarabanjina.
My brain had almost vanished.

On a burnt tank in Eritrea.

With Babe the Pig in the kitchen.

With Madame Butterfly on the Isle of Wight, December 2003.

Holding Jamie with cigarette: dress from Granny Takes a Trip.

Jamie's christening.

Polaroid by me of
Jamie aged 6.

Our wedding in Fort William – Jamie as best man.

Bafta night with Stevie, me wearing Betty Jackson.

Jamie on the beach in winter by his dad, Michael Claydon.

With Alice in the music room, 2003.

Pearts, past the shelf where circulars addressed to Finnish businessmen lay in misaddressed yellowing piles, outside round the dustbins and into the garden. The fronts of the houses in Addison Road are rather majestic, the backs a chaos of wrongly-placed windows and eccentrically ambitious downpipes. The garden had dull flowerbeds round the edge, neat square quarters of lawn, a bird-bath and a sort of dank sheltered seat. I've made it sound frightful, and it was; but it didn't matter – it was a garden for picnics, or early-evening drinks or tiny firework displays.

During our time there, a succession of dear hard-working girls came to live *en famille*, au pair: they all became members of the family and frankly they had to, as we had only one bathroom, no dishwasher, washing machine or freezer, a very old cooker, one telephone and hand-painted everything. We'd stripped the floors, and you could burn real wood in the fireplaces. The huge sash-cord windows opened wide over little parapets, and when the cushions were plumped up and fresh flowers were in a china jug it looked, to me, fabulous. We rented the flat; it seems strange now to remember the anxiety when it went up from £14 to £16 a week. In those days I always kept a pound note folded in half in my wallet so I couldn't see it and forgot about it; then, when the chips were down and the shadow of Newgate Gaol fell on your shoulders you could suddenly remember – a whole pound left! I used this trick on myself for years and never got wise to it. On films we were paid in cash for our daily expenses, our 'per diems': by keeping these in a carrier bag, along with the sixpences saved from the dimple Haig whisky bottle, and selling the odd lamp or chair, I managed to amass a king's ransom or, in any case, enough to pay for one term at Harrow School for

Jamie. Like people the world over, I would lie in bed at night and wonder how to make ends meet; but they did meet somehow, even if the elastic was stretched to resemble old string. Pick a leaf of mint and follow me through this huge glass door set in the wall: this is the music room.

Music Room

For two years we lived at 91 West Hill Avenue, Epsom, Surrey. I was just nine and still at Mickledene; my father was working for the War Office before going back to Malaya, and these were army quarters, that is to say it was a house found for us by the Army. The house was at the bottom of a cul-de-sac, with a neat little garden full of golden rod, apple trees, laurels and a large slabby rock garden with small indeterminate plants crawling out of the cracks. In the sitting room was a piano, so perhaps the house was rented half-furnished, or fully furnished, as we'd never had a piano. Our next-door neighbours had a television set and once or twice a week we were allowed to watch *Bill and Ben* with them, and circus performances and *Champion the Wonder Horse*. I can remember hearing a lullaby . . . was it sung by Shirley Abicair, sitting on her high stool plucking at a zither? Anyway, I tried playing it on the piano, and it sounded almost right, if a bit sparse. So I added some left-hand harmony and played it again. My parents heard me and I played it again for them, plinking and plonking in F-sharp major, which looked an easy place to work from and sounded nice to my ear. As a result, I was allowed to take piano lessons at Mickledene; but I'm afraid to report that from then on I went quietly downhill, a lamentably short trip which ended when I gave up lessons altogether aged about 12.

No matter how I tried I couldn't read music successfully, couldn't 'do the dots' as musicians say. I tried and tried, but a bit of my brain, the bit that copies numbers down wrong and puts decimal points in the wrong place, didn't seem to progress from Every Good Boy Deserves Favour to my fingers. If someone played a piece and I could watch their hands, I had a good chance of copying the music fairly well. But, as with touch-typing, many of my piano lessons seemed to involve putting a newspaper over my hands, which were bunched up like armadillos . . . 'Imagine you're holding a tangerine in your palm' . . . I could only stare at the miserable notes, gripping on to their telephone wires of staves, while my small chipolata hands bungled about in the newsprint gloom trying to make 'The Blacksmith's Dance' come alive. I didn't want to play the Blacksmith's anything; I wanted to play the theme from the New World Symphony! Or that bit from 'Ol' Man River'! Or something that sounded even a tiny bit lovely. The truth is this: I was not destined to be a musician, even a pathetically inadequate one. I could do galloping arpeggios and broken chords, and bang out some home-devised rendition of the theme from *Exodus* – and sometimes I'd even make up tunes of my own, although they were usually very derivative, and eventually sounded much the same. But I'm afraid that was it. I'm so sorry about this. It broke my heart not to be a musical person. I *feel* like a musical person because I've always loved music since the first day of my life I can remember . . .

Q. You don't have to go on like this. You love music and you're lucky enough to be married to a musician. Isn't that enough?

A. Yes; of course you're right. It's just that if I could have broken through that barrier of not being able to read the notes . . .

Q. That's rubbish. Paul McCartney can't read or write music. It didn't stop him. Stevie Wonder is blind. It didn't stop him. It's an excuse you've polished up over the years so you can evade criticism. 'Do you play the piano?' – 'I'm afraid I never learned to do the dots': what rubbish.

A. That's true. If you really want to do something you'll do it because you can't live with yourself *not* doing it. Stevie said that for him a day without music would be like being dead, i.e. it would be unthinkable. He said that he first loved music when aged five he held down two notes, a 10th apart, on the piano. The sound was so mesmeric, addictive and compelling that he started from then learning how to read music. He was extraordinarily gifted in what he could hear. He can still hear and discern anything. He can hear that silent echoey sound just before a gramophone record starts and tell from that *absence* of sound's echo what the piece is and in what key. He hears a person's voice, singing or speaking, and it slots away into his computer brain and he can recognize it 14 years later. He went to the Choir School at Canterbury, then on to the King's School – in both places he was in a seam of richly musically talented boys with inspiring, dedicated and demanding teachers. At 12 he was writing music for services in the Cathedral – they all were: it was expected of them. 'I want a Nunc Dimittis before 6.30' . . . and they scrawled and scratched the music down – having first *composed* it – and went off to play football. He blossomed and grew (he'll

hate me drooling on like this) and got yet another scholarship, this time to be Organ Scholar at Trinity College,
Cambridge. His whole life is music – except for the bits
that are cricket, wine, decent sports cars and leaving piles
of papers about in every room of the house. And, to some
extent, being married to me. I think I've rather compressed
his life here, just a few measly sentences for a preternaturally
gifted musical genius who is also my husband; I can see
that it's pretty unsatisfactory but I do promise you . . .

Q. . . . Ssshh!! Is that him? Coming down the garden? Listen!

A. No, don't be stupid, he's in Chicago; I told you, he's doing
Carmen in Chicago. Lord! That made my heart beat faster.
I promised I wouldn't write about him, us, our marriage.
It is both extraordinary and inevitable that we are together.
Shortly after Jamie was born, I spent a Sunday with Celia
and Tony Armitage, who had five children, and were close
friends. I'd stayed with them when I was expecting Jamie
and they'd become a second family to me. Their eldest
son, St Clair, had just started at the King's School, Canterbury; he was 13. He was bringing another new boy
from school back for lunch on the day I was there; but
at lunchtime only St Clair arrived. For some reason I've
forgotten, Stephen Barlow, the musical prodigy, didn't
come with him as expected. I do remember feeling dis-
appointed, which was odd as I was 21 and these boys were
only 13. But I would have liked to meet Barlow, who by
all accounts was black-haired, slightly difficult and very
good at games. Ten years went by; and St Clair, now a
young naval officer, was getting married in Dawlish. The
organist was to be his great friend the same Stephen Barlow.

With Celia and Tony, I arrived early at the church, where there was some anxiety as the sheet music for Zadok the Priest hadn't been delivered, putting Stephen into a bit of a rage. When I first saw him at the keyboard, very pale with black hair, I felt a huge jolt of recognition like an electric shock. That's all it was; but I talked to him at the reception and thought that although rather fiery he was good fun. It turned out that we had friends in common – John Caird, my flatmate Jane Carr's boyfriend, had formed a group called Circle of Muses with Stephen when they were both at university. We went to a play together in London directed by John, starring Jane Carr, and Stephen spent the night chastely in Addison Road in the tiny spare room. And left. It was of no consequence: I was with someone else anyway. Much later, I heard that Stephen had married a singer, and I felt as though something had gone wrong, although I couldn't think what or how or why.

Seven years passed; then out of the blue I got a note through the front door, propped by a neighbour on the pile of Yellow Pages and junk mail with unclaimed final demands for gas bills, saying, 'Do you still live here? I'm rehearsing in the school hall next door. Can I come for tea?' We talked for about four hours and I had the strangest sensation of absolute calm, as though I had arrived home, and recognized the harbour, as though I could speak the language; as though a long journey was over. We got married very secretly in Fort William in a register office with only a handful of family attending and Jamie as best man. Both of us had been married before, and this time we were both determined to make the marriage work for ever if possible: a quiet solemn start seemed a good beginning. Eighteen years have gone by since then. You never imagine you'll be able to say, 'Eighteen years ago, when we were driving back from Scotland . . .' I can now easily remember 50 years ago.

In my head I feel the same as I did when I was about seven. When I was three and in Hong Kong, I can remember thinking, 'I'm too short and I don't know enough words to talk properly to the grown-ups.' I can see the polished wooden coffee table by my face; and outside the windows in the streets of Hong Kong the air is grey and muggy. I think I can remember our nursery too – I can see twin beds and a bedside table, all rather plain stuff, army-issue – but when I look directly at it in my mind, it disappears. It is the strangest thing to look back over your life and see what you looked like to other people: just a child, a little girl with pigtails, a spotty lumpy teenager – when all the time inside I was somebody completely different. Here's a thing: I don't know if it's very common or not but I'll try to explain.

In my mind, the way I think and imagine things and try to sort out problems, in my mind I am not a woman or a man. Or a child. I'm a thinking thing with periscope eyes; and only in the presence of other people or mirrors do I remember who I am. I don't feel I think like a woman; just, or not even, a person. On the island of Tsarabanjina, after nine days of my not seeing myself (I saw my legs and arms, of course, as they walked underneath me and collected things), the sense of being isolated from my own identity was complete. The camera crew and the director, and Paddy from the Irish Guards, they were all men but they very civilly treated me like a bloke and didn't do or say anything that made me feel . . . well . . . feminine. I was just a character they had to record, and actually I didn't think of them as men, just as friends. Anyway, when finally the helicopter came to take me away back to Nosy Bé, the bigger island near the mainland of Madagascar, and I could look down on that tiny touching brilliant little jewel in the huge blue-green ocean, I thought how strange and scary it was to be going back to civilization. At our beach hotel, as I walked in with my shells and rucksack, the staff greeted me with pleasure. 'Better better,' they said, ruffling my sea-coiled ropes of hair and patting my dark brown arms. But when I stood in the bathroom and looked in the bathroom mirror before washing my hair I had a terrible shock. I was looking at a perfect stranger. I looked at the woman and she looked back at me and it was beyond scary: it was like the beginning of a serious nightmare. But I stood and stood and then smiled and then spoke some words and heard her saying them in the looking glass; and very soon, after about 10 minutes, I had fused my mind and body together again. I wonder if this is the 'inward eye' that Wordsworth referred to when he was lying on his couch, 'in vacant or in pensive mood'. His eye saw the daffodils, mine had been seeing fish eagles and flying foxes, dolphins, baby turtles, a million fish, a trillion stars, and six men. I felt like all of them and none of them at the same time.

Zoom! 'Whence is that goodly fragrance blowing / Stealing our senses all away?' – and now we are back in the school gym in singing class, holding our song sheets in front of us: 'The Elizabethan Serenade', 'What is life to me without thee?' and Handel's Largo – rather draggingly 'Li-i-ight of the Wo-oorld' – and music on the old school piano. There used to be, long ago, BBC *Music for Schools* on the wireless, with songbooks for every term. Because of those lessons, I knew many old English songs by heart and we used to sing them on long car journeys or on buses on the way to lacrosse matches. They've gone now: 'Green Grow the Rushes O', 'Dashing Away with a Smoothing Iron', 'The Lass of Richmond Hill'. 'Ah, leave me not to pine alone . . .' All children in all schools sang together every day; in assembly, usually, a hymn which I can understand now isn't suitable for our much more integrated inter-faith society. But a good song! Even if you couldn't sing well the music went in and performed its civilizing influence. Music is the opposite of élitism: everyone can hear the most sublime sounds ever created and by hearing them they cannot but be made better. Music appeals to that inner person; while you listen, you can escape the bodily carapace that sits around your mind and fly off into a world of your own making. Music is the senior service: of creative artists I rate composers at the top of the tree. Roald Dahl once said to me that he thought writing fiction was the hardest of all writing, poetry and plays included.

Q. What would he have said if he'd been around to read this?

A. I never think of anybody but you reading this. I'm writing this for you. At school one of the most inspiring teachers was Miss Hortin-Smith, who taught English literature and English language. Ælene was extremely good at both subjects, and I wasn't bad either. I didn't know until recently that when both my parents were in Malaya Mummy had asked Miss Hortin-Smith to keep an eye out for us. She liked us: she liked me because I was cheeky but rather good at English. When our school photographs were taken, 'Hooter', as we called her, ordered one of me for herself. It was an unprepossessing portrait but she kept it. Although in a letter home I expressed incredulity – 'Honestly! It's *frightfully* bad! For herself! Well, good luck to her' – and so on, I think I was very pleased that she rated me highly.

Was it Jane Taylor who had a little transistor radio? It was tuned in to Radio Luxembourg, snatches of pop songs screeing in and out of focus, awash with static and atmospheric alternations. Each of the common rooms had a gramophone: Felicity Alcock had the best and largest collection of 45s; but most of our 33 rpm vinyl records were classical. Every term brought a new craze, a different Beethoven symphony, Rossini and Wagner overtures (not the whole opera, no time to listen to the whole thing and indeed no money to buy them), Chopin and Liszt, Elgar and Grieg. On Sundays, when you got into the sixth form, you were allowed to use the clanging empty school kitchens to make high tea to eat in Pilgrim's Progress, the sixth-form common room. We usually made spaghetti bolognese and ate it sitting round the old wireless listening to *Top of the Pops* or what was it called . . . *The Hit Parade*? There was a film-review programme, too, on the Light Programme on Sunday afternoons: they would play scenes from films and I'd listen to the silences and rustles and footsteps between the words and try to imagine what the actors were doing and how I would ever in a million years be able to do the same thing with confidence.

Down the lower corridor, beyond the Barrow Way, where our lacrosse sticks hung in winter and our tennis rackets in summer, were the tiny cell-sized music-practice rooms. They each had a high window facing on to a tall bank, an upright piano with just enough room for a piano stool and a chair for the music mistress and that was it. Sounds mixed and tangled: 'Rondo à la Turque', chromatic scales and a vamped-up version of 'Blue Moon', all jumbled up together. Prep was taken in classrooms with a senior girl presiding. You would put your hand up – 'Please, Angela, may I go and practise?' – and you would escape from Cicero's speeches to wrestle with the Moonlight Sonata, looking glumly at the fingering recommended by Miss Montgomery. Sometimes people would come to the school to give recitals: that meant all the 4B girls had to carry 70 chairs into the gym and line them up in rows so we could hear some German *lieder* performed by Miss Peggy Stack.

We all had to learn to read plainsong for chapel – which was lovely but easier than it looked on the page – and the choir learned and practised anthems for special occasions. I was in the choir, and eventually became Head of the Choir. We had extra-large chapel veils to begin with, which were eventually replaced by blue cassocks and skullcaps. We had to assemble in Edgeworth, one of the classrooms, before processing up the path to the chapel between wallflowers and sweet williams, hanging on to our hair as the wind from the sea whipped round us from across the games field. My job was to recite a prayer before we started to get us into the right frame of mind: 'Defend us, O Lord, in all our doings with Thy most gracious favour . . .' and off we'd go, looking as powerful and matronly as only teenage girls can, ink-stained hands holding prayer books, heads full of the Everly Brothers and 'Cathy's Clown'. I met them, you know, the Evs – and Bill Haley and Little Richard and Chuck Berry. Shall I write a list of the famous rock stars and singers I've met?

Q. No, it would just read like a boastful catalogue. You may as well start from here until the end of the book just writing down all the famous people you've met . . .

A. I've met them all! I seem to have met everyone.

Q. . . . but you'd leave people out; and there wouldn't be room for all the stories that go with the meetings. It's just a pathetic suggestion.

A. You've rather changed your tune. But it's what children always ask me, 'Have you met Robbie? Have you really worked with Kylie?' Sometimes I pretend I know people so I don't disappoint the children. Nobody knows who knows whom. Quite often you forget you *do* know someone, because they're so famous you feel you know them anyway. If someone asks for Jennifer's autograph I sometimes fake it, because honestly her signature is little more than a demented scribble and no one would know or care.

Q. They *would* care – how awful that you admit to faking other people's signatures.

A. But she does mine! And she also dubs extra words in *AbFab*; when they can't be bothered to get me into the BBC to do such a little bit she just mimics my voice. I only know because she told me; I never noticed the difference.

Q. Did you ever collect autographs?

A. Not really. At school we all had autograph books, and schoolfriends would do a drawing of a horse or a bunch of flowers and write, 'By hook or by crook I'll be last in this book.' Some grown-up wrote in my book, 'Be good, sweet maid, and let who will be clever,' advice that soared over my head missing me on both counts. The photographer Roy Round gave me a 10×8-inch photograph of Nureyev at a curtain call, head thrown back, holding an armful of lilies. It's stupendous – and Roy's wife, the ballerina Georgina Parkinson, got Rudi to sign it for me: he wrote, 'To Joanna, Rudolf Nureyev.' I keep it in a reddish-pink wild-silk frame. But that's about it. If I'd collected autographs I might have become an anorak . . . but look at who I'd have got! Frank Sinatra, Ava Gardner, the Beatles, the Stones, the Dames and Divas, the Prima Ballerina Assolutas, the Who, the Presidents and Prime Ministers, the Sirs and Lordly Ones; the writers, the sporting heroes, the Maestros and Masterchefs . . .

Q. The world. But not Elvis.

A. That's true. I never got Elvis's autograph: but then I never got anyone's autograph as I've just explained. Also I own up to faking signatures of Patrick Macnee, Gareth Hunt, David McCallum and Rod Stewart. For a very brief time in the seventies I went about with Rod the Mod, who was just terrific fun to be with. He dedicated a song to me on *Smiler*, the album he was working on at the time. It was a Bob Dylan song called 'Girl from the North Country'; he brought a demo round to my flat after they'd recorded it and played it to me, and when it was over he said, 'There you go: I dedicate that to you.' It's not written down anywhere on the record sleeve that it's my dedicated song, so only I know this fact.

Q. Perhaps he dedicated that song to other girls as well as you.

A. No. I'm sure he didn't Anyway, when the album was released, I got about 10 to give away to charities and I signed them all 'Best wishes, Rod Stewart' as I'd seen him do. Is that bad?

Q. I really don't think it amounts to a hill of beans.

A. I think this whole thing about meeting famous people depends on what rung of the ladder you're perceived to be on at the time. If you are a lowly worm (as I was when I met Frank Sinatra and worked with Ava Gardner), if you are just starting out in your career, or struggling to make ends meet, to encounter a movie legend is utterly thrilling. If you've been a long time on the road and your own leathery features are fairly well-known it's a different thing. You go into parties and say, 'Hi Elton,' and give him a gorgeous hug, 'Hi Cliff,' 'Hi Shirley' . . .

Q. Please stop.

A. . . . and they're friends, friendly people – still superstar diva über-fab trail-blazers but actually just people as well.

Q. Have famous people been here? You know, famous friends?

A. What a strange question; of course they have. Because of our jobs, our professions, very many of the people we know are 'famous' in the general use of the word . . . and very many of our friends aren't. They, like you, are most welcome here, as we are welcomed into their houses and homes. The fame thing doesn't rank very highly amongst people who are well-known; it's seen mostly as a mild irritant. I have taught myself, as self-preservation, to love equally being recognized and not being recognized; that way, either way, you are as happy as a king.

Once or twice I have been invited to do live perform-ances with Stephen conducting: 'Peter and the Wolf', for instance, which I've known since I was a child. Musicians are very different from actors: we drift into the rehearsal room, putting down scripts, coats, collecting cups of coffee, having a bit of a gossip, whereas when we ran through 'Peter and the Wolf' Stevie just said from the podium, 'This is Joanna Lumley, who will be the narrator,' raised his baton and off they went, with me unable to make chummy, self-deprecating remarks and smooth over the mistakes I was bound to make. They have a far stricter discipline with very little talking, as music is the language used. We actors are used to stopping and starting, trying things out, discussing points of text; they *know* what to do and apart from writing a few notes on dynamics, tempi or bowing, they just stick to the score and watch the conduc-tor. And it's ensemble work from the outset: it's all utterly different. Although I can't read music I can follow it well enough to know when my part comes along. The more you've worked on it beforehand (like anything) the easier it is, and your speaking voice becomes another instrument in the orchestra. Singers are something else again. They arrive on the first day of rehearsals knowing their entire role by heart. Actors nowadays are 'on the book' to begin with, certainly for the first week or so. However, Noël

Coward expected his actors to arrive word-perfect on the first day, and to be elegantly dressed as well. Now we slouch in wearing shocking old track-suit bottoms and gym shoes, looking as though we've been sweeping the streets. This is the protective locker-room mentality: you can't be judged on what you've got on or how you do something because you have clearly been doing exercises or going for a run, so what do you expect.

I love this music room when musicians and singers come to rehearse here. The acoustic is good, and natural light comes down from the roof and through the garden doors. There's a kitchen and a lavatory; Stephen's study has all his miniature scores, CDs, sound decks and so forth; and it all doubles up as a huge dining room when we need it. That lovely line drawing of a woman's head is only a print but it's by Picasso. I thought it was so brilliantly clever, so few strokes of a pen bringing her calm face to life; only when I looked closer did I see that he had written on it '*1er mai 1946*'. Picasso was drawing this portrait of Françoise Gilot the very day I was being born in Kashmir. In France, May Day is special – children pick lilies-of-the-valley and give them to the grown-ups. Picasso put a crown of leaves on Françoise's hair. These enormously tall wooden candelabra I had made for Stevie's birthday – there are two of them, each supporting 18 thick church candles – and the lights are on dimmer switches, so with the sandblasted brick walls and plain oak floor the place looks golden at night-time. We've got art books and two sofas by the wood-burning stove . . .

Q. It doesn't look as though it actually burns the wood.

A. Well, it's gas flames and it looks real; flickering firelight is lovely when the wind is rattling away outside or the garden is white with snow. The room loves people: we've had big parties here, 90 people at a time, and there's no crowded feeling at all. These four school tables I bought from a catalogue – pushed together like this is how they are when Stevie is writing music, full-score paper spread out all over them so he can see what he's doing and where he's going. This piece is 'King', an opera he's writing to be performed at Canterbury Cathedral; it's about Thomas Becket and Henry II. Please don't touch it; just look at how it's done. All the orchestral parts are written on their separate staves all to be played at the same time. It's like three-dimensional chess only harder. Sometimes he will go over to the piano and play a few bars he's just written but mostly the composing is done in silence. I suppose I thought, like everyone else, that he'd sit at the piano with a pencil between his teeth, possibly Judy Garland at his elbow, playing a few chords and crying, 'That's it!' and she'd lean over his shoulder and sing it and in two weeks it would open on Broadway.

Q. You didn't think that.

A. No – but in my dreams! In my dreams, everything would happen more quickly, particularly films and plays. Everything grinds to a halt for lack of money. I rather like the French tradition of dragging a table into the street, standing on it and declaiming your poetry. We've got a bit cautious about putting on new work: can it be justified, how much will it make, will there be a sequel, are the exits clearly marked? This room is both a haven and a hothouse for invention. When Alice is old enough I shall teach her to dance here.

Q. That's a bit of a jump. Your mind moves very erratically.

A. I can't help it. I live in fits and starts. I want to take you now back through the garden and we'll climb to the top of the house which we haven't seen at all. But look, before we leave the music room, look at this huge grey sculpture of a flower on a bracket against the brick wall. It's not a sculpture – it is an actual fossil dug out of a riverbed in China. It's a sea lily, a crinoid; the tall waving stems supported these hugely veined petals, which look like an enlarged tulip with frilly edges. These soft feathery shapes closed around small aquatic beings, shrimps and plankton, and consumed them, rather the way pitcher plants or sea anemones do. They were alive 240 million years ago. They lived in shallow seas, anchoring themselves to floating logs, and they only died when the log became saturated, or the colony of crinoids became so heavy that the log was dragged down to the sea-bed. If they were not buried immediately in the soft mud they would disarticulate within a few hours. Swimming round them were ichthyo-saurs, 25 feet long, fish, sharks, turtle-like reptiles called placodonts, and nothosaurs, which were the forerunners of the plesiosaurs which ruled the seas for the next 150 million years. Mankind hadn't put on his first shoe, hadn't got a foot, wasn't even a man in those days – and now we can stroke the stem past which these huge creatures swam. Chris Moore told me all this; my mother had dragged me down to Charmouth in Dorset to his fossil centre, the Forge: for her, fossils are as Jimmy Choos are to others. If you can't think what to give someone of any age for a present, give them a fossil. This crinoid was expensive, naturally; but there are small fossils you can buy for a few pounds, each unique and breathtaking. At a recent fundraising dinner for Fauna and Flora International in the Natural History Museum, where the tables were set out under the skeleton of a dinosaur, we put a tiny trilobite into each goody bag as a surprise present. Chris Moore found them for me, it was my gift to all those generous people, to remind us how life goes on.

We're walking back down through the garden to the house: doesn't it look tall and thin? My cousin Maybe has a map of London drawn in 1850, and it shows this square as the last buildings before the country lanes and water meadows take over. They would have been very new when the map was made, as they were built in 1847 . . .

Q. You've said that before.

A. It has always interested me that the nearer you live to people, the less you infringe on their territory. 'Tall fences make good neighbours.' It has to be that way; you have to turn a blind eye, or deaf ear, to families living shoulder to shoulder, back to back, side by side. However, here we have struck gold: we know all our neighbours, and faces from people across the square, and all our local shop-keepers and families from the estates. We all live here all the time, so it's a real community with its own identity. Take a deep breath: we're going to climb up five flights of stairs now. I shall regale you with snippets of interest as we go.

Q. I had dreaded 'regale' turning up.

A. When I was talking on the telephone the other day to the actor Richard Griffiths, the conversation turned to Lee Marvin. I said how much I admired his work and that I'd met him in New York at the end of my tour promoting the Pink Panther films in the States. Michael Apted, casting for the film of *Gorky Park* and staying in the same hotel, asked me down for a drink to meet Mr Marvin – who had already got a part in the film. I told Richard how immensely charming and courteous he was to me, assuming that as I was an English actress I would have played all Shakespeare's heroines on stage. He quoted at length from several plays, his deep rumbling voice animated, his clever eyes ablaze with the Bard's poetry. Richard told me that he had worked with Marvin and that Marvin had told him that he, Lee Marvin, had worked with Spencer Tracy who had given him a tip on screen acting that he'd never forgotten and would now pass on to Richard. It was this: 'Never let the camera see you *not* thinking.' That's all. I love it. So now I pass it on from Spencer Tracy to Lee Marvin to Richard Griffiths to Joanna Lumley to you. Obviously it is of more use if you are a screen actor yourself.

Q. I take that on board. Up we go.

Stairs Again

One of the advantages of travelling alone is that you often sit next to interesting people who are happy to talk. Random conversations with complete strangers can be memorable, as long as you can work out a polite way to return to your book when there are still three hours left of the journey: you can't talk for hours on end to anyone.

On a flight to Mauritius, when planes still allowed smoking, my French neighbour lit up as soon as the NO SMOKING light was switched off and called for a large brandy. When the air hostess brought it to him she addressed him as Doctor. 'Doctor!' I said. 'I can't help feeling surprised that you smoke and drink.' 'But I know what kills people,' he said. 'I'm a heart surgeon. I've just attended a tragic case . . .' And here he named a French football team and their young star striker. 'His heart was in perfect condition, his body could not have been in better shape. But he was a worrier; he had worked himself up into a terrible state about this particular match – and the result was a massive and fatal heart attack. Stress. It is stress that kills people. I'm off to see my family in Mauritius. I am quite old and fattish, I smoke and drink, and eat very well' – here he patted his stomach and laughed – 'but I am completely happy. I will die one day but it won't be from stress.'

Travelling on aeroplanes was lovely when you were allowed to smoke. There was a feeling of the cocktail hour, time for chit-chat and courtesies and compliments. The air-conditioning had to work full blast to dispel the smoke, and in consequence all the cold and flu germs were blown out into the ether at the same time. Nowadays they hardly change the air at all, so almost everyone gets some sort of cold or bug during a flight, even on a short hop like London to Paris. London to New York is like eating bad shellfish: you *will* get ill. In the olden days there were non-smoking sections and you really weren't troubled by clouds of tobacco smoke as it was siphoned out of the fuselage as soon as it was exhaled.

On such a flight, from Cairo to London, I sat next to an old Egyptian banker, very well dressed and pleasantly talkative. My visit to Egypt had been fleeting, three days in all; but the country and its people had impressed me hugely and I said so to my companion. He told me a bit about his life and family; as he did so he packed strands of tobacco into a pipe, pressing them down and tamping them in with his thumb. He told me about Abdu, who had come to work for him as houseboy and cook at the age of 17; although largely unschooled, he had picked up the culinary arts from the French cook of his first employer. She was jealous of his youth and dexterity and complained to the lady of the house that Abdu was dirty, having herself first inserted two dead cockroaches into his stew. The lady pointed them out to Abdu with disgust, but Abdu, picking them out delicately, said, 'Merely braised onions – delicious,' and popped them into his mouth.

Such a bond of love and trust had developed between him and the banker that, on Abdu's marriage two years later, the banker had given him a house with a shop attached. '"But, Baba," said Abdu, "if I leave you, you will want your house back." "Abdu, it is a present. I have no children; money is no use to me when I am dead."' 'How lucky for Abdu,' I said to the banker as we flew up over Egypt. He turned to me, his eyes bright. 'But no! I am the lucky one! Abdu has taken the place of my son — now he has three children of his own. I am a happy man.'

The aeroplane was full and stiflingly hot. I thought the banker had nodded off, and reached surreptitiously for my book. His head snapped round like an old turtle's and, quaffing down the last drops of Omar Khayyam, he positioned the empty bottle on the rickety plastic table. Tapping the top, he said, 'Allah is here, let us say — some call him Allah, some call him God. I said to Abdu, "Some climb up to God this way, and they are Jews."' Here he traced his finger up the condensation on the bottle. '"Here are the Muslims, and here come the Christians, and here come the Hindus . . ."' Four wet trails now led to the summit; he regarded them with pleasure. '"When they get to the top, do you think Allah will say, 'Which path did you take?' No! He will say, 'What have you done with your life?'"' He applied a match to his meerschaum and puffed rapidly, twinkling at me through the clouds of smoke. 'I said to Abdu, "Do you think, after such a journey, Allah will say, 'Abdu, did you drink water during Ramadan?'"' His fingers absentmindedly tapped the Almighty's allocated seat on the bottle; he chuckled sadly. 'What do you think he replied? He said, "Yes, Baba, Allah *will* say, 'Did you drink water during Ramadan?'"'

'The important thing is to be happy,' the banker said. 'We have quite lost sight of this duty to our God. Spread around us in this dense and dazzling tapestry are all kinds of opportunities for joy; but we have stopped seeking them, and in England the people are glum. Glum!' He repeated the word several times, chortling to himself. 'Glummies! That's what I call them. Now, in Egypt . . .' He leaned towards me again, his face suddenly serious. 'In Egypt people are happy. They have so little but they smile and are happy. Oh yes, during Ramadan tempers are frayed and the crime rate rockets and cars crash more frequently, but still they will offer you the hospitality of their home. In Egypt they say, "If you are happy, then I am happy." That, I think, is good.' I said how pleasing it had been to be waved at by small ragged children with broad smiles, and to be greeted in the poorest village with courtesy and warmth. He nodded, acknowledging my compliment on Cairo's behalf. 'What we have also forgotten,' he added earnestly, 'is that you will always get what your heart desires. Always. It is written in the Bible. But take care! You must not want the wrong things or they will come to you and you cannot escape them. What is great wealth but a kind of prison, great power but perpetual fear? And great beauty but a flower that dies?'

Q. Here we are on the third landing of this thin house. White-painted wooden stairs, with the occasional nail still showing from where you ripped the carpet up. Why don't you get things done professionally? This is a lovely house, you're so lucky to be here, and now you've got enough money to get it done nicely and what's this? More hand-painted walls, curtains from three homes ago, things that don't fit . . . why don't you get in a designer?

A. Because we like it like this. I've told you before, I like doing things myself; and Gill and I are good at painting. I stand on a ladder and do the top because she doesn't like heights, and we use masking tape and work quickly and efficiently. We painted the bedroom in one morning and shortly we will do it again. This bookcase has been rather rammed in on this half-landing but what better place to sit and read, even if it's only for a few moments. Lovely tall sash windows; the Turkish hordes massing in two prints I brought back from Istanbul.

> As I was going up the stair
> I met a man who wasn't there.
> He wasn't there again today.
> I wish, I wish he'd stay away.

There's no need to go to the gym if you have this many stairs. I go up two at a time. The house has very solid walls and floors; to call from one floor to another you must stand on the stairs and yell. These old houses shift and resettle all the time, so largish cracks appear vertically in the walls. We just fill them up, paint over them and wait for them to open up again. The most attractive house shouldn't look smarter than the guest it's welcoming: tidy and clean but not too perfect. Palaces, yes; but they're built and decorated to impress and overwhelm. I've been in palaces, sometimes as a tourist (the Topkapi in Istanbul – no hordes or harems now), sometimes as a guest. You *want* to be overawed in a palace or castle, to gasp at the scale of its halls, stare at the throne room, admire its tapestries, sneak into its lavatories. The Palace of Westminster is rightly named: the central lobby, endless corridors, mind-boggling wallpapers and noble statues combine to make you trust, or want to trust, our representatives and feel proud of our constitution. A stately home is almost as good as a palace, but I hardly ever feel jealous of that lifestyle simply because of the amount of work and effort that has to go into keeping it all going. Ireland has some of the grandest houses in Europe: they're not pompous or over-embellished, but powerfully gorgeous and elegantly scruffy.

I'd like one day for Stevie and me to live in a huge old wild house where you could ride a horse into the hall, and have a whole tree chopped up for firewood – and if a room leaked you could decamp into another one, and some rooms you could leave completely empty except for a chair and a table or just one piano or one vast bed . . . The biggest house we've ever owned was the Parsonage in Kent; it was in fact quite huge: nine bedrooms to begin with and five rooms in the cellar alone. We converted some of the bedrooms – into a little bathroom, a dressing room and a study – but there was still space to put up hordes of friends. Our first house owned together, our matrimonial house in Wimbledon – which one newspaper rather accurately called our 'love-nest' – had been bought when neither of us was earning enough to pay off the huge bridging loan. We'd moved there from Addison Road but in only a year and a half we had to sell. In that time we'd stripped some floors, opened up a fireplace and dragged over the massive bath from the flat in Addison Road, which in turn had gone to someone who would give it the facelift it deserved (major surgery and implants, actually); but we hadn't had time to do more than fall in love with the house and then fall out again because we had to. So together we have owned three wonderful houses, not counting the little cottage in Scotland: Wimbledon, the

Parsonage and the one we're standing in now. Houses, like people, have their own characters, and the impact of the character of the Parsonage was undeniable: thrilling but turbulent.

Once on a freezing night, soon after we moved in, I was woken up by the moonlight. I got out of our bed and stood at the window, looking down on the rough grass below the soft tennis court, and saw a freshly-dug grave. The earth was heaped up by the side, the hole in deep shadow. It was very brightly lit by the moon; there was no mistaking what it was. The next day it was gone. We decided (I decided) to dig a pond in that place and so we did, lining it with carpet and then butyl and planting reeds and daffodils round it. I put the statue of the scholar gypsy there to calm unquiet spirits.

Q. Did it do the trick? Are we talking ghosts here?

A. The ghost-story writer M. R. James had been born in the Parsonage when his father was Perpetual Curate to the parish. He left as a little boy, four or five years old, but I think the house may have had some effect on him. We first saw it on a violently tempestuous day, the day of the night of the great storm of 1986. I noticed then that the village, although in full view over the fields and hedges, tended to appear and disappear. The road goes nowhere: when you leave the village you turn round and drive back out. It is, and was then, a bewitching place – almost as though it could still remember the Romans marching through the valley, or Thomas Cromwell planning his assault on Canterbury Cathedral, staying in West House, with his men billeted in the cottages. We experienced some strangenesses: lights that turned themselves on in the attic, no matter how often we turned them off; footsteps across the big spare room when we had friends to lunch in the kitchen below – and they *all* heard them – but when Stephen went up to look, of course there was no one there. Things disappeared and reappeared: my watch vanished from the bedroom and was found in an empty wastepaper basket in the other end of the house. I couldn't ever open the lock on the door to the big attic space; Stevie could open it with a struggle, Jamie never had a problem. Coldness would suddenly occur in the middle of a sunny day – once the kitchen seemed to be filled with a great chilly darkness so that I couldn't even see across the room to the back door.

One evening when Stevie was conducting in another country, I settled down with the cat to watch television in the drawing room. We never closed the big wooden shutters, as outside was only the garden and woods. I saw a man in a white shirt walking past the window in the darkness, round the house to a place where there was no way out. He didn't return and I was too unnerved to go looking for him. But the next day I thought I'd see if there were footprints, and it was only when I was standing outside the drawing-room window that I saw how high it was – the cellar underneath had its own windows visible at ground height. The man would have had to be a giant. I went inside and sat on the sofa and looked at the window and realized that the man must in fact have walked past not outside the window but *inside* – and moreover behind the sofa where I was sitting; his body had been reflected in the glass.

Q. This sounds spooky and terrifying.

A. The house, the village, the people were so lovely. We
loved it there. We made a terrace with a herb garden:
marjoram, sage, tarragon, thyme, fennel, poppies, roses
and lilies. We moved the old garage and oil tank, and built
a new double garage of Kentish bricks and a terrace with
steps down to the tennis court. We opened up the little
door at the end of a passage into double doors with glass
to let light into the hall. (When the work was going on, a
young plasterer arrived to make good the walls where the
new doors had been installed. Although it was midsummer and the garden full of flowers he stopped short, like
a mule, and couldn't be persuaded to go into the house.
He wouldn't even step inside.) Across the road was the
church which our near neighbours Jack and Ruby tended,
Ruby cleaning and dusting and keeping the key, Jack
winding the clock. At the end of the village street stands
Goodnestone Park, the home of Lord and Lady Fitzwalter;
in the Dower House lived Dan and Mathilda Taylor, both
now gathered in, but then the best friends you could hope
for. The village made us very welcome at once. On the
day we moved in, a dark, cold December morning, Frank
and Maureen came over from the pub, the Fitzwalter
Arms, to bring us bread and soup. There were summer
fêtes and cricket matches, bonfires on Guy Fawkes night,
Harvest Festival and carols in the church at Christmas.

Q. It sounds idyllic. Why did you leave?

A. It became almost impossible for me to work in London.
At the time the Channel Tunnel terminus was being built

in east Kent and all the roads were in chaos, making the journey time at least two and a half hours by road. The trains didn't run late enough to bring you back from town after a play, so if you were performing you had to drive, or use up all your salary renting a flat to live in. Stephen's work at the time was far-flung – operas in New Zealand, Australia, San Francisco, Vancouver – and when he was out of the country the house seemed extra huge and empty (but never quite empty. I had the beloved cat, Bee, who used to pad down the village street after me when I went to the village shop and chase the pheasants I fed in the garden. And then the rooms were never quite empty either: I could sense someone waiting or watching, hidden in the silence of empty stairs and landings, waiting for me to leave.)

I persuaded Stevie that we should sell up and go. We put the house on the market and dressed her up to look as beautiful as possible for people to view. I worked out a way of showing people round, starting with the five cool rooms of the cellar, from where a secret tunnel led under the road to the graveyard, then moving up to the kitchen and all the ground floor, up to the first floor and then up again to the attic rooms. One particular visit stands out in my mind. A couple came to see the house with their young daughter. I showed them the cellar, the flagstoned kitchen and one of my chief prides, a north-facing pantry with a zinc screen on the window and wide stone shelves, covered with bottles of fruit and home-made jams, a basket of eggs and a large Cheddar cheese. It looked like something out of a magazine. 'And here is the larder,' I said, opening the door – but inside the air was screaming with a cloud of bluebottles, buzzing over every part of the dim cool room.

I quickly shut the door and the woman laughed, 'Some larder!' and we went on upstairs. When we got to the attic space (whose door I had left slightly ajar as I still couldn't manage the lock), despite the great heat of that summery day, the little girl started to shiver uncontrollably. 'It's so *cold*,' she kept saying and she wouldn't go in to see my artfully arranged attic junk – an old toy fort, a wicker chair, a birdcage. They left quickly and I went back to the larder with some fly spray and a dustpan and brush – but when I opened the door there were no flies, not one bluebottle, nothing, not even a tiny corpse of a fly in my spick and span pantry. I went downstairs to the cellar and stood amongst the wood and coal and said very loudly, 'We're leaving.' At once the most delicious scent of roses filled the dark rooms, so thick and strong I nearly fainted; the smell of old English roses in hot sunshine.

Q. You haven't told me the most frightening thing of all; why didn't you tell that?

A. It's over now so I can. On that cold winter morning when we were moving in to the Parsonage, I had marked with Post-it notes where every box, suitcase and piece of furniture would go: Bedroom 2, Bathroom 3 and so forth. Then I labelled every door in the same way, to make it easier for the delivery men to find their way around. The cellar's rooms were harder to number, not having doors – there was the wine cellar, the wood cellar, the toolroom – and I positioned myself down there to direct all the fairly jumbly accoutrements of gardening equipment and old trunks into their rightful places. Men clomped down the narrow steps from the kitchen: 'Where does this go?' – 'There' . . .

'And this?' One man, having delivered his burden, turned to go back up the stairs. I was standing by the newel post and as he passed me he suddenly leaned his face very close to mine and said in a loud rasping growl, 'Leave – this – place!' I stood quite still and he stamped up the stairs. He wore an old leather jerkin, the type that coalmen have, and a whitish shirt and a flat cap. I couldn't see him very clearly by the dim light of the single bulb hanging on its bare stem. 'I shall report him to the supervisor,' I thought; my heart was beating in my throat and I couldn't tell if I was afraid or angry – both, perhaps.

But now you've guessed the end of the story: when I got up to the front drive where the removal lorry was parked there was no man dressed in that way, no man in a cap. So I kept it to myself. When, three years later, I went down to the same spot in the cellar to tell him we were going, he gave me the scent of a thousand roses to thank me.

We've been back to the house several times. Successive owners in their generosity and hospitality have asked us in at Christmastime, when Stevie plays the organ in the church for the carol service; and the thing, the feeling, has gone from the house, gone completely from every room. It won't return.

Q. How do you know?

A. Because it's sitting here on the stairs with me now.

Q. You make my blood run cold.

Spare Room

When I was modelling in the sixties, the photographer's assistant had to hold up massive polystyrene panels to reflect the light on to your face and clothes. This was hard work when the wind blew, and they'd sometimes be gusted off like people on sailboards, clinging on like bats as they were whirled away across the beach or park, feet barely touching the ground. Then someone invented a circular reflector, silver on one side, white or gold on the other, about the size of outstretched arms when open but . . . and this is the cunning part . . . when twisted and folded, reducing in dimension to a disc the size of a dinner plate which could then be stored in its zipped circular sleeve. When you took it out, it would prang open; when closed, you could dangle it from your belt. I suddenly thought that if the reflectors were refined so that they seemed as clear as mirrors you could make tiny versions and use them when travelling for make-up and hair. You would look a bit distorted, rather like a funfair Hall of Mirrors, but you'd be able to see if your hat was on straight. This is an adapted invention. I haven't invented it till now, so it is brand-new.

We have arrived at the spare room. Outside on the landing is a pretend tiger-skin rug, designed by David Shepherd for his wildlife foundation; and above it is this marvellous *thangka*, a silk wall-hanging depicting the

Buddha. It was given to me by the King of Bhutan at the end of our journey across his country. All over the house you will have seen Buddhas and Madonnas, and little tokens that aren't holy but bring with them a numinous quality from their own culture: Maori axes, beaded bracelets from the Masai, soapstone Inuit seals, that kind of thing. And just before we go in I'd like you to observe this collection of toy cars . . .

Q. . . . positioned unbelievably on yet another stack of small suitcases.

A. I've always collected cars; instead of a doll's house when I was small, I had a garage with petrol pumps and a lift to take vehicles to the upper parking area. I've still got my set of leaden road signs, although most of my original cars have gone. I've collected these over the years: a London taxi, a yellow New York cab, a Land-Rover for the rough terrain in Kenya, a huge Cadillac in lipstick-red and these wonderfully-made Citroëns fashioned out of insect repellent and baked-bean tins in Madagascar. The people there are too poor to have Dinky or Corgi toys for their children, so they make these from cans collected from rubbish dumps. They're perfect in every detail, even to the opening in the roof. I've gone through a few cars in my time, real cars: Minis, a Renault 5, a Rolls-Royce Silver Wraith, a Ford Granada; I had a Skoda for a year and have only recently sold my Ferrari; I drove a lovely green Nissan for ages and now zoom about in my little Smart car, with a Lexus for long journeys. I go by public transport when I can . . .

Q. You don't.

A. I do; but I prefer to be alone in my car if I'm doing voice exercises before a commercial dub, or am learning lines. Also some of my journeys that start in London, like taking stuff to the dry cleaners or buying stationery, continue from the town to the country to visit my mother or my aunt, or to attend a meeting outside the city. Very few country stations have taxis and I'm never certain whether buses are coming from or going to the name they show in the window, so all in all I'd rather drive. Also, if you're driving in the country and you see a sign saying 'Farm Shop' you can stop and buy home-grown produce. You couldn't do that from a bus; even if you got it to stop to let you off, another one wouldn't come along for six hours.

Q. How do you think people get about in the countryside?

A. By car or taxi, I expect. Let's go into the spare room now. The first thing you see is this large elaborate wooden bed. We bought it from neighbours when we were in the Parsonage. When we came to London I had it stripped and found it was covered with a thin walnut veneer which was coming off in places. So in an excess of découpage, in a frenzy of cutting things out of magazines, Christmas cards and gardening catalogues, I amassed an array of images – fruit, flowers, animals, angels, views of frosty parks, aspects of India, portraits of Byron and Shah Jahan, tea clippers, sands of Arabia – and made a collage on the headboard. Isn't it lovely? The only reason we don't have this as our bed is that it doesn't fit in our bedroom. When you lie back on the pillows and look up, you can see a cherub carved in wood at the very top near the ceiling, holding a quiver of arrows to smite your heart with love. He's leaning over to look down at you. And now you're lying here, you can see that the room is themed . . .

Q. After a fashion.

A. . . . well, the intention is that this is Abroad, mostly India and the Far East. Two paintings on cloth that I brought back from Mauritius, when I was doing a photo-shoot for *Fair Lady* magazine with Patrick Lichfield, hang over the fireplace and beside the bed. There is the photograph of the 5th Deccan Horse, all 500 of them mounted on their horses, given to me by Colonel Richard Smith who used to work for my grandfather. There are bamboo baskets on the cupboard, and the mantelpiece is covered with my bird collection and a few elephants – in particular, this astoundingly lifelike wooden elephant puppet, about 20 inches high, all his strings attached. I got him in the old puppet shop, which has now closed, off Kensington Church Street. (At the same time, I got a puppet of a rather wild-looking yellow-haired woman. I put her hair up, glued a miniature cigarette in her hand and gave it to Jennifer as a portrait of Patsy.) And the curtains are crewelwork from Kashmir. I made them; and though I say it myself they are easily the worst-made curtains in the house. I stretched the material out on the ground so that it looked evenly distributed; then I took my shears and cut it neatly, machined on the drawstring tape, whipped up the hems – and found that they were sometimes as much as eight inches different in length. But they're not lined, so frankly they could have been collected from different parts of Kashmir . . .

Q. Even though they came from Peter Jones.

A. My sister's Greek godmother, Helen Stavrides, started the first crewelwork factory in Srinagar. She made a scene for my christening present, of pine trees, mountains and a path winding through flowers in loop-stitch. It's up in the cottage in Scotland. Here, in this wooden chest from Morocco, bought when we were filming *AbFab*, here are more of my travel journals. Please listen to this one – it was a dream destination, to a part of the world that is presently reverberating to the unease in the Middle East and particularly in its neighbour Iraq: Syria, the centre of civilization. Twelve years ago, in some fluke of diary-window-of-opportunity for both Stephen and me, we set off for just a week together, arriving in Damascus in the late afternoon of a warm March day. 'Throwing our suit-cases into the hotel room, we ordered a car and drove up the twilight roads to a well-known viewpoint to get our bearings . . .' Shall I read on?

Q. Don't make it too long.

A. It'll fly by.

> Somewhere behind us, on the dark hillside of Mount Qassioun, thousands of years ago, Abraham was born. We stopped the car and got out to look at the lights of Damascus below. On various hilltops, just visible, were the President's palace, a prison and a military installation.

Patches of darkness in the glittering carpet marked the Chutah, the fabled green oasis of orchards named as one of four paradises on Earth. By the roadside were small cafés made of wood and corrugated iron, painted brightly and decorated with coloured bulbs, selling drinks, pistachio nuts and sweetmeats. Business was slack. The night was cold. Banner photographs of the President, Hafez Assad, snapped in the wind. Seven days in a country can give you no more than an idea of a place. Stevie and I had organized a gruelling itinerary. One morning in Damascus was all that we had allowed ourselves before setting off into the desert.

In daylight the city lost its *Arabian Nights* appeal. Yellow taxis, hooting ceaselessly, were travelling in sedate anarchy. Sometimes we were driven the wrong way up dual carriageways, and approaching cars passed on either side. Our driver, Abou Sharif, spoke no English or French; we spoke no Arabic. We set off for the Hamidiyah souk, the huge covered bazaar by the citadel, whose interior stretches in dappled gloom, criss-crossed by alleyways, right up to the Umayyad mosque. For sale were carpets, spices, silver, daggers, bed linen, crystallized fruit, goats' heads, cheap scent and brass trays. We watched two men making silk brocade on a hand loom, weaving seven colours into delicate patterns of flowers and birds. They worked all day to produce half a metre of cloth.

Sharif chivvied us on to the mosque, where we took off our shoes and I was given a black hooded garment, which eclipsed me completely except for my English feet sticking out palely from the hem. This has been a holy place for 3,000 years. Aramaean and Roman temples made way for a Byzantine cathedral. It, in turn, was replaced by mosques, which were sacked and looted by Mongols and by Tamerlane's men. Sharif pointed into a rich tomb, which was small, dusty and ornate. 'Yehia ben Zachariyha,' he murmured. 'Aaah,' we said, nodding and fumbling in the guidebook. The shrine contained the head of Yehia (St John the Baptist), revered by Muslims and Christians. Outside, I photographed the three minarets. Muslims believe that when Jesus returns, just before Judgement Day, he will arrive through the spire of the Jesus minaret to fight the Antichrist.

The sun had become much hotter as midday approached. Over the beige, boxy jumble of flat-roofed Arab houses and office blocks could be seen the dry, bare hills, pale against a hot, blue sky. We packed into Sharif's taxi and set off for Palmyra, city of palms. The landscape did not change much during the three-hour journey. Occasionally we saw a railway line, but in a week in Syria I saw only one train. The land appeared barren, but flocks of brown and black sheep grazed everywhere. The shepherds – children or old men in robes and Arab headgear – looked as though they had stepped from pictures in a Bible. Every so often a bump in the road indicated a police checkpoint. Young soldiers asked, 'Who? Where to? Why?' They were quickly pacified by Sharif's answers, and the sweets he gave them. A thin line of green appeared on the horizon. 'Palmyra,' Sharif said.

First we saw three or four old towers in the desert, tomb towers half in shadow as the sun set; then the modern hotel, a low building squatting between the oasis and Afqa, the sulphurous spring without which Palmyra would not have existed. Then, spread out like a massive stage set, the ruined city itself: colonnades, triumphal arches, temples, streets and pillars, ruined and standing. The sight was stupendous. Palmyra rose to its greatest heights in the first century BC, when the Romans invaded Syria. For 400 years it was the most important and prosperous centre of trade in the Middle East. Through its gates flowed silk, spices and ivory from the East, glass and statues from Phoenicia, goods and perfumes from the Arabian Gulf. Great caravans arrived there, unloaded, bargained, paid their tithes, feasted and moved on to the coast.

One of my earliest and often recurring dreams is set in a Middle Eastern harbour at first light of dawn. The hills around are baked dry, creamy-white against a sky that is already hazy blue with the heat of the coming day. I am swimming quietly between the great wooden ships lying at anchor; in fact I am swimming from one anchor chain to the next, in the shadows of the great vessels. Underneath me the water is fathoms deep and crystal clear and I can see the chains almost reaching down to the sandy sea-bed. Then my dream ends.

According to legend, the god Bel and his acolytes, the sun god and moon god, were ousted by Christianity there in Palmyra. Zenobia, a descendant of Cleopatra (she said), took over the kingdom when her husband died (some said she killed him). She conquered Lower Egypt and had coins minted with her newly assumed title, August. This was too much for the Roman emperor Aurelian. He put together an army, marched across Anatolia to Palmyra, besieged the city, which fell after a few weeks, and captured Zenobia. He took her back to Rome and forced her to ride in his triumphal parade, bound in chains of solid gold. Palmyra never recovered. Zenobia's likeness was erased from statues and paintings; by AD 700 the once mighty metropolis was home only to peasants and goatherds. Palmyra slept in the sand for a thousand years.

The next morning we got up at 4 a.m. Village dogs were barking as we stumbled along in the darkness to catch the sun rising over the ruins. The earth was paler than the sky, and the stars were out. We sat on a fallen pillar by the entrance to the central avenue and, as the light came up, buzzards which had spent the night in the oasis wheeled up, then swooped down over the remains of the city. We walked into the ruined amphi-theatre and counted out how many people could sit in the huge tiered semicircle in comfort – about 3,000, we reckoned. 'Say something on the stage,' said Stevie. I trotted down and turned to face the audience: only my husband in the very back row. Speaking in a normal voice, I started, 'Shall I compare thee to a summer's day . . .' and at once Stevie's distant figure said, 'I can hear every word.' I've been in modern theatres a third that size, and had to yell to be heard. An Arab castle stares down from a hilltop at the agora, where the camels were unloaded. The banqueting hall is decorated with flowers and swastikas, and at the theatre itself and at Bel's ruined temple are carvings of signs of the zodiac with angels, pomegranates and pine cones. Each capital of every pillar is carved with palms.

The sun was up. Our guide, Moffaq, led us into the valley of the tombs. Moffaq has 12 camels, which were all in calf. He plans one day to have 50, to open a souvenir shop and start three-day trips on camels, camping in the desert. The tombs are tall – one is four storeys high. Bodies were stacked on shelves, and each shelf was sealed with a plaque carved with the occupant's likeness. A whole room in the small museum is given over to the plaques. Like those in a photograph album, the faces stare out and the years in between melt away. Women in their best clothes – dangling earrings, bracelets, elaborately-dressed hair – rest fingers lightly against their cheeks, like a picture from *Country Life*. Men with moustaches and curled fringes are shown with their favourite horses and weapons. I think Patsy would like to be portrayed with her biggest Ivana Trump hairstyle, a glass of Bolly and a cigarette; I'd like lots of junk jewellery, a penknife and quite a lot of mascara. And a light chiffon scarf round my rather scraggy neck. Suddenly, rain poured down and four huge white birds flew overhead.

Back at the hotel we drank Bedouin coffee – very strong and deliciously flavoured with cardamom seeds. We drove north to Aleppo in a few hours. The rain had broken into the earth and brought out blood-red poppies, scabby little blue and yellow flowers, flashes of purple. All along the highway, tiny trees grew in serried rows – some the size of a crow's feather, others nearly waist-high. A sand-coloured Bedouin tent showed its dim interior, hung with patterned carpets. I'd love to live in a tent like that. The earth around Aleppo is dark red. The fields are full of rocks, but the land is lusher than at Damascus. The museum has cabinets of treasures from the past 7,000 years – delicate dishes, fine ivory carvings, and animal images of lion, deer, sphinx and hedgehog. A crocodile of schoolchildren pattered past, calling, 'Hello! Hello!' Some had green eyes and fair skin; most of the girls were too young to have their hair covered. Looming over the town is the giant citadel of Aleppo, with its five impregnable doors. Inside, work goes on to reclaim the castle from dereliction. There are steam baths and markets, reservoirs with cooling air-ducts, and a throne room of enormous proportions with spy-holes through the floor and walls from which to watch for enemies. Wild flowers and weeds clamber over the ramparts, which boiling oil once turned into a skating rink of death.

On the road to St Simeon Stylites martyrium, the Qalaat Semaan, we passed women dressed in cerise and orange, sitting in a field and eating sweet cakes and fruit spread on cloths. The air got cooler as the road rose, and fir trees brought an alpine feeling to the meadows of boulders. At the sanctuary, flowers carpeted the ground: roses, scarlet anemones, herb robert, lupins, buttercups and cow parsley. Mustapha, who showed us round, has planted 2,000 trees in the 34 years that he has worked there, and has taught himself English, French and German. The church was built after the saint's death, to accommodate the thousands of pilgrims who continued to flock to the place where Simeon spent 42 years of his life chained to the top of a column, preaching twice a day, winter and summer. Mustapha said that the most-asked question was how did the saint go to the loo: 'I tell them he used baskets to move things up and down the column,' he murmured inscrutably. A great stone marks the exact spot where the column stood, and around it stretch the remains of the basilica and the monastery, which housed 500 monks. As you look from where the west door would have been, the arches down the aisle go out of alignment, symbolizing the fallen head of the crucified Christ, just as they do in Canterbury Cathedral.

The hazy blue valleys reached Lebanon and, to the north, Turkey and the once-treasured Syrian town Iskenderun, birthplace of Alexander the Great. I pointed to some ruins a few miles away. 'Just more old towns; too many old towns round here,' Moffaq said. We headed south, to Hamah, where all the women are veiled, and wooden water wheels fill the air with their groaning. We bought ice-creams, and walked in quiet streets where lemon trees leaned out from courtyards and small boys played marbles with bottle tops. We had taken Bosra off the list, as we wanted time to see Ebla, Apames and Maaloula.

Ebla is approached through a village of what look like big, mud beehives. These are the traditional houses of the region. The contours of the land are irregular, with huge barrow mounds and hillocks. The excavations of Professor Matthiae lie like an empty ice-tray embedded in the earth. In 1964, as a young man, he started digging there. He found a statue marked King of Ebla, but he only knew for sure that he was on target when he unearthed 17,000 tablets, written with reeds on clay in Eblaite, cataloguing goods, cotton and gold. There are five cities here, one on top of the other, the first built in 2400 BC, a second in 1890 BC, these two using each other's walls as foundations, streets above streets. The excavations spread over only half an acre, but the old city wall must measure four miles around, with four great gates leading north, south, west and east; to the Euphrates, Egypt, Anatolia and the eastern gate to Babylon and Arcadia. In the museum, there were lumps of unfashioned clay in the bottom of jars, waiting to be patted into shape and then written on. This must have been how the Ten Commandments came, not carved out of rock (which would have been far too heavy) but on clay plates marked in clerical cuneiform.

Grey rain was pouring down on the morning we visited Krak des Chevaliers. It looked absolutely colossal, squatting on its hill, the greatest castle that ever existed, a fortress within a fortress, built by crusaders for crusaders. We were in the company of 2,000 schoolchildren on a holiday outing, feet drumming in the clammy arched corridors and sleeping quarters of the knights, sweet papers fluttering where the round table had been. I suppose we had become rather spoilt, expecting to explore Krak in the solitude we found at Ebla and Palmyra. Krak had become a dream goal for me, and I had wanted to sit on a parapet looking out over the vast plains of the Homs gap and imagine Saladin's army circling for four days before retreating without even attempting an attack.

The last day arrived, and we walked round the old town of Damascus – down the Street Called Straight, where Ananias was sent to find Paul and restore his sight, and where my father bought a silver powder compact in 1942. The silversmith imprinted 'Beatrice', written in my father's hand, on the lid. Tiny scenes of Syria appear round the rim: camels, palm trees and Arabian dhows in full sail. He gave it to my mother in Abbottabad when he returned to India a year later, in August 1943. I had always longed to see the Street Called Straight; now we were wandering through ancient alleys winding between lath-and-plaster buildings, arches cobbling mosques on to Roman temples, coffee shops sheltering between church and souk. This is a city built on former cities, older than time, the oldest inhabited city in the world, under a cobalt sky. Every man of culture (it is said) has two countries: his own and Syria. We turned a corner and there was the Eye of the Needle, a tiny door in the huge gate of a caravanserai. Two children were standing beside it. The door is very small – the rich man has not got a chance.

Q. I don't quite get that very last bit.

A. The name of the little door is the Eye of the Needle. It would be virtually impossible for a camel to squeeze through it. So, it would be easier for a camel to pass through the Eye of the Needle than for a rich man to enter the Kingdom of Heaven. Meaning you can't get to heaven if you're rich. Meaning 'sell that thou hast, and give to the poor'. You can't take it with you. There are no pockets on a shroud, all that.

Q. But you're rich now. What are you going to do about it?

A. I think all you can do is keep earning it and keep giving it away. I'm not sure if there is such a thing as a level playing field: no sooner have you rolled it flat and put up sunscreens and windshields, and weighed the teams, something happens to make the playing field tilt again, yawing over to one side so it's unfair again, and one side romps home. Perhaps just the chance of equal opportunity is all that can be offered. I'm fascinated by the theory that if you gave 10 people £100 each, by the end of the day someone would be flat broke and someone else would have made his £100 into £300 or £400. 'To him that hath it shall be given': that always seemed a wretched recommendation, until I realized it was instead just an *observation* of how life is – lucky, rich, happy, fit people hitting the jackpot again and again, while people who really could do with a break, one lucky break, become poorer and more downtrodden. Philosophically it's a conundrum; and perhaps all we can do is keep on trying to balance the scales.

Q. You've never been really poor, have you.

A. No. In the old days I've been boracic, not had a penny to my name, walked because I couldn't afford the tube, washed my sheets in the bath, lived on toast and been unable to pay off a £30 overdraft for a year, but that isn't poor. I know what poor is, now that I've travelled to countries where people – like Satel in the hills behind Rora Habab – have nothing, next to nothing at all: a saucepan, a knife, a piece of cloth – nothing. We are poor in this country in a different way; the poverty hurts just as much, but so many First World must-haves have edged into the screen that you can be thought poor if you don't go away on holiday, or if you have the cheapest trainers or second-hand furniture. Because of our ways of measuring achievement, i.e. by wealth, people lose respect for them-selves if they're poor, and admire those who are rich. The 'Rich List', published every year in British newspapers, is an example of the illness in our society. Richness is now seen to be a good thing. I swear I am not going to turn into an old raving hippy but in the time of flower power, money was considered rather vulgar. Those who had it didn't mention it, and dressed as insanely as the rest of us whilst quietly paying the bills. Dreams, philosophy, creativity and curiosity were kings in those days; now it's money's turn to rule, and the world is duller, darker and more dangerous for it.

Q. Will you get rid of some now? You'd better.

A. I shall write a cheque as soon as we go downstairs and send it to one of my charities. We're going to go up to the attic now.

Q. You always try to leave before I've finished peering round. A huge empty frame leaning against the wall . . . what's that for?

A. You see above the writing desk the portrait of the actress Kate Fahy? I painted that of her years ago when we were both between jobs; she's sitting in a big pale-green armchair in a white shirt with a patterned scarf twisted round her neck. She's got a wonderful face to paint: good sharp bone structure, a big mouth and dark eyes. At school we didn't use oil paint till the last year, and I'd never liked it until I started to do portraits of people. I bought this empty frame in a junk shop and I plan to do a painting of Stevie to go in it. Rather obviously, I've decided to paint him in maestro gear, that is to say a tail-coat; but perhaps the white tie can be left off and the collar would be open. Although

I hardly ever get to paint nowadays, from sheer lack of time, I think about it every day: how I would get the light on the knuckles, whether to paint the background in any detail, if the eyes should look at me or away. If I were a real artist I would carry a sketch-pad with me at all times. Toulouse-Lautrec used to have his pencils cut into tiny inch-long sections so he could draw people on a pad in his pocket without their knowing. Anyway, the painting of Stevie will be fairly monochrome but I'd love a Francis Cadell orange-red screen or blind in the background to denote the wild temperament of my husband.

Q. He puts up with you, and doesn't seem wild at all. He seems to be more even-tempered than you are.

A. Precisely what I was trying to say about the civilizing effect of music. I shall do the picture on hardboard or maybe wood panelling. Anthea says you can get a good surface for oils by pasting sheets of the *Financial Times* on your board. She says it's interesting to see and use the newsprint as it shows through. Anthea hasn't changed at all, to my eyes, since she left school. Painting is her life (apart from her family, obviously). Being with a painter makes you look at everything in a different way: a positive way, a way of thinking, 'How can I make this work?' – trying, not giving up. And as you settle down to work, putting down what you see (if you are painting from life), you experience respect and empathy for the subject; just as when you're acting, you have to love the subject you're portraying even if it's unpleasant. We are all advocates, putting a case for our subject or character. Come on; let's go upstairs.

Q. And this is the *en suite* bathroom, is it, with holes in the floorboards and tiles painted over with emulsion –

A. Just come on! You've been reading too many style magazines. It's a bathroom, it works; now let's get on. I love this part of the house; the stairs reach the uppermost landing and there is a skylight, and banisters around the edge here to stop you dropping like a stone to the floor below. But look out of this window! The view! Lean on the windowsill here and let's look out over London.

Attic

London is crammed with surprises: I've lived here now for nearly 40 years, and every day I see a street name I don't know or glimpse an alley going unexpectedly from a busy road to a builder's yard. I don't like sanitized London, where the buildings have windows all the same size. It's gone a bit mad at the moment with road bossiness too: painted lines and concrete islands make it very hard to drive or ride anything safely, as you lurch up and down over speed cushions (between which bikers zoom at 70 mph). But it will soon settle down. Roads are for driving and riding on, pavements are for walking. That's all. But the essence of London lives on, and like most eternal love affairs it's a bit lopsided. London doesn't care if I live or die, if I stay for ever or leave tomorrow. I love London with all my heart but it doesn't know who I am; some of its people do, but the town itself doesn't trouble to learn our names. It has seen it all – fire, plague, bombings, celebrations, heat waves and months of ice. It has seen coronations and beheadings, demonstrations and victory parades, funerals, fun-fairs and the ordinary daily grind of millions of people over hundreds of years. I feel privileged to live here, proud to say I live in London.

Here on the top floor of our house we hear Big Ben clearly, particularly when 'the busy world is hushed, and the fever of life is over, and our work is done . . .' It's become more audible, strangely enough, since they built the enormous apartment blocks, St George Wharf, at Vauxhall Cross. The muffled clang of the great bell cannons off the new green glass windows and is redirected towards our house. Let me show you round: three little bedrooms and a bathroom leading off a wide bright landing, with light pouring in from above – there is a window set in the roof. There is an old cradle filled with toys, mostly mine as Jamie has taken his for Alice (if they're suitable: obviously not Action Man with Gripping Hands who sits defiantly in a cupboard clamped on to the snare drum, but the Pink Panther has gone and so have lots of nursery books). Stevie didn't keep many of his things, just cricket balls, boxes of paper and the robes he was given when he was made a Fellow of the Royal College of Organists at the age of 17. This attic is a bit of a backwater; things drift in on the tide and become firmly silted in, and although we make the bedrooms as charming as possible when people come to stay there is an undeniable feeling that one of them is actually a junk room.

This is a place for reflection: sometimes when I come up here, ostensibly to hunt out a rucksack or track down a book, I lie on one of the beds and dream. In the old days I imagine a servant girl slept up here, in her tiny room with the same little iron Victorian fireplace, perhaps with one measly lump of coal burning; she would have had to tend to the fires on all five floors, panting up and down with a heavy coal scuttle, careful not to touch the walls with her sooty hands. When Alice can walk (and there may be others! our grandchildren!) she will come and stay with us and the bedroom facing the garden will be hers. It's a long way up for little legs to climb; but she'll grow so fast that she'll soon be leaping up, two at a time, and we'll sit on her bed and read night-time stories. Most of Jamie's baby clothes have gone, passed on to younger cousins, but this I kept: it used to be my dressing gown, and it was made for me in India of pure cashmere, pale green with patch pockets. My mother kept it when I grew up and gave it to me for Jamie when he was three; and now I've kept it for Alice to wear if she likes. There's the old desk that I used in Addison Road as my beside table and dressing table combined; my Aunt Toona gave it to me 35 years ago, and opening the drawers I can see that there's some repair work to be done. With glue and a bit of judicious cabinet-making I'll make it as good as new. Could you move, do you think? I'm afraid you're sitting on the clothes I'd ironed so carefully for my next trip. I'm off to India, to Dharamsala in the foothills of the Himalayas which is now the home of thousands of Tibetan refugees.

Q. I didn't recognize these as clothes.

A. Well, they're lovely colourful scarves and cloths, and these gigantic patchwork trousers . . .

Q. You can't be serious.

A. . . . which will be comfortable to wear as it's already 90 degrees in the daytime, although cooler in the evenings. I have been granted an audience with His Holiness the 14th Dalai Lama; I'm travelling with the journalist Kate Saunders and the photographer Tom Stoddart: we're going to try to highlight the problems these exiled people have, and see if there are ways we in the West can help. I've met His Holiness before, outside the House of Lords. He's very kind and wise and good-humoured; it's extremely exciting. Taking a tip from Flora Robson I'm going to give him a present of some dark burgundy knee-high socks; and a rather marvellous Tibetan Buddhist scripture, given to my grandfather by the 13th Dalai Lama in 1930. As most of their holy scriptures were destroyed in the Chinese invasion, my mother was anxious that this one should be returned. It's written on separate slips of handmade paper and is enclosed by two heavy carved wooden panels.

There's nothing more thrilling than packing for a trip. As I've said earlier, I try to make a plan involving clothes-co-ordination, but I always pack an empty bag or case to stuff with purchases from wherever I go; and quite often I give away a lot of the clothes I've taken. These pretty sarongs are from Malaysia, from Sarawak which is on the island of Borneo. I was there to make a documentary film about the White Rajahs of Sarawak, an English family called Brooke who for a hundred years ran that remote part of the world like a country estate, banning headhunting and trying to broker peace between the warring tribespeople. I loved Sarawak: the sleepy brown rivers with their suddenly whirling rapids, the sweaty rainforests, thunderstorms and spicy foods. During the filming, we made our way up the Rajang river, using poles to push ourselves along over-grown waterways, and we stayed in longhouses as guests. Longhouse life is extremely methodical: each family has its own room, or 'door' as they're called; there is a communal veranda divided for walking on, for drying peppercorns and chillies, and for sitting on. The young men and women go out to work in the paddy-fields and forests each day, leaving all the children in the charge of the grannies, maiden aunts and people who aren't able to work. At quite a young age the children go downriver to a boarding school; day schools here are impractical as there are no roads in these jungles and going everywhere by river is slow and rather tiring. So then the grannies are left with the babies, which they put into hammocks made of sarongs tied on to the veranda railings; and the grannies chatter and gossip and make things. If a baby cries (but I never heard a baby or child cry, not even once) there's always a wise old pair of hands and a kind old wrinkly brown granny-face to shush it. All the children belong to everyone: as the young men go off to work, walking barefoot into the jungle, they ruffle the hair of any child standing around. I loved that way of living. The first sip of any drink was tossed to the wainscoting of the stilted bamboo houses as an offering to the spirits. The shrunken heads, which hung on beams above us, were treated with great respect, even though they had been attached to the bodies of enemies when alive.

We were at one of the longhouses when an ancient villager died. As a customary courtesy, we, as strangers, left the longhouse for three days; but when we returned they invited us to the last night of the wake. Friends and relatives had travelled miles on foot or by boat to be there, and when we arrived at the feast shortly after midnight the party was in full swing (and it would go on till dawn). We had been advised to bring a gift of some sort; having none we offered money, which was received well. In Sarawak society, when others are seated you never stand upright, so, bent double, we crept around to the bereaved family, who had dutiful looks of melancholy on their faces when they remembered their loss – but the air was shaken with gossip, and laughter, and the loud plaintive lament of the hired mourner who was extolling the virtues of the departed soul. It was one of the grannies who had gone. She lay peacefully on a bed of plaited mats in the midst of the festivities, with offerings for her to take with her on her travels to the next world. There were a few coins, some flowers, sweetmeats, a bracelet, and someone had thoughtfully put two cigarettes and a box of matches on a banana leaf for her. She would be taken downriver to the burial ground at dawn, with everyone piling into boats to accompany her on her last journey; and she would be buried standing upright, like her forebears. It made death seem very natural and ordinary and friendly. Someone had done her packing for her, as it were; putting in everything she might need – rather as I'm doing now for my trip to India.

I don't know whether it's because I'm growing older, and can see the sunset from the top of my hill, but I find things more and more fascinating nowadays. Everything opens up avenues of discovery, and with alarm you realize you won't ever know a trillionth of what there is to know; and that the more you know about anything the more interesting it becomes. Making things interesting to children is one of our duties, and I plan to be a good grandmother, because the other merciful thing that happens to ancient people is that they become more patient and don't mind picking up titchy little plastic soldiers and saying 'Boo!' a hundred and forty times a day. I don't want you to leave yet because there seems so much still to talk about. The world is changing fast, but in many ways, in most ways, it stays the same as it has always been. People collect their children from school, crops are harvested, houses are built and pulled down, leaders of men come and go and the birds fly south in the winter. I expect the truth is that *we* are the changing factor, how *we* perceive things. This feels like my world and its history is my history; but when I've gone it will bowl on for thousands more years. Perhaps there will be some major changes – climates warming up and behaving unseasonably, whole species becoming exctinct before our eyes, travel getting even quicker. But we've been here before and survived; if we can do our part, maybe we can prevent catastrophes from happening to the natural world. There will always be room for plays and films and books, which reflect and inform us on the way things are going and give us an escape route if reality is too harsh.

I hope to go on acting till I tumble over, but like Robert Morley, who in later years accepted parts only if they lasted two days and a car was sent to collect him, I shall become pickier about the roles. (But not too picky: you can be too wise in our profession, and a really bad part in a dreadful play is not so much a breath of fresh air, more a major enema and very good for you.) Not too much good taste, then; and as the great actor Michael Kitchen once told me, the last thing you should say to yourself before you go on stage is, 'Don't try too hard.' I'm going to aim to get a bit more discipline into my life and learn to concentrate completely on the matter in hand rather than starting 17 things simultaneously – except I like multi-tasking. Like most women I feel I do things more efficiently if they're all happening at the same time, like learning lines while planting bulbs, with a telephone under your chin and a pie blackening in the oven, a bath running and hair dye streaking down your neck. In my new efficient world I shall factor in quite a lot of travelling; but this time there will be the odd week marked 'holidays', either in Scotland or driving across Europe, exploring the Far East, or taking the golden road to Samarkand.

I won't get ill: from Joseph Corvo I have learned some of the techniques of reflexology – how to keep well and flexible, how to cure headaches and colds and how to be happy with the body I've been given. Perhaps I'll plant an orchard of delicious exotic fruit trees in Sarawak. When I returned from Malaysia with a big leaf from a tree known only as *buah ambang*, the Royal Botanic Gardens at Kew identified it as *Mangifera pajang*, wild mango; and another tree I had described they named as Sang Dragon or Burmese rosewood, whose tiny yellow heavily scented flowers gave off the sweetest smell ever to drift across a lagoon. I will plant an avenue of trees somewhere, and I'd like to live in a tree-house, even for a short time. Perhaps I shall invent a wheelchair that can rise on telescopic legs to bring the sitter up to face height when stationary, so people don't bend down as if looking into a pram. In this I shall go to parties and art galleries . . . but my life-line seems to go across my palm, round my thumb and start at the beginning again, so perhaps I'll be alive for ages – perhaps for ever. Now, back to my packing. When I'm in India I plan to buy a *chuba*, a traditional Tibetan dress, to wear for my audience with His Holiness.

Q. Please don't take those colossal trousers. Is that a bell ringing? Who's ringing the bell?

A. Don't get in a flap. That's Stevie coming home from

Chicago. He must have caught an earlier flight. He's probably packed his keys at the bottom of the suitcase. Shall we go down? It will all be very familiar to you by now, the long staircases and glimpses into rooms, views from each landing of the garden, the books and suitcases – except it all looks slightly different when you're coming down from above. We've seen it all: we've seen all there is to see. Come on; I'll pour us a glass of something delicious and you can stay as long as you like. It's been a pleasure having you here.

Acknowledgements

I would like to thank very much those people whose letters I have quoted: in no particular order, Helena Williams and Gladys Warren, Pete Goss, Robin Hanbury-Tenison, Blake Edwards and the dear departed David Niven, Dirk Bogarde and Emily Chitticks. Added to these are the teachers who wrote my school reports, namely Mrs Nancy Cuddy, Sister Barbara Allen CHF and Miss Hortin-Smith. The Imperial War Museum was, as always, helpful and kind, particularly Penny Ritchie Calder and Rod Suddaby. Everyone at Penguin and Michael Joseph deserves a bouquet, but the largest by far should go to Louise Moore, who supported and cajoled me along the way. My agent, Anthony Goff, has never failed to believe in me, for which I'm humbly grateful. Thanks are due to Susan Close, who typed out every word deciphered from my scrawling longhand at breakneck speed and with awesome efficiency. I want to thank all the crews and fellow travellers who are unnamed here, from my travels to Sarawak, Kenya, Tsarabanjina and Eritrea, not to mention Switzerland, Syria and all of Europe and the rest of the world. I want to thank everybody for everything.

There are photographers whose names are absent from my brain but ever-present in my heart: there are all my old school friends and family members mentioned in other books but omitted from these pages. And all those people who listened to endless deliberations, suggested titles and made sounds of interest have my deepest gratitude, especially Stevie, who said, 'Do we have to go on thinking up titles even when the book is published?' We don't: it's done.

★

The author and publisher wish to thank all copyright holders for permission to reproduce their work, and the institutions and individuals who helped with the research and supply of materials.

Text Sources

'Arms of Mary': words and music by Iain Sutherland © Universal/Island Music Limited. (100%)

'Rainbow Valley': words and music by Buzz Cason and Mac Gayden © 1967, Sons Of Ginza Publishing Inc., USA
Reproduced by permission of Keith Prowse Music Publishing Co Ltd, London WC2H 0QY.

Extract from *Collected Short Stories* by W. Somerset Maugham published by Heinemann. Used by permission of The Random House Group Limited.

Extract from 'Business Girls' by John Betjeman. Reproduced by permission of John Murray Publishers.

Pictorial Sources

'Me at 18. Test shots for my photographic book.' Crispian Woodgate.

'Me at 19. Very horrible hairstyle worn by no one before or since.' Roy Round.

'Royal Hospital Gardens in the 1960s, Chelsea.' Michael Claydon.

'Getting my first film part in *Some Girls Do*.' © Plunket-Greene Ltd.

'Me as a Bond Girl in *On Her Majesty's Secret Service*.' Bob Penn. © 1969 Danjaq, LLC and United Artists Corporation. All rights reserved.

'With Charlotte Cornwell and Siân Phillips in *Vanilla*.' John Haynes.

'Miriam Margolyes as Aunt Sponge, producer Jake Eberts and me as Aunt Spiker with rat's teeth in *James and the Giant Peach*, San Francisco.' Lucy Dahl.

'With Gareth and Patrick on *The New Avengers*' first trip to New York, 1975.' © Mark 1 Productions Ltd.

'Episode One.' © Mark 1 Productions Ltd.

'Giving Graham Norton a Golden Globe in New York.' © Anita & Steve Shevett.

'Promoting *Pink Panther*.' © Brian Aris.

'With Gareth, judging Purdey lookalike competition. Extreme right won.' *Sunday People*.

' "Lost in France." First series.' © BBC.

'Patsy in Val d'Isère.' Brian Ritchie. © BBC.

'Rehearsing *AbFab*: Jennifer, Julia, me and June.' Sally Soames.

'With the Bee in the garden.' Harry Cory Wright.

'With Ken Frogbrook: behind, Frogmat deployed as oil-spill protection.' Peter Taylor.

'Modelled by Steve Swales for Madame Tussaud's.' Courtesy of Madame Tussaud's.

'Me with shell ring, coconut and Paddy's knife on Tsarabanjina. My brain had almost vanished.' Brian Ritchie. © BBC.

'On a burnt tank in Eritrea.' Fraser Barber.

'With Babe the Pig in the kitchen.' Iain Raydon.

'With Madame Butterfly on the Isle of Wight, December 2003.' © John Wright/www.johnwrightphoto.com.

'Jamie's christening.' Celia Armitage.

Acknowledgements

'Jamie on the beach in winter by his dad, Michael Claydon.'
  Michael Claydon.
'Bafta night with Stevie, me wearing Betty Jackson.' Doug
  Mackenzie.

Every effort has been made to trace copyright holders and we apologize in advance for any unintentional omission. We would be pleased to insert the appropriate acknowledgement in any subsequent edition.